Philosophy, Et Public Policy

What makes a policy work? What should policies attempt to do, and what ought they not do? These questions are at the heart of both policymaking and ethics. *Philosophy, Ethics and Public Policy: An Introduction* examines these questions and more. Andrew I. Cohen uses contemporary examples and controversies, mainly drawn from policy in a North American context, to illustrate important flashpoints in ethics and public policy, such as:

- public policy and globalization: sweatshops; medicine and the developing world; immigration
- marriage, family, and education: same-sex marriage; women and the family; education and intelligent design
- justifying and responding to state coercion: torture; reparations and restorative justice
- the ethics of the body and commodification: the human organ trade; factory farming of animals.

Each chapter illustrates how ethics offers ways of prioritizing some policy alternatives and imagining new ones. Reflecting on various themes in globalization, markets, and privacy, the chapters are windows to enduring significant debates about what states may do to shape our behavior. Overall, the book will help readers understand how ethics can frame policymaking, while also suggesting that sometimes the best policy is no policy. Including annotated further reading, this is an excellent introduction to a fast-growing subject for students in philosophy, public policy, and related disciplines.

Andrew I. Cohen is Director of the Jean Beer Blumenfeld Center for Ethics and Associate Professor of Philosophy at Georgia State University, USA. He is co-editor (with Christopher Heath Wellman) of *Contemporary Debates in Applied Ethics* (second edition, 2014).

Philosophy, Ethics, and Public Policy

An Introduction

Andrew I. Cohen

Routledge
Taylor & Francis Group

LONDON AND NEW YORK

First published 2015
by Routledge
2 Park Square, Milton Park, Abingdon, Oxon OX14 4RN

and by Routledge
711 Third Avenue, New York, NY 10017

Routledge is an imprint of the Taylor & Francis Group, an informa business

© 2015 Andrew I. Cohen

British Library Cataloguing in Publication Data
A catalogue record for this book is available from the British Library

Library of Congress Cataloging in Publication Data
Cohen, Andrew I.
Philosophy, ethics, and public policy : an introduction / Andrew I. Cohen.
pages cm
Includes bibliographical references and index.
1. Policy sciences--Moral and ethical aspects. 2. Social policy--Moral and ethical aspects. 3. Economic policy--Moral and ethical aspects. 4. Public welfare--Moral and ethical aspects. I. Title.
H97.C624 2015
172'.2--dc23
2014015473

ISBN: 978-0-415-81416-4 (hbk)
ISBN: 978-0-415-81417-1 (pbk)
ISBN: 978-1-315-77201-1 (ebk)

Typeset in Garamond
by Taylor & Francis Books

Contents

Acknowledgements

For comments, conversation, or suggestions about various chapters, I thank Nigel Ashford, Jessica Berry, Bob Brecher, Andrew Jason Cohen, Maxine Eichner, Christie Hartley, Tim O'Keefe, Peter Lindsay, George Rainbolt, James Stacey Taylor, Peter Vallentyne, Kit Wellman, Larry Wilkerson, and Matt Zwolinski. I am grateful for the guidance and encouragement of my editors at Routledge, Tony Bruce and Adam Johnson. Several anonymous reviewers for Routledge were generous to offer extensive and constructive feedback. Many students were kind to comment on various chapters. Among them were Mason Arline, Cameron Boone, Maria Caruso, Chelsea Coleman, Harold Crowe, Alexander Davis, Darla Greaser, Matthew Hiltman, Callie Hollander, Jess Hullinger, Taylor Jones, Judith Kim, Ayesha Kirk, Alexis Koutrelakos, Ryan Le, Joshua McCormack, Caitlin McCoyd, Jamie Moon, Taylor Mumford, BaoChau Nguyen, Maryum Rabia, Evelyn Richardson, Joseph Shively, Leman Tatari, Kevin Thurston, Sarah Vogt, Andrew Weyant, and Anastasiya Yashchuk. My thanks to Carson Young for research assistance, and to Megan Hiatt for careful and patient copyediting. I am especially grateful to Elizabeth Dwyer for immensely helpful research assistance and copyediting. In many ways, I can trace this book to Anthony Pennino, who inspired many people with his contagious passion for ideas. A special thanks for the love and support of J, S, & M: almost done!

Introduction

Discussions of public policy often consider how policies are made, how well they connect to intended goals, and how to evaluate their effects. A proper understanding of public policy would then require close attention to how the world works and to how things became the way they are. Who are the relevant actors? What institutions are in place to achieve various goals, and how well do they function? Why are institutions designed the way they are, and why do they work as well—or as poorly—as they do? Policy theorists and other social scientists devote their careers to investigating these and related issues. They sometimes propose various models for understanding the motives of policymakers, the content of the policies, and how to assess the consequences. Their work is complex and often controversial. Even the most highly regarded experts disagree about the causes of events and policies, what is currently happening, what might happen, and how best to proceed.

As if such complexity and uncertainty were not enough, policy discussions sometimes fail to make clear what it should mean for a policy to "work" and how to understand which consequences *count* when considering what a policy does. Sometimes we lose sight of what policies *may* attempt to do or what they *ought* to do. Approaching policy disputes without a sense of the legitimate scope of political action may then miss a vital part of the discussion. This is not a question of effectiveness, though that is crucial to policy discussions. It is a particular type of normative issue: It is a matter of understanding the *moral* possibilities available to anyone considering competing policy proposals.

A central function of ethical principles is to indicate what we *may* do alone or together through institutions. These principles can also tell us what we *ought* or *ought not* to do. Ethical principles guide our behavior, constraining or marshaling our conduct by offering special reasons that encourage or discourage (or, more forcefully, compel or forbid) our actions.

Ethics is then that part of philosophy that considers, among other things, what makes for a good human life, what people owe to one another, and how human beings ought to behave. The institutions we create and inhabit crucially shape what sorts of lives we lead. Since ethics guides our actions, it offers a framework for evaluating the merits of rules, norms, or institutions. Ethics can indicate how to construct, change, or assess key social and political institutions. As a part of philosophy, ethics also helps us to explore deeply held commitments and traditions. It urges us to expand our imaginations to consider morally enriching possibilities. It can then be a crucial part of the policy theorist's toolkit for at least two reasons. First, people care about doing the right thing. Second, despite disagreements, ethics can be a way of framing policy disputes and possible institutional responses in a way that might achieve greater consensus.

Policy theorists care about what ethics has to say. People who act within and for public institutions care. Of course, ordinary citizens care, too. We all care because we want to be sure to support and do the right things. Often it is not entirely clear just what that right thing is. Sometimes there are many possible right things to do. Even though there is sometimes uncertainty and disagreement about many fundamental ethical questions, ethics can still help us in part by making a bit clearer what is at stake in policy disputes. It can deepen our appreciation of what matters and why. This book uses philosophical ethics to lend clarity to policy disputes and to help us determine what constitutes good reasons in policymaking.

Bringing ethics to policy might seem an uneasy marriage. After all, policy is concerned with getting things done. Ethics may just threaten to get in the way. That might be why some people would be suspicious of ethics. It seems to stand for the parent wagging a finger at us, admonishing us to stop doing something we like doing or to make us do something we really do not want to do. Perhaps this worry has something to it. Perhaps ethics sometimes is a chore. However, it might also help us to understand what our values are, what they could be and should be, and how to go about realizing them. It can even help us to understand together what our shared values are or should be. Ethics might then be an important part of understanding and shaping policy.

What is public policy?

Let us back up a second. Think for a moment about public policy. What is it? It is tempting to think that a public policy is anything a state does. But that definition is too broad. Think about why. States, through their governments, do many things that are either not public or not a policy. When a county government decides to lower the speed limit on a local road, it sends out a county employee in a county vehicle to install a new sign. When Chris, the county employee, removes the old sign and installs the new one, Chris acts on behalf of the county government. Acting through Chris, the county does many things, including some that seem inconsequential. When Chris tightens the bolt on the new speed limit sign, that action is not a public policy. But tightening the bolt is something the county does (through Chris). So, "public policy" cannot be *anything* a state does.

When Chris the county employee installs the new road sign, plenty of public policies are still afoot. The lowering of the speed limit is a (new) policy. It was enacted through procedures that are set out in various public policies, such as those governing open meetings, public hearings, the election and appointment of officials, and rules defining what makes something a traffic regulation. Chris also drove a county vehicle as part of official county business to the place where the sign is posted. Chris had tools that belong to the county and used them to install the new sign. The existence of *county* vehicles and tools, and the existence of funds to purchase a new sign, are all licensed by various public policies. There are rules that describe how to raise the revenue to do such things. There are rules, norms, and institutions for holding, allocating, and dispersing such funds. There are also rules regarding the maintenance of county property. There are many other rules regarding how someone such as Chris can have a job working for the county and who can tell Chris what to do.

Therefore, public policy can be defined as any institution, norm, or rule that the government of a state upholds *to guide people's behavior*. States, through their governments, have many tools for guiding behavior, such as laws, regulations, various norms and procedures, budgets, regulatory directives, executive orders, and so forth. These are all ways of making people do things, or not do things, by providing or signaling reasons to act or not to act in certain ways.

What makes a public policy *public*?

What makes policies public and what makes them policies? Consider first the *public* part. Public policies are not private preferences or choices, even if they reflect, encourage, or celebrate private choices. Suppose Pat is a vegetarian. Even if Pat is very public about this dietary choice, it is not a public policy. Pat is not the government. Even if Pat were the president or prime minister, Pat's vegetarianism would not be a public policy. Being a vegetarian is something Pat does as a private citizen. If, however, Pat were the head of state and somehow issued and enforced an order that everyone must become a vegetarian, then vegetarianism would be a public policy.

The choices and policies of privately held companies are not public policies. Coca Cola's policy to keep Coke's formula a trade secret is not a public policy, but not because it is a secret. It is not a public policy because it is a choice made by a privately held corporation. There are public policies *about* trade secrets, such as those that enforce non-disclosure agreements. However, Coke's policies, just as the policies of any non-governmental entity, will not count as public policies as this book will understand them.

The norm among many observant Jews never to eat pork is not a public policy. It is not a public policy even if it is promulgated by Jewish religious officials, and even if it is informally enforced in Jewish families and communities through social pressures. If a government were to enforce an order that no one (or at least no Jews) may eat pork, then that would be a public policy.

The practice of shooting fireworks on the Fourth of July in the United States is not a public policy but more of an informal social custom. However, there are plenty of public policies relevant to the Fourth of July. It is an official holiday, so most government offices are closed. In some communities, there are public policies that provide for publicly funded fireworks displays. Nearly all communities have policies regarding when, whether, and how private citizens may set off fireworks, and which ones.

What makes a public policy a *policy*?

Next, consider the *policy* part of public policy. A public policy is not a one-off; it must be some rule, norm, law, or institution. The general idea here is to exclude renegade acts as public policies. When officials act beyond their official roles, their actions do not constitute or express public policy.

Suppose some officers in a police department were to single out members of a particular racial group for mistreatment. Their acts are not public policies. There are still plenty of policies relevant to such officials' acts, however. There are policies regarding how to discipline such officials and how to undo any effects of their acts.

Some cases show blurry lines between actions that are authorized by public policy and those that are not. If a police department's institutional culture supports singling out certain persons for arrest, such norms may amount to a sort of public policy. Sometimes there are norms that guide what public officials do even if they are not explicitly articulated. Great journalism investigates institutions to discover such norms when there seem to be problems with what public officials do or do not do. Whether such norms amount to public policy depends on how much we press on the "public" part of public policy. These sorts of borderline cases should not distract us from the general idea that a public policy is any institution, norm, or rule that the government of a state upholds *to guide people's behavior.*

The scope of the state

States do many things and touch our lives in countless ways. A discussion of ethical considerations can help us to understand how the state may go about doing what it does. Indeed, ethics may sometimes suggest that the state ought to have different policies (or that it ought not to have policies at all) about some things people do or the choices they make. Ethics might also suggest that sometimes it is best to let people figure things out on their own by letting them make choices and face the consequences. Sometimes it might be best to allow people to generate, uphold, and revise certain norms in their various groups and associations. Perhaps, in short, it is sometimes best not to have much of a policy about certain things people do.

Perhaps we do not need, and perhaps we should not have, a policy about some things. There may be good reason for government policies to be silent on certain domains of choice. This silence may be an important expression of commitments to various central ethical values.

Consider an example.

Are there public policies about sexual partners and what we do with them? In many senses there are. There are policies that restrict who may be your sexual partner. As an adult, you may not have children as partners. There are public policies that define what it is to be an "adult" and what it means to be a "child." In most jurisdictions, you are forbidden from having nonhuman animals as "partners." But, in Western representative democracies, there are rarely any policies about whom you pick as a partner in the context of a relationship among consenting parties. The only relevant public policies *constrain* our choices. For instance, the partner must be *willing*—and the law defines what "willing" means.

There are many public policies about what you may not do with your partner. Various policies forbid us from nurturing intimacy with partners by engaging together in recreational arson with other people's property. You also may not celebrate your love for your partner by painting a romantic poem on the side of your neighbor's home (at least, not without your neighbor's permission). There are some policies about sexual relations: the sex must be *consensual* (and the law determines what that means). There are even policies determining some things about consensual sex. For instance, it may not happen in certain places, and the sex may not be so loud as to disrupt neighbors' peaceful enjoyment of their homes. Many of these constraints forbid violating other people's rights or imposing undue costs or burdens on them. Within those and similar constraints, when it comes to who is your partner and what you do with him/her and how you do it, you are free to do as you please.

Are there public policies about when, whether, and how you might present flowers to someone? There are informal norms about such matters. We offer flowers to partners to commemorate their being a part of special occasions such as proms, weddings, recitals, or plays. We bring flowers to friends to brighten their days when they grieve for the death of a loved one or when they recover from surgery. Sometimes we simply wish to say that we care about someone by sharing something lovely. These customs and norms are not public policies. To be sure, there are policies that set the background for choices about giving people flowers. There are policies that forbid assaulting people with flowers. There are policies regarding the minimum amount an employee of a florist may be paid and regarding his/her working conditions. There are policies regulating the manufacture, use, and composition of some chemicals that preserve the flowers. There are public policies governing the shipping industry that transports the flowers from the greenhouse to the store. There are policies for taxing the purchase of the flowers, forbidding the sale of certain endangered flowers, and licensing the florist who sells the flowers. There are policies governing the utilities that bring crucial water and electricity to the store for keeping the flowers fresh. There are also laws (all of which are public policies) governing liability and recovery from loss in the event the florist somehow misrepresents the flowers or if the flowers are somehow causally connected to some injury.

Even though all these and many more public policies define the boundaries of permissible conduct regarding the growth, transport, delivery, and sale of flowers, there are no specific policies about when, whether, and how one is to give someone flowers. We welcome some such space of choice, and we welcome the constraints. This space and the policy constraints that define it open opportunities to define our world and our relationships in a mutually acceptable and safe environment. Ethics has a lot to say about how best to shape and describe the space for such choices. This book will offer illustrations by taking specific policies and topics as springboards for reflection.

Ethics and public policy; political philosophy and public policy

Philosophy is invariably concerned with exploring arguments: it considers what are better and worse reasons for particular conclusions and why. Among philosophy's many subfields are those exploring arguments with specifically practical conclusions about what to do, how to think, or how to evaluate. Ethics often focuses on what we as persons may do, what we may not do, and what are better and worse ways of living. Ethics will help with policy disputes by considering how we should assess the competing values from which they arise.

Political philosophy does some of the things ethics does: it explores what to do and think. But political philosophy focuses mainly on political matters—particularly the state. Though theorists dispute the precise tasks and boundaries of political philosophy as a discipline, we might say that, among other things, political philosophy considers the justification of the state, the proper extent of state authority, and how and whether citizens are obligated to do what the state tells them to do. These sorts of issues certainly come up in policy disputes. This book will not insist on rigid boundaries among philosophy's subfields. Though it will not provide a detailed discussion of issues of political philosophy such as when and how a state can impose duties on citizens, these sorts of issues do matter for many policy disputes. If political philosophical themes come up when considering policy possibilities, then we need not turn away from them, especially if understanding them can help sharpen our sense of what is at stake.

The book considers what sorts of ethical presuppositions there are to policy controversies. When questions of the proper extent of state authority come up, as they often do in policy disputes, this book approaches the issue not with an eye to resolving theoretical differences in political philosophy. Instead, it considers arguments regarding what we owe to each other and how we may or must live together. It considers how a grasp of arguments about such issues will help us to formulate clearer and more compelling policy arguments.

Who is the "we" formulating and grasping arguments about policy? The "we" can be anyone who needs to consider the scope, extent, and possibilities for public policy. Policy controversies arise for many of us in different ways. They arise for persons who are active in various policy fields, be they public or otherwise. Researchers for NGOs, planners for multinational corporations, and functionaries for government agencies all face policy challenges. All of them confront *public* policy controversies, though certainly in different ways. Policy controversies also arise for us as thinkers and as citizens. Ethics can help concerned persons by clarifying what is at stake and what moral possibilities and constraints mark the landscape for public policy.

Consider, for instance, how Médecins Sans Frontières (MSF) has various policies for promoting public health, including those for delivering and administering antiretroviral treatment to different areas of the world. MSF policies are not *public* policies, at least as this book understands them. However, which policies MSF has will depend crucially on the actual public policies that are in place. MSF researchers or planners think carefully about which public policies to support when consulted by governments, other NGOs, the media, and advocacy groups. No doubt, they face unique challenges when assessing how to shape policies for their own group. But just like anyone else, they must consider which policies if any to endorse for public entities.

Policy challenges obviously confront policymakers and researchers who work for and consult state agencies. But again, such challenges are not unique to state functionaries. Residents of any representative democracy also have the responsibility and opportunity to determine which state actions to support and which ones to oppose.

Of course, there are many policies whose details might be secret or elusive. There are also more public policies than even the expert can master. Meanwhile, people have their own lives to live. So we cannot and perhaps should not have an informed opinion about many public policies. However, sometimes we must decide how and whether to support the use of state resources and power (including state coercion) for the measures governments take to guide or influence behavior. This is not the unique responsibility of government officials. It is something we confront as voters or as contributors to public discussions. So public policy challenges can arise for many of us. The tools and concepts of ethics can help us to sort through such challenges.

Ethics can help us to frame what we owe to each other as we choose and act in our various roles. Policymakers (public, nongovernmental, or private) must sort out what states can, should, or should not do in shaping or guiding people's behavior. Similar challenges confront any of us when we expect states to justify to us what they do or do not do. Though there is a greal deal of dispute among theorists about what to make of this growing emphasis on "public justification," the general idea seems to be that a state that may claim authority over us must have reasons each of us can accept for what it does or does not do. Considering whether public policies can be supported by such reasons may help us to distill some of the relevant controversies.

Ethical theories and principles can frame policy disputes

Policymakers of any sort, activists, citizens, or other concerned persons often need to assess what the state may or should do to guide people's behavior. Whatever options seem to be (or not to be) available, there are many ways to frame the ethical stakes. Different ethical theories will privilege (or, alternatively, rule out) certain options over others. These different theoretical frameworks matter for understanding what might justify policy or policy reform—including reducing the reach or scope of policy.

This book is not intended to give an exhaustive survey of the theoretical possibilities for rooting policy. It will typically offer a glimpse of some of the different ways to frame people's moral concerns and aspirations. More comprehensive surveys are available elsewhere (such as in Darwall, 2014, or Rachels & Rachels, 2011). Through discussions, we can point to sample compelling ethical theories and principles to illustrate competing understandings of what seems to matter. Different ethical theories can root different *political* moralities, namely, a theory that (among other things) justifies what if anything states may do to guide people's actions. And sometimes different ethical theories can converge on similar political moralities. This may open the door for a possible consensus on policy controversies among persons who seem at first to have different policy positions. Perhaps they share commitments to some ethical views that might support a policy resolution—including one where there is no one policy resolution.

To illustrate some of the variety of ethical considerations available, one class of ethical theories treats morality as a function of the consequences. There are many varieties of such consequentialist theories. When justifying a political morality and its application to particular policy possibilities, a consequentialist theory justifies state action or inaction by appealing to consequences it deems most valuable. Specific consequentialist theories will differ, among other things, according to which consequences they deem valuable and why, whether one should attempt to *maximize* the values the theory upholds, who should apply or implement the theory, whether one should apply the theory to acts or to rules/policies, for whom the relevant consequences matter morally, whether things are justified according to what one expects or what actually happens, what the time frame is for assessing the relevant consequences, and many other factors. So, there is no single consequentialist theory. Even consequentialists who agree on a theory might differ on which policies are morally justified.

Another class of theories might morally privilege the status of a certain class of persons. Such *prioritarian* theories variably target different groups of persons and different features of their status. Some theories, for instance, hold that improving the situation of the least well-off should take priority in a political morality. Different versions of such theories have different accounts of what it means to "improve" and how broadly we should understand the "least well-off." A prioritarian justification for policy might, for instance, say that a policy is justified by addressing the situation of persons in the lowest X percent of some category. Or it might say that a certain group lacks access to certain goods and opportunities needed for a minimally decent life and so must be assisted in some way.

Other theories may hold that equality is a key moral value that should be expressed in political moralities determining policy. Versions of such *egalitarian* theories differ considerably according to, for instance, what is being equalized and how. An egalitarian theory might then justify various policies that aim to reduce or eliminate inequality according to some measure. But the devil is in the details: much depends on the specifics of the theory, especially including for whom something is to be equalized and whether national, class, ethnic, or racial groupings matter.

Another class of theories stresses the significance of treating persons as beings with a dignity worthy of respect because they each have lives of their own to define and live. A political morality arising from such a view might forbid, for instance, using people merely as a means to advancing goals they do not share. These sorts of theories (sometimes called *deontological*) might still differ, for instance, according to what counts as a person and what it means to "share" or endorse an end.

Still another class of theories takes political morality (if not morality itself) as justified by a sort of agreement among free and equal persons. There are again important differences among such *contract* theories, especially including the scope of beings whose agreement supposedly justifies some ethical norm or political institution. Contract approaches also differ according to what if anything limits the agreement.

There are still many other enduring ethical traditions, theories, and principles. This was only a glimpse and nothing near an exhaustive survey of various ethical considerations, principles, and theories. We should also note that these considerations are not necessarily in conflict; they might justify similar policy prescriptions, and a fully spelled out theoretical position might draw on different parts of these and many other considerations. The point here is *not* to offer a selection that might conveniently justify whatever conclusion one wishes to support. It is to help us get a sense of the variety of issues that might be at stake.

This book need not commit to any one specific ethical theory. It also need not commit to any specific political morality. Political moralities vary according to many measures, such as whether and how they endorse principles that justify active roles for the state in regulating an economy or a culture. Some political moralities might hold that among the state's proper tasks is promoting the moral development of the citizenry. Others might maintain that a state ultimately must guarantee certain basic goods for its citizens. And still others would defend the state's responsibility for enabling its citizens to maximize their freedom, however understood. Whatever the specifics and labels we might attach to such positions, the point of this book is not to defend any one of them but to indicate how some appeal to ethics might fruitfully frame policy disputes.

Sometimes this book indicates the reasons for what some might call a sort of conservative view of politics, which tends to prize economic liberty but worries about the impact of unrestricted individual liberty. At other times, the book might allude to a sort of modern liberal view, which notes the drawbacks with stressing economic liberty but nevertheless warns of the perils of discounting individual liberty. And in some chapters, the book considers whether policy progress might be possible were the state to do less or nothing at all in a particular domain. Perhaps this latter view shows some affinities with what some authors call a libertarian view, which upholds among its tenets individual freedom, suspicion of state power, and voluntarism. But the point of the book is not to defend any one particular political morality or to crowd out important alternatives by imposing labels. If policy progress is possible by drawing on considerations some might describe as "liberal," "socialist," "feminist," "libertarian," or any other view for which there are various labels, we need not balk for fear of crossing some ideological or party lines. The point is to explore what resources ethical considerations and reflection might offer for approaching policy disputes.

Addressing policy controversies might not then require resolving theoretical differences. Those differences might rest not on error, bias, or misunderstanding, but stem from reasonable disagreements about fundamental values. This sort of disagreement might be a permanent part of our moral community. Given such differences, people who want to achieve some policy progress can still appeal to some shared values as a reason in favor of some policy possibility. When some values are not shared, people can still offer *reasons* for their views. This process of giving and attending to reasons is part of a process of justifying what we do (or ask others to do) for each other. This is especially important when it comes to *public* policies, since they concern institutions that claim authority over all of us and rest on the coercive powers of state institutions. Surely brute force is not its own justification; we offer and expect reasons for why the state does what it does. Appeals to ethical principles can be one part of that process of achieving policy progress in a way that is mutually acceptable.

Applied ethics vs. public policy

Philosophers continue to have a lively debate about whether and how they should be involved in "applying" ethics. Over the past 50 years or so, applied ethics has seen the growth of increasingly sophisticated literatures on increasingly numerous subfields. There are scholars specializing in business ethics, environmental ethics, journalistic ethics, medical ethics, legal ethics, and the ethics of many other fields. The growth of this part of philosophy has been controversial. Some worry that philosophy becomes pernicious ideology when put in the service of applied ethics. Part of the reason for such worries is that there is no consensus on what the right ethical theory is or whether we even need ethical theories to determine how to make the best choices. There are further continued disputes about whether there is a distinct method of applying ethics and which content is the appropriate one to apply. It may then seem, for instance, that applying ethics to any particular controversy simply begs many important questions and does little more than offer tools for constructing arguments on behalf of some desired conclusions.

Despite this controversy, philosophers have much to offer people with an honest commitment to respecting what ethics suggests or requires of them. Philosophers' stock in trade is the careful argument whose conclusion must resist counterexamples. The philosopher might then help people to avoid mistakes in reasoning and, by encouraging moral imagination, help people to be sensitive to alternative theoretical approaches. This increased openness to alternatives may be a crucial tool in policy discussions.

Ethics can be a tool at least for avoiding mistakes and perhaps for getting closer to better answers to the policy problems we face. When it comes to *public* policy, among the problems are: What, if anything, should the state do? What should the state not do? Ethics here would not merely have us go through a mechanical exercise of avoiding undesired conclusions. Sometimes we desire the wrong things. Ethics can help us to see why. Ethics and the enhanced moral imagination that comes with ethical thinking can help us come to better justified conclusions about the proper scope and content of public policy. The chapters in this book will illustrate how ethics might then fruitfully add to the conversation about policy disputes.

The organization of the book

Many empirical complexities dominate current policy controversies, but no chapter attempts to resolve them. Instead, the discussions treat ethical considerations as a way of framing the disputes. As the book indicates in its discussions of various topics, ethics offers ways of prioritizing some policy alternatives and encourages imagining new ones. It helps us to understand what makes for good reasons in policymaking. Each chapter approaches any given controversy from a perspective that should be accessible to nonexperts. Each chapter explores how we might make some fruitful progress by considering the ethical stakes.

Policy theorists and philosophers sometimes argue that in any controversy ultimately there has to be a policy. This book explores the possibility, however, that sometimes the best policy is no policy. Or, if there is already a policy in place, perhaps the better policy is a different and less ambitious one. Sometimes it may be best to let people figure out what to do without the state setting a policy on the matter, or sometimes people may do best when the state has less of a role in shaping their conduct. But this alternative view requires careful qualification; the chapters in this book explore some of its contours and how and whether the view makes sense for any particular controversy. Sometimes we do indeed need a policy resolution to some controversy. But perhaps sometimes we do not. Indeed, sometimes, part of the reason there is a controversy is because of attempts by policy to resolve some matter of social consequence.

There are countless public policy controversies, and selecting any of them invariably omits crucial others. This book focuses on ten leading controversies, but we must acknowledge that many issues will remain outside its survey. The policies highlighted here are nevertheless windows into enduring significant debates about what if anything a state ought to do to shape people's behavior. Each chapter uses some specific policy as a platform to meditate on what we can and should expect of the states that claim authority over us.

The book selects topics that highlight many dimensions of current policy controversies. Among them are themes in globalization, state coercion, markets, and privacy. These are key issues that arise in many policy dilemmas, and they come up in different ways for each of the issues in the book. And though some controversies might be especially timely, others point to more enduring challenges about what we should expect, demand, and support regarding the states that claim authority over us. In each case, the controversy highlights the challenge of figuring out whether, why, and how the state ought to privilege certain norms for how people may live. What can we support in our various roles and responsibilities? Examining such questions matters for nearly all of us, whether we are policymakers in any capacity, educators, or simply human beings considering what we might legitimately expect of our state.

The chapters are modular; none necessarily requires familiarity with the conclusions of the others. The reader might then rearrange depending upon her interests or needs. However, readers who are especially interested in globalization might focus on the chapters about sweatshops, immigration, and pharmaceuticals. Readers curious about the justification and limits of state coercion might look to nearly any chapter, but such issues come up pointedly in the discussions of torture, restorative justice, and women and the family. Readers looking for some insight into the proper extent and regulation of markets might focus especially on the chapters on sweatshops, human body parts, factory farming of animals, but also the chapters on immigration and pharmaceuticals. If you come to the book first interested in the contours of policies about privacy and the family, consider looking initially at the chapters on same-sex marriage, women and the family, and education and intelligent design.

All the chapters offer narratives to encourage asking what sorts of reasons we have, in the roles we occupy, for supporting, opposing, or shaping public policies as they guide human conduct. Some policies might be better supported by reasons than available alternatives. Sometimes viable alternatives to current policies include a less ambitious policy or none at all.

Further reading

The introduction briefly discusses the idea of "public justification." Public justification typically arises when free persons in a political community have reasons to support state acts. Among the many sources on this rich idea are John Rawls, *Political Liberalism* (Columbia University Press, 2005); T. M. Scanlon, *What We Owe to Each Other* (Harvard, 2000); Jonathan Quong, *Liberalism without Perfection* (Oxford, 2011); and Gerald Gaus, *The Order of Public Reason* (Cambridge, 2012). The introduction also mentions a central theme in the book: perhaps sometimes it is best when the state does not impose a single policy. Among the many writers who consider what role if any the state needs to have for resolving problems facing persons living in a society are Elinor Ostrom, *Governing the Commons: The Evolution of Institutions for Collective Action* (Cambridge, 1990) and the many essays in David Beito *et al.*, eds., *The Voluntary City: Markets, Communities, and Urban Planning* (University of Michigan Press, 2002).

References

Darwall, S. (2014). Theories of Ethics. In A. I. Cohen, & C. H. Wellman (Eds.), *Contemporary Debates in Applied Ethics* (2nd ed., pp. 13–32). Malden, MA: Wiley-Blackwell.

Rachels, J., & Rachels, S. (2011). *The Elements of Moral Philosophy* (7th ed.). New York: McGraw Hill.

1 Sweatshops

The conditions that laborers face in developing countries may seem horrifying. By Western standards, the work is long, grueling, dangerous, and poorly compensated. Many stories document the tragic loss of life and limb by workers, who may include young children toiling long days in garment factories instead of attending school. Striving for maximal profits in a globally competitive environment, employers hire unskilled and desperately poor workers and sometimes disregard safety, rarely offer workers health care, and often fire those who initiate talk about unions. Unfortunately, workers seem to be in no position to negotiate for better conditions.

Exploiting a vulnerable workforce, some employers demand overtime or simply withhold pay. Sometimes they confiscate workers' official documents, effectively denying them the chance to leave. Deaths from devastating fires in factories with blocked or locked exits, crippling injuries from repetitive work, no bathroom breaks—these and other harsh conditions are commonly cited in reportage about "sweatshops," where workers also live in fear of losing their jobs if business conditions change or they are insufficiently productive. Despite all of this, plenty of poor people eagerly take factory jobs that often represent their families' only chance of survival.

Low-cost production plays a crucial role in the developing world's process of turning out an abundant variety of inexpensive goods for Western consumption. But there are many critics of such common global sourcing practices. They ask whether it is fair that Western lifestyles seem to depend on the grueling work of anonymous poor persons abroad. Perhaps, if their challenge is successful, some public policy remedies would be appropriate to improve working conditions in the developing world.

Proponents of sweatshop jobs draw on economic arguments about labor costs, business arguments about comparative advantage, and moral arguments about workers' choices and employers' discretion. Sweatshop labor, they say, is a way out of poverty and a step toward cultural advance. It respects the workers as individuals who can choose how to improve their lives. Critics, however, denounce sweatshop jobs as exploitative. The jobs, they argue, unfairly deny workers their rights or present them with unconscionable choices. On such critics' views, the jobs are but one part of a global economic system where everyone races to the bottom to extract profits no matter what the human toll.

This chapter addresses the background of low-wage labor in the developing world. The first section considers current policies and practices regarding working conditions and surveys some leading candidates for additional measures. The second section discusses some ethical stakes framing the controversy and indicates how the economics of some proposed policy reforms matter. The third section considers policy options and challenges. The fourth section closes by highlighting the potential pitfalls in making moral progress without harming those one most wishes to help. Much hangs on empirical issues, but moral discussion can help to frame the controversy and how one might attempt progress.

Background

What is a sweatshop?

Nowadays, manufacturing features global chains of exchange. Production might originate with factories in the developing world, but—as Jill Esbenshade (Esbenshade, 2004), Luisbeth Sluiter (Sluiter, 2009), and others have noted—distribution and sales are largely the task of multinational corporations that target customers in the first world. The companies "source" their goods in developing economies with low labor costs, where workers have low expectations for job benefits, and where there is little pressure from organized labor. Developing world nations nevertheless welcome this production model as a way to bring needed resources into their countries.

This driving search for the least expensive locations for manufacturing bothers some writers. Critics have described globalized manufacturing as a "race to the bottom" (Tonelson, 2002). Not committed to staying anywhere, multinational enterprises go wherever they find the increasingly lower costs demanded year after year by their buyers or their buyers' agents. Manufacturers, perhaps unduly pressured to comply, face perverse incentives to cut corners on quality or worker safety.

Sources with the lowest costs win contracts. Wages are part of production costs, which are among the most important of overall costs. Manufacturers who keep all costs low are more likely to secure contracts consistently.

Consider, for example, a Chinese garment factory that must compete with factories everywhere for the chance to provide goods to the West.

The lower its wages, and the fewer and cheaper its safety measures, the less it must charge buyers. This sort of global competition seems to have changed the shape and structure of economic progress in poorer countries (Esbenshade, 2004).

Over time, previous waves of industrialization had raised wages and living standards as factory jobs provided workers the money and skills that would build economic and social capital for a resilient civil society. But because much manufacturing in the developing world nowadays is oriented to export, critics question whether the current model of global sourcing similarly fosters lasting economic improvements. Skills acquired by workers and management are sometimes not easily translatable into domestic-targeted production (Hobsbawn, 1999, pp. 39–40).

For the moment, we can set aside moral and economic disputes about the merits of global sourcing. Consider now the employment practices that are and have been controversial. Because of the difficult working conditions and low wages, writers dubbed them "sweatshops." The term evokes images of poorly paid workers toiling for long hours in unsafe conditions. In the 1800s, writers spoke frequently of "sweated labor" employed by "sweaters," who were intermediaries between retail buyers and garment workers. According to the nineteenth-century British writer Charles Kingsley, the sweaters typically ran shops where workers were paid so little and kept in conditions so stark that they were often on the brink of starvation (Kingsley, 1850).

Today the term "sweatshop" is a pejorative to convey working conditions that strike many observers as unfair, degrading, or exploitative. It is nevertheless unclear precisely what "sweatshop" means. Building "exploitation" into a definition of sweatshop risks a tendentious account at the start. Perhaps appealing to legal standards would help? The General Accounting Office of the United States defines sweatshop as "an employer that violates more than one federal or state labor law governing minimum wage and overtime, child labor, industrial homework, occupational safety and health, workers' compensation, or industry registration" (United States General Accounting Office, 1994). For our purposes, however, this definition focuses too much on employers in the United States. The definition is too narrow for another reason. US laws—or the laws of any nation—are not a foolproof indicator of what makes something a sweatshop. Even though factories in developing nations violate no local laws, they might qualify as sweatshops.

For the purposes of this discussion, let us stipulate that a sweatshop is any place of employment where workers labor under some combination of the following: (1) long hours, (2) low wages, (3) few opportunities for alternative employment, (4) workplaces lacking some available safety or comfort conditions, and/or (5) low opportunities for collective bargaining.

Rarely would a sweatshop feature just one of these conditions, but those things people call sweatshops often show all five features in some way. All of these conditions involve some comparative measurements such as "low," "long," "few," or "some." We should then note two points. First, what makes something a sweatshop is significantly a function of departure from some norms. We need not settle here whether those norms can evolve in a way that what is now a sweatshop would not count as one in the nineteenth century. Second, though we can understand what a sweatshop is by comparison with some other workplace environments, the term *sweatshop* may be a function not so much of a comparison as it is of a failure to meet some threshold(s). The thresholds of acceptability might themselves evolve, but they need not. We need not specify what these levels are and what combination of features is sufficient to make for a sweatshop. But this thin sketch should avoid question-begging accounts of the merits of sweatshops while giving us enough to begin analyzing the ethics and policy challenges of sweatshops.

Sweatshop conditions

Concerns about sweatshops are hardly new. Nineteenth- and early twentieth-century writers worried about the conditions for low-wage workers (Bender, 2004). Several notorious incidents galvanized public concern and legal action. Among them was the infamous 1911 Triangle Shirtwaist factory fire, in which 146 garment workers perished when they could not escape through exits managers had locked to prevent theft and unauthorized breaks (von Drehle, 2004). Upton Sinclair's 1906 novel, *The Jungle*, is widely read as reporting abuses in the US meat-packing industry. Among the responses to perceived or actual abuses were legislation to promote unions, minimum wage legislation, overtime regulations, and regulations intended to promote workplace safety.

Moving forward into recent times, the developed world still has its share of workplaces with substandard conditions. Reporters sometimes uncover stories of alarmingly unsafe and low-paying jobs in garment districts (Chin, 2005). Workers sometimes do not merely labor in difficult conditions. They die avoidable deaths. In 1991, for instance, 25 workers in Hamlet, North Carolina, died in a fire in a food-processing plant. Management had locked the fire exits to keep workers from stealing chickens (Tabor, 1991). Other recent publications highlight the alarming persistence of child labor and sex trafficking, which reinforces the vulnerable status of children from the developing world.

While discussions of sweatshops often flag illegal conditions in the developed world, by far most of the press and scholarly debates focus on factories in the developing world. Some of these stories highlight wages or working conditions illegal in the source factory's nation. But the conditions are not always in violation of local laws. Wages and working conditions were the subjects of much controversy about Nike's source factories in the 1990s. (See e.g. Ballinger, 1992, Clancy, 2000.) Sometimes the workers in Indonesian Nike factories had been paid beneath the national minimum wage or allegedly intimidated into asking to be exempt from such regulations (Roberts, 2013). Safety conditions are often the basis for tragic stories. In 2012, 112 workers perished in a fire in the Tazreen Fashion factory in Bangladesh. In 2013, over 1100 persons died in the collapse of the Rana Plaza, a Bangladeshi building that held several garment factories. In China, Foxconn factories employ hundreds of thousands of workers manufacturing electronic goods for sale in the West. The hours are long. Workers sometimes complain of physical problems, and several have attempted suicide. Conditions are sometimes unsafe. For instance, some workers have been hospitalized for exposure to the fumes from a chemical they use to clean iPod screens (Branigan, 2010, Duhigg & Barboza, 2012). Foxconn chose this chemical over alcohol because it evaporates faster and so speeds up production.

Despite the working conditions and low pay, workers eagerly sign up for the jobs. For many workers, the pay seems to be an opportunity to improve their standard of living. Often these jobs are the only options available to avoid a life of starvation or abject poverty.

Intermediaries and oversight challenges

In the early 1990s, Nike faced bad publicity for the conditions in factories manufacturing its products. But, then as now, often a multinational corporation that markets consumer goods does not own the factories that prepare its products. The corporation typically purchases products from suppliers to which they provide manufacturing specifications. Suppliers then find factories that can source their products, or they find other intermediaries who find providers in various locations to manufacture the goods. There are often many layers in a supply chain, and often several independent parties separate a multinational corporation from the manufacture of its goods.

A good example of the intermediaries who are crucial links in current global supply chains is Li & Fung. *The New York Times* details the significance and power of this company (Urbiner & Keith, 2013). Li & Fung connects multinational corporations to companies worldwide. It handles the logistics for many major retailers such as Sears and Kohl's. Its agents have the local knowledge and connections to bargain for the best prices. They also know how to respond to conditions on the ground. They strive to anticipate bad weather, transportation delays, labor unrest, and political instability. Their business model supports working with source companies with a reputation for reliable delivery and compliance with local laws. Li & Fung agents will investigate allegations of noncompliance (such as child labor or blocked fire exits). Because these agents have such extensive local knowledge and represent lucrative possible sales, they have formidable bargaining power. They can often get better prices for manufactured goods than a retailer would if it were to try to negotiate with sources directly.

There are some potential drawbacks with this global sourcing model. One is that oversight depends on Li & Fung's interest in ensuring compliance. Their main interest is to stay in business, which requires that they reliably connect buyers to providers. Some people complain that their drive for maximizing profit and minimizing costs inevitably crimps the company's concern with ensuring compliance with local laws. Plus, the providers they deal with do not want to air their dirty laundry. They want the contract. Critics worry that this encourages a further "race to the bottom." As one labor advocacy leader remarked, "Every extra penny you squeeze from a factory ... is a step closer to that factory cutting the kind of corners that lead to deadly disasters" (Urbiner & Keith, 2013).

In this global sourcing model, multinational enterprises outsource the efficient manufacture and transport of goods. The additional links in the supply chain seem to promote efficiency. But this suggests a second potential problem about transparency. Retailers are insulated from the manufacturing conditions for their products. More precisely: retailers depend on intermediaries to make sure they do not have to answer embarrassing questions about manufacturing conditions. The multinational enterprise does not want any unfavorable news coverage. One way to ensure that this does not happen is for there to be no such conditions. Another way is for the source factories to hide such conditions when they exist.

A third potential problem with this global sourcing model concerns the consumer. Because of all the intermediaries, it is difficult to hold accountable the most visible entity, which is the multinational enterprise selling the goods to consumers. The consumer rarely knows about the manufacturing conditions of the goods she purchases. One example is the market for sandblasted jeans. Workers who manually sandblast jeans sometimes contract fatal forms of silicosis. Now, machines can blast the jeans in conditions that reduce the risk to workers, but this is more expensive for manufacturers. Retailers have pushed for safer conditions for workers, but enforcement is lax and it is difficult for consumers to verify manufacturing conditions (Muller, 2013). Even when consumers do learn of problems in source factories and then demand change, the multinational enterprise that owns the retailer can slough off responsibility to its intermediaries or, perhaps worse, simply direct the sourcing companies to find new factories. The conditions that seem troublesome might then go uncorrected. Some reports suggest this is a feature of Wal-Mart's oversight of its manufacturing conditions. When it learns of poor conditions, it asks for improvements, but it may allow poor conditions to continue for lengthy periods. If the poor conditions persist, it might eventually abandon that manufacturer and switch to another, which may feature similarly poor conditions (Frank 2008, Silverstein 2010).

In reply, apologists for multinational enterprises would likely point to the significance of reputation. A company that is known for selling goods made by people who cannot escape their burning factories might suffer a significant loss, both in terms of tangible sales and intangible public confidence. Moreover, specialized global supply chains can curb tendencies to corruption. The local knowledge that source companies cultivate is an asset. As *The New York Times* reports, Li & Fung will "send undercover informants into factories to check for blocked fire exits, for example, or arrive early for scheduled factory inspections to check for child labor violations" (Urbiner & Keith, 2013). Those companies want to maintain contracts, and their customers—the multinational enterprises—do not want adverse publicity. This provides a very strong incentive to ensure that source factories comply with local laws. Of course, much here hangs on empirical details about which practices minimize treacherous or unfair working conditions. There may yet be room to adjust, through policy, some features of current models of global manufacturing. (We will consider alternative monitoring regimes later, in the third section on policy options.)

What are some of the ethical stakes?

People are working long hours in dangerous conditions for low pay. Why does this matter? Consider some of the ethical stakes that might justify policy reform. This section highlights a few—though not all—of the important moral issues this controversy engages. In this space we cannot give an exhaustive survey of the various positions in the debate and how people cast them, but with some examples we can begin to illustrate how moral consideration might *constrain* policy aspirations.

Welfare

Workers' jobs sometimes jeopardize their *welfare*. This matters because poor persons seem to be suffering on behalf of richer ones. That juxtaposition bothers people. It does not simply make them uncomfortable. It strikes them as unfair.

There is a great deal of debate among philosophers and social scientists over what counts for welfare and how to measure it. There might be no consensus definition. On most common accounts, however, being free of disease, getting enough calories to survive, and remaining alive with one's limbs intact seem to be important parts of any reasonable notion of welfare.

Before considering possible policy remedies, however, there are reasons to pause and note the welfare *benefits* of sweatshops. Sweatshops are often a device to improve workers' welfare. Workers choose these jobs because they see them as a way to improve their lives. And often (though not always) the jobs do just that: they give workers the wages that are crucial for escaping desperate poverty. With such jobs, workers can acquire the capital and skills to run their own businesses and send their children to school (Read, 2010). Those wages give them opportunities they would not have had otherwise. This is not to deny that some employers abuse their employees, or that some do not pay promised wages, or that some employ children for long hours. It is to say that sweatshops can and often do benefit workers.

The welfare benefits that workers receive take two forms. One is that workers are earning wages, which can help them to save money and reach for a better life. Another is that the workers are getting what they want. This second sort of benefit is a bit more abstract and requires supposing that the satisfaction of preferences can in itself count as a sort of benefit. Critics will point out, though, that sometimes preference satisfaction is not a benefit. It depends on what one's preferences are. Sometimes people prefer things that are bad for them, either because of weak will or poor knowledge. Perhaps then there should be policy remedies to counter the poor choices workers might make when taking unsafe jobs.

The difficulty with exploring policy remedies for poor choices is that it supposes policymakers know which choices are poor. Now, sometimes policymakers in the developed world purport to act on such knowledge. They impose "sin" taxes on goods or activities that they think are bad, such as gambling or cigarettes. They require people to save for retirement. But are such policies warranted for the poorest persons abroad?

We must ask who is best in a position to decide what is best for a worker in the developing world. From the standpoint of policy, allowing people to make their own choices allows them to do what they believe is best. In employment as in other exchanges, the parties choose based on their anticipated benefits. The exchanges are part of what some writers call a "discovery process" of what works and what does not. Knowledge of what works continually develops, and there may be multiple answers. One of the important processes for discovering what works is trade. The choices trade offers, and the experimentation and mutual adjustment that occur over time, allow people to explore alternative tradeoffs based on what they believe is in their best interests. (See e.g. Powell & Zwolinski, 2012.) What works for some persons and communities might not work for others.

Of course, saying that policymakers are fallible and should not short-circuit fruitful local institutions is not the same as saying they should make no policies at all. There may yet be room, for example, for policies to prevent or remedy clear injustices (such as worker coercion). Here too caution seems appropriate. Conditions that strike developed world readers as grueling do not obviously amount to such injustices. And when workers eagerly seek out the opportunities, we must ask whether policy should constrain the available options.

Policy remedies imposed by the developed world risk raising costs in a way that harms the workers they intend to help. Policy remedies might unintentionally increase labor or production costs and so make manufacturing more expensive overall. The South Asian ship disassembly industry is an example. Breaking retired ships into pieces for scrap involves numerous safety hazards. The yards in Alang, India, and else-where, can do this at low cost. But it could also be done in the West in conditions that are much safer for much higher paid workers. The Western process, however, is vastly more expensive (Langewiesche, 2000). Policymakers could insist that the West take care of its own trash in safer conditions, but such a requirement would deny Indian workers the jobs they might otherwise get and so undermine the economy local ship disassemblers might otherwise sustain. Any policy that sets conditions on production can raise costs, and when costs go up, there is the danger that fewer workers will have jobs. When they do not have jobs, they are denied opportunities to improve themselves by earning wages.

Some Westerners might object that such wages and conditions are morally problematic. But we need to consider what the workers' alter-natives are. Their alternatives are often far worse than sweatshop labor. Often they must choose between sweatshop jobs and subsistence agriculture, where the income is less secure and the hours even more grueling (Norberg, 2003). As Benjamin Powell (Powell, 2014) observes, typically workers overwhelmingly prefer these sweatshop jobs, and they often prefer to take their compensation as wages rather than as safety or other benefits. (See also Powell & Zwolinski, 2012.) Indeed, sweatshop wages are typically above the World Bank's US$2/day median poverty line for developing countries, and they are often much higher than wages available elsewhere (World Bank 2012; Powell, 2006). When well-meaning policymakers require certain production conditions in the developing world, they risk increasing costs, which could come at the expense of workers' jobs. Those jobs are crucial for enhancing workers' welfare—and that of their families and communities.

To be clear, this is not an argument against imposing such production restrictions or conditions. It is a cautionary note. Much hangs on empirical details. If policies can be designed to encourage better conditions abroad without jeopardizing jobs, then there may be a reason to consider those in light of other moral concerns.

Appeals to welfare do not resolve the controversy over sweatshops. They help to frame it. Complicating matters is that appeals to welfare do not simply come in one variety. Some such approaches defend as morally required minimizing the number of persons in desperate poverty. Others defend a moral view that gives priority to certain minimal working conditions (including wages), even if this might mean fewer jobs overall. Still others may say that whatever produces the greatest welfare for all (or for compatriots in the developed world) is morally best. Sometimes these sorts of views may converge on a particular policy recommendation. Sometimes they will not. But understanding whose and what sort of welfare is at stake might help clarify some of what matters in disputes about sweatshops.

Dignity and basic humanity

Sweatshop workers may choose to take jobs with wages and conditions that some residents in the developed world find unconscionable. It might seem exploitative to take advantage of these workers' vulnerable position. This arrangement might even disrespect their dignity. As some labor activists assert, "Labor is not a commodity." Taking advantage of desperately poor workers may seem to deny their humanity and treat them merely as a means.

Those who defend sweatshop arrangements might argue that low wages can be an improvement for workers. They insist that mutual agreement means there is no exploitation. But critics find this defense unpersuasive. They deny that workers' consent eliminates worries about mistreatment. (See e.g. Arnold and Bowie 2003; Meyers 2004, Carson, 2013.)

One way of understanding the heart of this challenge turns on the possibility of wrongfully benefiting someone. Chris Meyers (Meyers, 2004) and others have argued that sweatshop jobs give workers an unfair choice. Prospective workers must either continue to endure their gloomy status quo (such as subsistence farming), or they can take jobs in the difficult conditions sweatshops offer. This might seem an *unconscionable* offer that no one should be in a position to make.

Imagine, for instance, a terrible storm destroyed sailor Sam's boat, leaving Sam clinging to some floating wreckage for days. Pat spots the wreckage and comes to investigate. On discovering Sam, Pat makes the following offer: "I will rescue you if you agree to ... " What Pat then proposes is something that strikes us as unconscionable. Perhaps Pat offers rescue conditional on sexual servitude, or signing over vast sums of money, or some other costly choice. If Sam agrees, some might say both parties to the exchange are better off. Sam, in particular, chooses something over death. Critics will argue, however, that Sam should not have to make such a choice. Pat's offer might strike those critics as unfair.

Chris Meyers and others criticize these and similar offers as soliciting a form of "forced consent" (Meyers, 2004, pp. 325–8). Pat's offer *wrongs* Sam, who simply needs rescue. Pat's offer victimizes Sam; it exploits someone's vulnerable position.

There is much dispute about what exploitation means. Some authors understand the term by appealing to unequal bargaining positions. Others speak of any case where someone profits excessively from another's need. Some respond by narrowing the notion to focus on treating someone *merely* as a means. Among many of these and other views is often a general idea: it is exploitation when one person turns another into a victim by wrongly profiting from desperate vulnerability.

When people object to exploitation, they often appeal to the idea that human beings are not things to be manipulated. Each of us has a dignity that forbids such treatment. Different views might vary on what dignity means, and what it means to profit wrongly, what it is to treat someone merely as a means, and what desperate vulnerability is. While ethicists work through the theoretical details, perhaps public policies ought to acknowledge and institutionalize an entirely plausible view that forbids inappropriate profit from desperation.

As it turns out there are various laws that do forbid offers such as Pat's on the high seas. More precisely, the offers are not enforceable (Parent, 2010). We might take that as a cue to say that some offers are such an affront to decency and express such disrespect for humanity that they must be forbidden by the laws of all nations. Without passing judgment on the merits or nuances of the unconscionability doctrine, here we need only consider whether the analogy of sweatshops to rescue is apt.

There is a problem with the analogy as a basis for formulating policy. Easy rescue of drowning persons is a one-off event in which any decent person would unhesitatingly provide the rescue. When conditions are chronic, however, things change. Among the things that change is the moral logic. In the case of the desperately poor abroad, helping them is neither a one-off event nor is it an easily improved situation.

The developing world's poor may be desperately eager for work. But such desperation is not an emergency. It is a terribly unfortunate chronic condition. As a chronic condition, individual and policy responses call for careful reflection about how best to improve things. This is different from an emergency. In emergencies, decent persons provide easy rescue without giving it much thought. Chronic problems, however, call for plenty of thought, especially about the danger that some policies might slow the process of improvement or derail it altogether (Cohen, 2014).

Multinational corporations sourcing their goods abroad are more like businesses specializing in salvage and rescue rather than random boaters happening to find needy persons adrift (Powell & Zwolinski, 2012, p. 467). Providing such rescue services costs resources. Allowing the providers to make money helps them to afford to devote the resources to providing this valuable service. Allowing profit in such circumstances is also important because of what it does *not* do. It does not stop people from making exchanges they both find acceptable, and it does not discourage potential rescuers from pursuing rescues. These rescues save lives.

Of course, it is one thing to say that people should be allowed to make some money. It is another to allow them to make the most money from people who are desperate to exchange with them. Perhaps then there should be policies that provide certain limits on the terms of such exchanges. This may allow for wage floors and/or caps on high-end compensation. The upshot might then be that no one has to endure unconscionable working conditions.

One challenge is arranging policies—or more precisely, *not* enacting policy barriers—so that people can come to mutually beneficial agreements. Return again to the case of rescue on the high seas. Surely we do not want policies to discourage rescue services from being available in the first place, otherwise, people needing rescue will die. But more basically, we can all agree that if possible, institutions and policies should minimize the number of people needing rescue in the first place.

In the case of developing world workers, we should be alert for trade-offs when policies hoping to reduce what some call exploitation might prevent welfare gains to workers. When policies increase costs of doing business in another country, multinational enterprises may take their business elsewhere or simply not create the business in the first place. If there is much chance policies might help the situation of the least well off, people would and should seize on it. But people first need to reflect on how and whether ethics might constrain a vision of how to help. Is this an issue of maximizing the number of least well off whose situation might improve? Is it instead a matter of guaranteeing as best as possible that more people enjoy some minimal threshold of working conditions? Perhaps ethical principles will commend protecting the opportunities to contract for all parties, including the employers? And there are many other ethical considerations that might give priority to some policy possibilities over others.

One part of the challenge of fashioning policies where many people are destitute is not obstructing the value-creating choices people might make. When people may make exchanges that leave them all better off, they can advance welfare over where they started. For those concerned with the dignity of workers, some might argue that allowing people to choose how to improve themselves respects and promotes their dignity by allowing them the opportunity to define and live lives of their own. And they might also point to previous seeming success stories where under-developed nations grew their economies and the wealth of the poor through manufacturing oriented to export. This might be the start of an argument that policymakers should be leery of unintended consequences that might have ethical as well as economic costs.

This hardly settles the matter. As critics of sweatshops might note, carefully designed policies might promote growth while abiding by important ethical concerns. For instance, perhaps import restrictions in developed countries might require improved conditions in poorer countries' source factories. A requirement that there be certain wage floors in poor countries, for instance, might provide some persons a higher wage than they might otherwise receive. No doubt, regulators and activists might then point to such persons as success stories. But, as critics of wage floors might say, we could not then point to the many persons whose jobs were not created because of the corresponding increased production costs. These never-created jobs are invisible, and so is the resulting continued desperate poverty of the persons who never got those jobs.

Social scientists dispute what sort of effect regulatory wage floors have in labor marketplaces. It is difficult to measure in domestic circumstances and even harder to determine globally. There is a risk, however, that imposing conditions on manufacturing abroad may cause unemployment there or otherwise stifle the creation of jobs. Given that the people whose jobs are at stake are often among the poorest persons anywhere, any policy attempting to improve their situation should be careful not to prevent the gains that might help them most, namely, acquiring the means to feed themselves and their families.

Complicity in injustice

We might say that sweatshop workers and their employers freely and voluntarily agree to an employer/employee relationship. Sweatshop workers take jobs at low pay and in unsafe conditions because they are better than the available alternatives. But why are their alternatives so bleak? This is of special concern for prospective workers whose alternatives seem to be a bare subsistence (if even that) or, as might be common for females, a life of prostitution.

Consent is often taken to change the normative situation. What was once impermissible can change because of an agreement of some sort.

(Sexual contact is one example.) But now, defenses of voluntary transactions among consenting adults might take us only so far. In the case of sweat-shop jobs, some of those consenting adults are *desperate* to consent. This is a potential serious problem for the legitimacy of any supposed consent. Sometimes the reason for desperation may be partly because of something a prospective trading partner has done.

Suppose that A offers B an exchange that B finds appealing. But suppose it is the only one available to B because A had credibly threatened all others with bodily harm should they attempt to exchange with B. Alternatively, suppose that A had bribed public officials to enact policies that restrict sellers' licenses to everyone but A. In such cases, A should not be able to profit from wrongdoing. Public policies can stop that, but not necessarily with anything new or special. They can prevent, not encourage, or punish the initial injustices that made the exchange possible.

Things become murkier when someone enters a market and benefits from the questionable acts of others. May someone benefit from policies that only afford individuals from his or her ethnic group the opportunities to engage in some business? Some writers suggest that a person may take part in systems providing such illegitimate benefits on the condition that she opposes the policies that provide them. What it means to "oppose" is difficult to disentangle. Indeed, opposition is not always easy. Sometimes dissent from dominant norms risks violent pushback. Much hangs on the debates of social and political philosophers regarding a person's responsibility to forswear injustice. (See a related discussion about whites' complicity in slavery and its legacy in Boxill, 2010.) It may be tempting to structure policy to prevent particular actors from benefiting from injustice—whether or not they support the perverse norms.

In the case of low-wage labor abroad, multinational firms benefit from a variety of policies, and sometimes not entirely innocently. Many developing countries are deficient in rule of law, distribute various benefits by arbitrary political privilege, or restrict people's opportunities to start their own businesses. Sometimes, as Thomas Pogge argues (Pogge, 2008), the developed world is complicit in the wholesale subjugation of peoples. The West avoidably supports an unjust global order in which kleptocratic leaders in the developing world enrich themselves with Western support at the expense of their disempowered and desperately poor residents. Policy remedies may seem appropriate to restrict how and whether multinational firms may benefit from the low-wage labor these conditions encourage.

One way policy can bring about improvements is by not facilitating unjust subjugation. For instance, until recently it was common for developed nations to offer tax benefits for the costs a company incurs in bribing foreign public officials. An international convention in 1997 restricted bribery. The convention calls for prosecution of persons who are involved in corrupt dealings abroad. Unfortunately, enforcement and supporting policies have been inconsistent. (See the various documents in Organisation for Economic Co-operation and Development, n.d.)

Should policy go further and discourage sourcing in countries that do not meet certain minimum wage or working conditions? As indicated earlier, it can be difficult to know whether this will avoid jeopardizing the welfare of workers one intends to help. But one avenue that might be available is to stop policies that facilitate the conditions that unjustly disadvantage workers abroad. Besides eliminating the tax deduction for bribery, policymakers in the West can reconsider both the privileged trading status some oppressive countries enjoy, as well as their eligibility to purchase military and police supplies. Of course, specifying what counts as "oppressive" is quite contentious. We need not resolve that here. (But see, for instance, Wenar, forthcoming.) We might nevertheless at least be in some position to make improvements by removing impediments to progress.

None of this is to deny the challenges and complexities of policy reform. Sometimes the norms in the developed world are importantly unlike norms elsewhere. In some cases, for instance, bribery does not smack of corruption so much as an ordinary way of doing business (Loughman & Sibery, 2012, ch. 10). Sometimes, the only way to do business is to break the laws of host and origin countries. Matt Zwolinski and Ben Powell defend some such lawbreaking if it benefits the least well off. They further argue that when sweatshops offer workers some gain over their current situation, it is deeply problematic to use policy to restrict such offers (Powell & Zwolinski, 2012, pp. 461–3, 468). Sweatshops, they argue, can provide mutually beneficial arrangements for workers and the consumers who purchase the products they manufacture.

Some policy options

The previous sections discussed some of the ethical considerations at stake and how policy intended to improve the condition of workers in the developing world may, if poorly designed, risk setting back some workers' interests. Perhaps there is room for altering policies in some fruitful way? Those policies would need to be designed with an eye on not deepening the desperation of sweatshop workers, not propping up oppressive leaders, and not encouraging Western firms to be complicit in the subjugation of workers who have no political voice and few economic alternatives.

Framing policy options

Some defenders of sweatshops appeal to prospective gains in opportunities for the poorest workers. They might warn that measures intended to raise the lowest wages will reduce the number of available jobs. They may also offer moral arguments that appeal to the freedoms of workers and employers. Critics may say that the difference in wages between the highest and lowest paid workers (or in standards of living between the richest and poorest peoples) is morally problematic. They may defend some policies that require minimum working conditions even if they raise prices. They may argue that dignity, which should have no price, requires making some minimum available for everyone with whom one interacts.

Much will depend on what works, and what works may vary from one circumstance to another. Certainly much then depends on empirical issues. But framing the issues are background commitments to moral principles, which constrain the available options and mark out certain options as salient possibilities. The biggest concerns are not with advancing the wealth of multinational enterprises. The main concerns are with the situation of the poorest workers abroad.

There may very well be objectionable exploitation at work in providing sweatshop jobs. But we must ask whether making such jobs available is better than doing nothing at all (given the alternatives), or whether making some better jobs available is better than more with worse conditions. Things might not be so easy. If a public policy were to require that goods from abroad must be manufactured with certain minimum working conditions, the jobs might not materialize at all. But this is not an argument against policy regulation. It is an alert that policies should not undercut the goals many of us share, which is to allow improvements for the worst off.

Trade agreements and trade sanctions

Among the tools available to policymakers are trade agreements. For instance, Cambodia gained greater access to US apparel markets when in the late 1990s it agreed to ensure better working conditions and better protections for labor rights in domestic factories. Monitoring by NGOs such as the International Labour Organization helps to make sure conditions exceed certain minimum thresholds. The apparel industry is among the leading employers in Cambodia. While many industry observers praise Cambodia as a model for improvement, others complain that conditions have stagnated. (See, for instance, Silverstein, 2010; and O'Keefe, 2013.)

It may be possible that policy levers available to officials overseeing trade might inspire lasting improvements in industries. Sometimes they seem to bring about concrete changes. The US Dog and Cat Protection Act of 2000 forbids the use of dog and cat pelts in products sold in the United States. The act provided steep fines for selling such products (Dog and Cat Protection Act of 2000). Why not then use policies to inspire improvement not just for critters but for human beings?

The problem here again is that the policies may hurt the people they are intended to help. Much hangs on the findings of social scientists who investigate the impact of regulatory regimes. If they find that some policies can improve the lives of workers without jeopardizing their chances for employment, this may be the start of an argument in favor of considering such changes. However, there are reasons to be leery: some preliminary findings about Indonesia, for instance, suggest that raising the minimum wage there adversely impacted overall employment (Harrison & Scorse, 2010, p. 263). Here, as elsewhere, causes are difficult to diagnose, and in the Indonesian case, the problem might not be with raising the minimum wage but with raising it too quickly.

Much still hangs on what sort of policy improvements are morally permissible (if not required). Flagging how different moral views commend different sorts of improvements might help people to understand the heart of their dispute. It may also help them to see that they have less disagreement than they seem to at first.

As Powell and Zwolinski note, there are many opportunities for reform that do not demand additional public policies. "A filtering process that allows reforms to take place where they help workers but does not mandate them where they do not is necessary to find out what can work and what would unemploy workers. The market's competitive process is precisely that filter" (Powell & Zwolinski, 2012, p. 459). Powell and Zwolinski here defend sweatshops partly by claiming that a relatively unrestricted market is the best way to find out what will help workers. They seem to believe that establishing one policy for all cases crimps the experimentation that might discover ways to improve conditions. And they seem to worry that imposing minimum working conditions will cause unemployment. Each of these is an empirical claim and can be tested. Public policy options may yet be available to achieve gains for workers better than an unrestricted market. Much now hangs on which approach seems better tuned to bring about those welfare improvements. There may even be room for experimentation among different policy regimes to see which might help the worst-off workers.

Monitoring

Talk of allowing people to discover what is effective may strike some critics as inappropriate when, in some cases, we know very well what should be ruled out: slave labor. In some cases, workers are forced to work at the point of a gun or threatened with beatings should they not perform up to employers' expectations. Critics correctly note that such practices are unjust and should be forbidden by policy. They should be forbidden even if somehow they produce welfare gains for the workers themselves.

Developing nations do not have laws that permit worker coercion, but public authorities sometimes quietly tolerate such practices. The challenge is whether the developed world's public policies might take steps to curtail such practices. Some policies, the argument might go, need to be in place to be sure that some basic human rights are respected.

Scholarship on various forms of monitoring shows the inconsistency of monitoring companies and practices. Some monitoring is public (by various governments); private firms provide other monitoring services. As indicated earlier, multinational firms often expect their intermediaries to handle monitoring. There are monitoring firms that cater to various industries' needs for oversight. The journalism and scholarship on this unsurprisingly show that you get what you pay for. If companies want the stamp of compliance, they can hire someone to provide it. If they want more reliable oversight, that will cost more money. (See e.g. Silverstein, 2010; Frank, 2008; and Clifford & Greenhouse, 2013.) Some audits are superficial checking of boxes on forms. There are cases where employees are primed to respond to questions in certain ways. But other cases involve surprise inspections and preemptive monitoring.

There may yet be room for experimentation with different forms of monitoring, both to ensure compliance with basic human rights and perhaps to improve workers' conditions. In Brazil, for instance, there had been difficulties with securing economic growth while ensuring compliance with local laws and human rights norms. Inspectors who wielded both carrots and sticks were able to achieve lasting compliance and seeming improvements. Government regulators and private industry experimented with how to enforce safety requirements without damaging employment prospects. They discovered that promoting workers' consortia minimized costs for employers and provided workers more reliable employment (Pires, 2008). The particular blend of market measures and regulatory oversight that works in one circumstance might not work in another. When a developed world nation imposes one policy on all trading partners, it risks cutting off that discovery process. Of course, it may seem there are cases where there is nothing to discover, such as the impermissibility of enslavement. This turns on what monitoring can uncover, but it is hardly clear that one policy is best for uncovering such abuses. When they are uncovered, there is room for thoughtful policy restrictions regarding conditions abroad.

Closing thoughts

Sweatshop conditions alarm many persons who appreciate what makes possible the inexpensive abundance they enjoy. People sit in Western cafes sipping high-priced coffee beverages while workers far away harvest the beans for a miniscule fraction of the costs of that coffee. Helping distant workers in such circumstances is no easy matter. What might help them least of all is to close off their opportunities to work at the jobs that provide such consumer goods.

Of course, public policy is not the only way to achieve progress. Plenty of grassroots organizations work tirelessly to improve conditions abroad and raise awareness in developed nations. There is the risk that their activism may also have unintended consequences, but their work does highlight the challenges of figuring out how to improve workers' conditions.

It is sometimes not clear what to do to help them. This uncertainty is not unique to sweatshops. It is common to many cases of chronic need. Figuring out what works is partly a discovery process whose results are not final. While people experiment with what works and what does not, perhaps workers in the developing world should have the opportunity to improve themselves by taking the jobs that are available to them.

Before considering policy options, appreciating what is at stake ethically can frame which options are live possibilities. People can reflect on which should take precedence: respecting the rights of corporations to maximize profit and determine how much to pay for the goods they source abroad, or respecting the desperate poor's access to jobs with certain minimal conditions, or advancing the opportunities for the poor overall, or guaranteeing the lowest prices the market will bear for Western consumers, or allowing the poor to act on what they take to be their best interests. Sometimes these and other ethical concerns will be in tension and so uphold obstructive conclusions. But sometimes they will not. Sorting through competing arguments about the merits of such considerations will show that they must sometimes clash. Working out the meaning and justification of such and other considerations will help to frame the controversy.

Public policy may yet increase opportunities for minimally acceptable working conditions. Empirical investigation is needed to sort out what might work in any given circumstance. Clarifying the ethical principles rooting views about sweatshops might help make explicit what is at stake and push disputants to focus on fundamentals.

Further reading

The literature on sweatshops is vast and often deeply unsettling. Among pieces more accessible to lay readers is Kelsey Timmerman's *Where Am I*

Wearing? (John Wiley & Sons, 2012), in which the journalist/author explores the sources of his clothing and finds out a little bit, on the ground, about what works and what does not. Virginia Sole-Smith explores the dangerous, low-paying, and unstable work involved in the Mexican squid harvest industry in "Mexico's Squid Sweatshops," from the May, 2010 issue of the *Progressive*. Among some surveys of monitoring are some findings that are not especially flattering for Wal-Mart source factories. See, for instance, Andy Kroll's "Are Walmart's Chinese Factories as Bad as Apple's?" in the March/April, 2012 issue of *Mother Jones*. A discussion of early-twentieth-century working conditions and the changing cultural norms about work, activism, and class is available in Nan Enstad's *Ladies of Labor, Girls of Adventure: Working Women, Popular Culture, and Labor Politics at the Turn of the Twentieth Century* (Columbia University Press, 1999). This chapter only touched briefly on the challenges of child labor. One working paper that highlights the challenges of policymaking in this controversial area is Eric V. Edmonds' "Child Labor: IZA Discussion Papers, No. 2606," available at http://nbn-resolving.de/urn:nbn:de:101:1–20080422146.

References

Arnold, D. G., & Bowie, N. E. (2003). Sweatshops and respect for persons. *Business Ethics Quarterly, 13*(2), 221–42.

Ballinger, J. (1992, August). The new free-trade heel. *Harper's*, 46–7.

Bender, D. E. (2004). *Sweated work, weak bodies: Anti-sweatshop campaigns and languages of labor*. New Brunswick, NJ: Rutgers University Press.

Boxill, B. (2010, December 14). *Black reparations*. E. N. Zalta (Ed.) *Stanford Encyclopedia of Philosophy*. Retrieved September 9, 2013, from http://plato.stanford.edu/entries/black-reparations/

Branigan, T. (2010, May 7). Chinese workers link sickness to n-hexane and Apple iPhone screens. *The Guardian*. Retrieved August 28, 2013, from www.theguardian.com/world/2010/may/07/chinese-workers-sickness-hexane-apple-iphone

Carson, T. L. (2013). Free exchange for mutual benefit: Sweatshops and Maitland's "classical liberal standard". *Journal of Business Ethics, 112*, 127–35.

Chin, M. (2005). *Sewing women*. New York: Columbia University Press.

Clancy, M. (2000). *Sweating the swoosh: Nike, the globalization of sneakers, and the question of sweatshop labor*. Washington, D.C.: Institute for the Study of Diplomacy, School of Foreign Service, Georgetown University.

Clifford, S., & Greenhouse, S. (2013, September 2). Fast and flawed inspections of factories abroad. *The New York Times*, A1. Retrieved September 9, 2013, from www.nytimes.com/2013/09/02/business/global/superficial-visits-and-trickery-undermine-foreign-factory-inspections.html?pagewanted=all

Cohen, A. I. (2014). Famine relief and human virtue. In A. I. Cohen, & C. H. Wellman (Eds.), *Contemporary debates in applied ethics* (2nd ed., pp. 431–46). Malden, MA: Wiley Blackwell.

Dog and Cat Protection Act of 2000, Public Law 106–476, 114 Stat. 2101, codified at 19 U.S.C. 1308. Retrieved September 9, 2013, from www.nlcnet. org/admin/documents/files/Dog_and_Cat_Act.pdf

Duhigg, C., & Barboza, D. (2012, January 25). In China, human costs are built into an iPad. *The New York Times.* Retrieved 28 August, 2013, from www.nytimes.com/2012/01/26/business/ieconomy-apples-ipad-and-the-human-costs-for-workers-in-china.html?pagewanted=all&_r=0

Esbenshade, J. (2004). *Monitoring sweatshops.* Philadelphia: Temple University Press.

Frank, T. (2008, April). Confessions of a sweatshop inspector. *Washington Monthly, 40*(4), 34–7.

Harrison, A., & Scorse, J. (2010). Multinationals and anti-sweatshop activism. *The American Economic Review, 100*(1), 247–73.

Hobsbawn, E. (1999). *Industry and empire.* New York: The New Press.

Kingsley, C. (1850). *Cheap clothes and nasty.* London: W. Pickering.

Langewiesche, W. (2000, August). The shipbreakers. *The Atlantic Monthly*, 31–49.

Loughman, B. P., & Sibery, R. A. (2012). *Bribery and corruption: Navigating the global risks.* Hoboken, NJ: Wiley.

Meyers, C. (2004). Wrongful beneficence: Exploitation and third world sweatshops. *Journal of Social Philosophy, 35*(3), 319–33.

Muller, D. (2013). *Breathless for blue jeans.* London: Clean Clothes Campaign. Retrieved August 30, 2013, from www.waronwant.org/attachments/Breathless %20for%20Blue%20Jeans,%202013.pdf

Norberg, J. (2003). *In defense of global capitalism.* Washington, D.C.: Cato Institute.

O'Keefe, K. (2013, July 5). Cambodia falls short as garment-industry model. *Wall Street Journal*, A9. Retrieved September 9, 2013, from http://online.wsj. com/article/SB10001424127887324423904578521240151597504.html

Organisation for Economic Co-operation and Development. (n.d.). *Bribery in International Business.* Retrieved September 9, 2013, from www.oecd.org/daf/ anti-bribery/oecdantibriberyconvention.htm

Parent, J. (2010). No duty to save lives, no reward for rescue: Is that truly the current state of international salvage law? *Annual Survey of International & Comparative Law, 12*(1), 87–139.

Pires, R. (2008). Promoting sustainable compliance: Styles of labour inspection and compliance outcomes in Brazil. *International Labour Review, 147*(2–3), 199–229.

Pogge, T. (2008). *World poverty and human rights* (2nd ed.). Malden, MA: Polity.

Powell, B. (2006). Sweatshops and third world living standards: Are the jobs worth the sweat? *Journal of Labor Research, 27*(2), 263–74.

Powell, B. (2014). *Out of poverty: Sweatshops in the global economy.* Cambridge: Cambridge University Press.

Powell, B., & Zwolinski, M. (2012). The ethical and economic case against sweatshop labor: A critical assessment. *Journal of Business Ethics, 107*, 449–72.

Read, R. (2010, March 6). Chinese factory workers cash in sweat for prosperity. *The Oregonian*. Retrieved August 30, 2013, from www.oregonlive.com/business/index.ssf/2010/03/chinese_factory_workers_cash_i.html

Roberts, G. (2013, January 15). *Nike workers claim military paid to intimidate them.* Retrieved August 28, 2013, from ABC (Australia) News: www.abc.net.au/news/2013-01-15/nike-accused-of-using-military-to-intimidate-factory-workers/4465058

Silverstein, K. (2010, January). Shopping for sweat. *Harper's*. Retrieved 30 August, 2013, from http://harpers.org/archive/2010/01/shopping-for-sweat/?single=1

Sluiter, L. (2009). *Clean clothes: A global movement to end sweatshops*. New York: Pluto Press.

Tabor, M. B. (1991, September 6). Poultry plant fire churns emotions over job both hated and appreciated. *The New York Times*. Retrieved August 28, 2013, from www.nytimes.com/1991/09/06/us/poultry-plant-fire-churns-emotions-over-job-both-hated-and-appreciated.html?pagewanted=all&src=pm

Tonelson, A. (2002). *The race to the bottom: Why a worldwide worker surplus and uncontrolled free trade are sinking American living standards*. New York: Basic Books.

United States General Accounting Office (1994). *Efforts to address the prevalence and conditions of sweatshops*. Washington, D.C.: United States General Accounting Office. Retrieved August 28, 2013, from www.gao.gov/assets/230/220498.pdf?.

Urbiner, I., & Keith, B. (2013, August 8). Linking factories to the malls, middleman pushes low costs. *The New York Times*, A1. Retrieved August 29, 2013, from www.nytimes.com/2013/08/08/world/linking-factories-to-the-malls-middleman-pushes-low-costs.html?hp&_r=0&pagewanted=all

von Drehle, D. (2004). *Triangle: The fire that changed America*. New York: Atlantic Monthly Press.

Wenar, L. (forthcoming). *Clean trade*.

World Bank. (2012, February 16). *Poverty & equality data FAQs*. Retrieved September 2, 2013, from http://web.worldbank.org/WBSITE/EXTERNAL/TOPICS/EXTPOVERTY/0,contentMDK:23012899~pagePK:210058~piPK:210062~theSitePK:336992,00.html

Zwolinski, M. (2012). Structural exploitation. *Social Philosophy & Policy, 29*(1), 154–79.

2 Pharmaceuticals and the developing world

Each year, tens of millions of people die from all kinds of causes. Some, mainly in the developed world, die simply because their bodies wear out from old age. In the developing world, however, many deaths are tragically premature because they are so easily preventable—at least according to Western observers. Economic, political, and logistical considerations conspire to keep medicines, treatments, and preventative measures out of the hands of the people who need them.

Critics worry that a significant portion of the world's poor have little or no access to the essential medicines that can help them fight or prevent disease. Many of these persons are vulnerable to diseases that seem easily preventable or treatable. But the health of many other persons is avoidably in jeopardy—though it is harder to see these individuals. That is because such persons face health challenges for which there might be cures, treatments, or preventions, if only the right medicines existed. Those medicines *might* exist if pharmaceutical innovators had the right incentives. But those medicines do not yet exist, and so people might be suffering needlessly.

The patent system gives some protections and incentives for pharmaceutical companies to do the hard work to create and distribute essential medicines. Many critics, however, believe current institutions for defining and protecting property in pharmaceuticals disadvantage the neediest persons. Patents, for instance, permit pricing products out of the reach of the poorest. Patents might also protect stagnant manufacturers who can claim state protection for their monopolies.

Pharmaceuticals are but one of the resources that determine opportunities for health. Among the many other crucial factors are: availability and training of healthcare providers, public health campaigns, education and literacy levels, rule of law, war, access to birth control, the penetration of foreign investment, and infrastructure (including roads, drainage, sewerage, and communication). The price of pharmaceuticals is nevertheless a common target in discussions about healthcare in the developing world. Crucial medicines or vaccines are often too expensive for the poorest and sickest. It may seem that pharmaceutical manufacturers have the resources to price their products differently and so could offer opportunities for immediate public health improvements. Public policy might encourage or require changes to the prices and distribution of essential medicines.

Current international policies provide strong protections for various forms of "intellectual property," including formulas for essential medicines. Those who patent a drug or a vaccine enjoy a near worldwide monopoly on its manufacture for a term of approximately 20 years. During that time, they may charge whatever the market can bear. But critics complain that such patent policies protect profits over human lives.

This chapter explores pharmaceutical public policy with an eye to its impact on the developing world. According to nearly all observers, the current system is deeply flawed. It features inefficient regulatory oversight, costly protection of stagnant monopoly privilege, and stifling of innovation. These problems do not uniquely impact the developing world, but they are particularly costly for the poorest and sickest populations, who tend to be concentrated in the developing world. Reforming pharmaceutical policy calls for reimagining how to encourage innovation. A discussion of pharmaceutical policies engages many other issues about the moral status of opportunities to access healthcare and the significance of national borders in the distribution of healthcare resources. This chapter starts by considering various arguments about the status of intellectual property. It surveys some of the relevant policies and institutions for pharmaceutical oversight. It considers some alternatives to the current system in light of widely shared ethical commitments but highlights the significance of addressing ethical disagreement for figuring out how to approach this complex issue.

Background

In developed countries with a pharmaceutical industry, bringing a new drug to market requires years of intensive research, development, and testing. The pharmaceutical compound must prove to be safe and effective. This requires clinical trials and preparing for reviews by regulatory bodies. The cost for doing all this is in the hundreds of millions of US dollars (DiMasi, Hansen, & Grabowski, 2003). As pharmaceutical firms point out, many of the compounds they test turn out not to work. The time to identify a disease, test possible compounds, and bring effective treatments or vaccines to market can be as much as 8–12 years (Natz, Gerbsch, & Kennedy, 2011). For some medicines that treat cancer, it can take as long as 15 years to bring the product to market (Stewart, Whitney, & Kurzrock, 2010). The time commitment and costs vary, but the point is that discovery and invention are not free.

It matters that pharmaceutical innovation requires resources. The money has to come from somewhere. If there are insufficient resources available for creating the medicines that can save or improve lives, then there will be fewer such medicines and greater numbers of sick or dead.

Speaking quite broadly, there are three possible sources for the funds needed to create vaccines and essential medicines: private industry, government, or philanthropy. Typically, private industry does the bulk of research, development and distribution, and it provides the largest source of funds. Governments in many developed countries do subsidize or fund a significant amount of pharmaceutical research through direct grants or public/private partnerships. Philanthropy also furnishes some resources through private foundations or nonprofit support organizations, such as the Bill and Melinda Gates Foundation or the American Cancer Society. Some commentators call for increased public funding, especially for diseases common to the developing world. Before considering which sorts of policy reforms might promote access to essential medicines, we should glance at what has shaped the current controversy.

Poverty and medicines

Every state that is a member of the United Nations has agreed to a set of ambitious "Millennium Development Goals," among which are reducing desperate poverty, curbing child mortality rates, improving maternal health, and reducing the impact of HIV/AIDS (United Nations Millennium Development Goals, n.d.). There has already been great progress toward these goals. Extreme poverty has substantially declined since 1990. Hundreds of millions of persons no longer suffer from abject hunger. But several diseases still claim millions of lives in the developing world—and avoidably so. Essential medicines exist now or could be created to help.

Healthcare has become increasingly expensive and occupies a greater portion of the GDP of developed countries. Pharmaceuticals are an increasing portion of that growing expenditure. Public sources pay for more than half the cost of pharmaceuticals. The Organisation for Economic Co-operation and Development reports that around 19 percent of healthcare expenditures among developed nations in 2009 were for pharmaceuticals. The total amount spent on pharmaceutical products is over US$700 billion across all such countries, and it has been steadily increasing.

Increased pharmaceutical spending is not necessarily a bad thing. More money spent on medicine may prevent more expensive hospital stays and it might lengthen or improve quality of life. (See OECD, 2011.) Compared to developed countries, however, poorer countries devote considerably less money to healthcare. Unsurprisingly, the incidence and impact of disease in such countries are far worse.

The "disease burden" for any given condition varies depending upon the illness and the country. For instance, heart disease and diabetes are more common in developed countries. This might be a function both of Western diets and the reliable control of other diseases. Richer people tend not to die from tropical diseases and they tend to have good access to food and healthcare. The diseases they do suffer from afflict the well (and sometimes overly) fed and longer lived.

Many diseases are not found in the developed world, or the mortality rates for such diseases are vastly higher when they strike poorer persons in the developing world. Pneumonia, various diarrheal diseases, malaria, measles, and HIV/AIDS are especially devastating for the poorest persons in the poorest countries. (See e.g. World Health Organization, 2013; Lozano *et al.*, 2012.) Sometimes, the medicines that can help are unavailable to, or priced out of reach of, the sick (Banerjee, Pogge, & Hollis, 2010). Moreover, the diseases that disproportionately impact the developing world often receive much less research and development funding than the burden they impose (Pogge, 2005, p. 190; Trouiller *et al.*, 2002).

Pharmaceuticals as "public goods"

Pharmaceuticals are goods that, though often expensive to create, are inexpensively replicated. This feature of pharmaceuticals generates some challenges for people hoping for rewards for their creative efforts. The challenges are also for prospective users. They want access to the drugs once they exist, but they also want the drugs to come into existence in the first place.

Drugs are a good that people create, and they can become a form of property. We can get a sense of the challenges of making them property by comparing them to other goods. A useful way to classify goods draws on two distinctions, one between *rivalrous* and *non-rivalrous* goods, and another between *excludable* and *non-excludable* goods.

Many goods are "rivalrous" in the sense that one person's use excludes others' use. For instance, when you wear a shirt, this typically means others cannot wear that shirt—at least not at the same time. The same is true of many other material goods: your use comes at the expense of others' opportunities to use them.

When someone enjoys goods that are "non-rivalrous," she does not take away from others' opportunities to enjoy them. This is often true of many immaterial goods. For instance, you can usually enjoy a passerby's audible song or the sunlight shining on your face without restricting others' opportunities to do something very similar. This is also true of many forms of knowledge. Knowing how to start a fire, what time it is, or how to perform a life-saving procedure are all non-rivalrous goods. Your knowing how to make a tourniquet, for instance, does not come at the expense of someone else knowing how to make a tourniquet.

Some goods are what economists call "excludable." When a good is excludable, it is possible to keep people from having access to it, such as only on the condition that they pay for it. Many material goods are excludable (such as a computer, a shirt, or a restaurant meal). Some immaterial goods are excludable, such as the performance of a song in a concert hall. Goods are "non-excludable" when it is very difficult if not impossible to keep people from having access to them. The fish in the open sea and the services of lighthouses are common examples of goods that are supposedly non-excludable.

There are usually no problems finding incentives to produce or conserve an excludable good. A producer takes the risk of investing resources in creating a good. If people wish to have access to the good, they negotiate with the producer to find mutually acceptable terms. None of this is unusual; this is what happens in any marketplace. Economists note, though, that it is often challenging to give incentives for the production or conservation of non-excludable goods. Such goods are especially vulnerable to overuse, and people who do not wish to pay for any such goods can "free ride" on those who do pay.

When goods are non-excludable *and* non-rivalrous, it is especially challenging to find reasons to produce or conserve them. Such goods are sometimes called "public goods": they can provide great value to people, they can often be consumed at little or no expense to others, but they can be expensive to provide. National defense, for instance, strikes many people as a public good. When you enjoy the protective credible military threat of your nation state, you do not do so at the expense of your neighbor's enjoying the same thing. But it is difficult to exclude people from enjoying this good. If a citizen lives in a nation state's territory, she benefits from military protection against foreign aggressors regardless of whether she pays for it.

Ideas are neither excludable nor rivalrous. If one person discovers how to make a fire, that person's knowledge does not come at the expense of others knowing the same thing. As Thomas Jefferson once wrote:

> He who receives an idea from me, receives instruction himself without lessening mine; as he who lights his taper at mine, receives light without darkening me. That ideas should freely spread from one to another over the globe, for the moral and mutual instruction of man, and improvement of his condition, seems to have been peculiarly and benevolently designed by nature, when she made them, like fire, expansible over all space, without

lessening their density in any point, and like the air in which we breathe, move, and have our physical being, incapable of confinement or exclusive appropriation.

(Jefferson, 1813)

Ideas might then be the sort of thing that cannot and should not be owned.

The availability of any pharmaceutical depends significantly on an idea. A particular pill, or a particular dose of a vaccine, is excludable and rivalrous. Only one person can swallow some particular pill. A provider might then charge people to have access to such a resource. In the case of pharmaceuticals, the non-excludable and non-rivalrous *idea* is the formula for the drug and the procedure for making it. If Abdul knows how to synthesize aspirin and what aspirin is good for, that does not keep Felicia from knowing the same things. But some people worry that unless we can find some way to give creators reasons for coming up with and synthesizing medicines, we will all have fewer medicines.

"Intellectual property" is one of the key institutional frameworks for producing some non-rivalrous and non-excludable goods. Treating some ideas as property supposedly ensures the production and distribution of the goods made from such ideas. Creators can acquire patents that give them a monopoly for a period of time over the production of any goods based on their idea. The specific policies vary from one country to another. In general, patents are only given for new and useful inventions that provide some advance over what is sometimes called the "state of the art."

Various international organizations and trade agreements provide greater unity among different sets of patent laws. The World Trade Organization (WTO), for instance, includes among its members the bulk of the world's nation states. Each member provides reciprocal openness to markets. Each member also participates in a common framework for resolving disputes. WTO guidelines permit some limited special protections for developing markets and allow for exceptions from usual practices because of public health emergencies. The Trade-Related Aspects of Intellectual Property Rights (TRIPS) agreement provides that WTO members will abide by and enforce certain definitions and protections for intellectual property, including patents. Generally, patents provide state protections for certain inventions for 20 years. This means that something patented in the UK, for instance, will enjoy patent protections in Australia.

Problems with patenting medication

Speaking very broadly, there are two types of moral argument in favor of any patent—including those for pharmaceuticals. One sort of argument is a consequentialist argument, which holds that it is better overall and in the long term for there to be patents of some length. Another family of arguments is nonconsequentialist. These tend to say that crucial principles of political morality require upholding patents. Both sorts of arguments face significant challenges.

Consider the consequentialist defense first. We might think, with Jefferson, that ideas should flow freely. But inventors might not share their creations—or even bother to invent in the first place—if they will not be compensated in some way. This is a special problem for pharmaceuticals since the creation process is difficult and expensive. Patents give inventors the opportunity to recoup their investment expenses. After all, as proponents of patents would point out, HIV/AIDS medicines do not grow on trees. Someone has to produce them. It takes years of experimentation, many frustrating failures, controlled clinical trials, and careful scientific analysis to discover what might work. This is expensive. Patents thus seem justified by bringing about the desirable consequences of greater beneficial pharmaceutical innovation.

This argument leans heavily on the promise of future payoffs. Granting patent owners monopoly pricing privileges for a time supposedly promotes future innovation. Moreover, just as with many innovations, while initially the well-heeled are better placed to enjoy them, over time, prices come down, availability goes up, and welfare improves for everyone. This was true for innovations such as automobiles, homes in the suburbs, air-conditioning, refrigeration, telephones, televisions, and so on. Buyers pay for the privilege of being early in line. A defense of such early price premiums then seem to be this: If sellers cannot charge such premiums to people eager to get in line first, there may be nothing for which to get in line.

Pure consequentialist arguments for patents must balance access now against access in the future. The arguments turn crucially on whether patents incentivize innovation better than feasible alternatives. Critics will note, however, that historically climates of invention flourished without patent protections (such as in nineteenth-century Holland and Switzerland) and that many major twentieth-century inventions were not patented, including the transistor, the laser, the jet engine, the cyclotron, and the zipper (Ridley, 2010; Stiglitz, 2013). Sometimes the inventors were motivated simply by the quest for knowledge. Sometimes, by freely disclosing their inventions, they might have been strategically trying to change the "state of the art" to prevent others from cornering the market with patents of their own. (One cannot patent something that is already common knowledge.) But in any case, the consequentialist argument must deflect concerns from critics: *patents might slow innovation by giving patent-holders government-backed monopolies, which lets them focus more on protecting their patents and fees rather than innovating* (Boldrin & Levine, 2008).

Perhaps pharmaceuticals are a special case where innovation requires the reward of brief monopoly privileges. Given the immense upfront costs, patents might be the best way to encourage innovators to invest the resources to invent the medicines to help others. However, any such argument must face an important challenge. Once the medicine is available, it may seem churlish at best, and grotesquely inhuman at worst, to deny needy others access to an essential drug.

Once a formula for some drug is available, production is usually comparatively inexpensive. Suppose Company A develops a formula for a pill(s) to control HIV/AIDS. Perhaps A invested US$800 million to invent the pill. Company A now wishes to charge US$25,000 for a year's supply of the drug. Company B can get a hold of the drug, reverse engineer it, and start selling copies at US$100 for a year's supply. But patents would prevent Company B from doing this. Until the patent expires, Company A may charge what it believes is necessary to recoup its costs. This seems to generate unnecessary and perhaps devastating losses. Economists call these "deadweight losses." These are lost opportunities to enhance welfare when people who might otherwise be willing to buy the product (say, from the imitating Company B) are prevented from doing so. In some cases, their suffering or death might have been prevented by the medicine. This is not mere theoretical speculation. Under current international policies, governments are required to remove copycat products whose manufacturers do not pay license fees to patent owners. In India, for instance, enforcement of patents for a vital class of antibacterial medicine may be responsible for significant losses to Indians without comparable gains to patent holders (Chaudhuri, Goldberg, & Jia, 2006). This is then another major problem with consequentialist arguments for patents: *patents seem to deny people, at this moment, access to essential medicines.*

Of course, it is easy to point to sick people now who cannot afford expensive medicines. It is harder to point to avoidably sick or dead people in the future who might otherwise have been healthy had pharmaceutical innovators had a reason to invest the resources to make the medicines to help them. Sometimes drug company executives mention this, almost with the tone of a threat. Sidney Taurel, CEO of Eli Lilly & Co., once remarked, "Cutting out pharmaceutical profits might make today's drugs slightly more available to people, but it would also certainly make sure that tomorrow's newer, vastly more effective cures are a very long time coming. In other words, cheaper drugs today, mean more disease, disability and death tomorrow" (Bailey, 2003). These companies sometimes make such threats quite explicit. International agreements allow countries to grant "compulsory licenses." Such licenses permit lower-cost sales of drugs in cases of public health crises. Indeed, some economists argue that expanding the use of such licenses might be better for everyone—including the pharmaceutical companies (Flynn, Hollis, & Palmedo, 2009). But when countries take steps to confer such licenses, pharmaceutical companies sometimes threaten to pull other drugs from those markets (Amara & Aljunid, 2012). This is yet a third seeming problem with patents: *patents give their owners the power to stop people from helping others.*

This quick discussion of consequentialist accounts is certainly not exhaustive, but it suggests that such arguments have significant burdens to overcome before fully justifying patents. These arguments stand or fall on whether they bring about the best consequences over feasible alternatives. And because of these alternatives (some of which we discuss in the next section), patents—especially as they are currently construed—might not be the best way to bring about the innovation they supposedly seek.

Many of the challenges facing consequentialist arguments for patents return with nonconsequentialist arguments. Speaking very broadly, arguments in this family often appeal to significant principles of political morality as a justification for patents of some sort. Ayn Rand, for instance, defends patents as an institution that acknowledges a person's control over the products of his or her own mind (Rand & Branden, 1986, p. 130). On this view, protecting patents is a way of acknowledging a person's proper sovereignty over the fruits of his or her labor. A related sort of argument takes a cue from the natural rights approach of John Locke. In Locke's view, a person acquires property in something by "mixing" labor with it and so adding value. But Locke cautions that one can only acquire property in a thing provided there is "enough, and as good, left in common for others" (Locke, 1988, sec. 27). Locke also warns that property may not be allowed to "spoil," though the invention of money allows people to accumulate more than what they can consume (Locke, 1988, chap. V). There is much debate about how to interpret the Lockean "proviso" and other restrictions, especially as they might apply to patentable inventions. Robert Nozick, for instance, argues that a researcher who creates a new drug but "refuses to sell except on his terms does not worsen the situation of others by depriving them of whatever he has appropriated. The others easily can possess the same materials he appropriated; the researcher's appropriation or purchase of chemicals didn't make those chemicals scarce in a way so as to violate the Lockean proviso" (Nozick, 1974, p. 175). Nozick is certainly right that, short of appropriating all the raw materials needed for a drug, others have an opportunity to invent the drug themselves. But the problem with such an argument is that patents take a non-rivalrous good—here, the idea behind an invention—and make it scarce, giving an inventor the power to deny others access to a good.

Following Jefferson, it may seem odd to deny people the chance to act on ideas they have—even if they observed them elsewhere. Suppose someone invents something that can provide substantial improvements for the lives of others. Imagine, for instance, one among a group of cave-dwellers invents a method for making a hut. If he insists on a fee whenever anyone else builds a hut, that might seem to give him some inappropriate claim over other people's goods (Kinsella, 2008, pp. 27–8). Many people might find it bizarre that he should be in a position to prevent others from building their own huts. (This is not to deny he might succeed in that if he were strong enough!) But this is precisely what patents as public policies allow. They permit inventors to stop people from acting on ideas they have. In particular, they permit people to call on the coercive powers of many nation states to stop others from acting on their ideas. This seems to be one problem with patents that nonconsequentialists must overcome. *Patents restrict freedom.* They keep second and third parties from acting on their knowledge. This is not to say that such restrictions cannot be justified. But if we take freedom seriously, such restrictions must be somehow supportable in light of moral costs elsewhere. And just as with consequentialist defenses of patents, any nonconsequentialist appeal to principles of political morality must discount the seemingly avoidable deaths and suffering *now*.

Complicating the problems with either consequentialist or non-consequentialist defenses of patents is a commitment to a principle of Samaritanism. It seems that any decent persons would lend a helping hand when they can do so at little cost to themselves. In just the way we might fault someone who walks past a child drowning in a shallow puddle, so too it seems tempting to condemn pharmaceutical companies who fail to provide the essential medicines that can prevent or alleviate suffering or death. When they exercise the rights their patents protect, they, and the states that enforce patent regimes, seem complicit in easily avoidable misery.

The problem with this line of thinking is that pharmaceutical companies are not like passersby happening upon a single drowning baby. Pharmaceutical companies devote significant resources to inventing ways to keep people from suffering and dying. It is important that they keep innovating; otherwise, there might be even more suffering and dying. If they cannot price their products in a way to cover their costs, they will not incur the costs (Maitland, 2002). They will not create the medicines.

This sort of appeal to unseen costs returns us to the tradeoffs involved in fashioning any public policy regarding intellectual property. We want to make sure any restrictions on freedom are justified. We also want the medicines to keep us healthy. We want to minimize sickness and death (now and in the foreseeable future). Are patents part of the public policy picture that appropriately expresses our commitments to such goals? The next section considers some possible reforms or alternatives that might better promote and protect health. Many such policies involve getting out of the way of people who can help others. Some may call for reconsidering the structure of the institutions that promote pharmaceutical innovation.

Pharmaceutical policy: doing more by doing less

Commentators regularly point out the perversities of the drug industry: lengthy and costly reviews, "me-too" drugs, failure to focus on small market segments, high prices, and inattention to the diseases of the neediest and sickest persons abroad. The current system for patent protection and regulatory review may seem to invite many of these problems. Some people have proposed reforms. Others have proposed abolition. This section discusses several leading proposals and suggests that, minimally, governments can do more by doing less. First, let us consider the prospect of abolition of patent protection and what impact that might have on access to essential medicines in the developing world.

Abolish patents?

Patents protect a monopoly privilege. They allow owners to block access to useful inventions. They permit owners to concentrate on accumulating what economists call "rent" from their monopolies instead of devoting resources to further innovation. Patents impose steep enforcement costs on governments, regulators, and patent owners. Expensive attorneys, bureaucrats, and law courts focus exclusively on investigating, creating, enforcing, and litigating patents. The immense costs of patents provide diminished incentives to innovate when the return is likely to be modest (such as, say, drugs for rare conditions). Patents seem to keep people from helping others now. They also seem now to give people the opportunity to deny others easy rescue from diseases they need not suffer. For these and other reasons, some experts and scholars have called for abolishing patents altogether.

There are various possible alternatives. In a world without patent protections, people could copy others' products and not be subject to legal reprisals. Why then would anyone bother to innovate? Among the reasons are to secure a "first to market" privilege. Businesses who are first movers often gain market dominance. They establish brand recognition. They create business relationships that, at least for a time, exclude others simply by having been first. They set a standard that others must match or exceed.

In the case of pharmaceuticals, the company who is first to market with a new drug or vaccine establishes distribution networks, builds a reputation for safety and effectiveness, and so can corner the market and reap significant profits ... at least for a time. Economists, business theorists, and policy analysts debate the merits of the first mover advantage. Some argue that first movers actually suffer a *disadvantage*. By being first, they let others free-ride on their hard work in innovating, testing the market, exploring business relationships, and testing the product. There is evidence that many leaders in other industries enjoyed a second-mover advantage. The market leaders among computer operating systems (Microsoft), online booksellers (Amazon), and search engines (Google), to name just a few, were not first to market. They studied what pioneers did before them and improved on them. Some of the costs involved in creating their markets were borne by first movers who have since fallen behind or disappeared. In the case of pharmaceuticals, it is then unclear whether first movers would enjoy sufficient advantages that would give them an incentive to innovate—especially when the development costs for a new drug can be in the hundreds of millions of dollars. If the second mover can copy the innovator's design and free-ride on its studies of safety and effectiveness, that seems to undermine any incentive to create new medicines.

Some scholars warn against discounting pharmaceutical first-mover advantages. In a series of controversial publications, economists Michele Boldrin and David K. Levine question the idea that patents are needed to protect innovation. They note that copying a drug takes time, and establishing brand recognition and a reputation for reliability are not easy (Boldrin & Levine, 2008, 2012; Clement, 2003). First pharmaceutical movers might then recoup their costs by selling prototypes to others, who could then distribute copies of the drug to their markets. Boldrin and Levine suggest a number of reforms, among which are exploring treating pharmaceuticals as regulated public utilities, establishing prizes for successful creation of a drug, and adjusting patent lengths according to the needs of different industries.

What might work here requires extensive and careful empirical analysis. There are two significant challenges to the idea of abolishing patents or adjusting patent lengths. The first is simply a function of the numbers: if first-mover advantages do not reliably promise sufficient rewards to cover the immense upfront research and development costs, companies will not bother to innovate. The second problem is a function of current institutions: the global economic order is built on a common system of intellectual property norms. Unless there is significant evidence that the costs of the current system are egregious and can be easily reduced by a feasible alternative, it seems plausible opportunities for improvement must first start elsewhere.

Reduce research and development burdens

Because pharmaceutical research and development is so expensive, only a few organizations such as large universities and pharmaceutical companies have the resources available to investigate new drugs. These costs may discourage new entrants to the pharmaceutical marketplace. They are also a key reason in favor of patents, since they provide opportunities for investors to recoup their great costs.

The costs are so steep for at least three reasons: (1) overly conservative state regulators, (2) state monopolies on certification, and (3) requiring proof of effectiveness as well as safety. Considering each of these reasons will suggest some potential opportunities for reform that do not require wholesale destruction of current institutions.

State regulation and conservative bias

Under the current system for certifying drugs, state agencies decide on the drugs' safety and effectiveness. In the United States, for instance, various policies give the Food and Drug Administration the unique right to determine whether a drug will be allowed into the marketplace. But as many industry commentators note, state officials face certain incentives that tend to discourage them from efficient approval of new drugs.

A certifying body can choose to approve a drug—or not. Or it can choose to delay certification. The drug can turn out to be beneficial or harmful. This creates the possibility for two sorts of errors. A "Type I" error occurs when a certifying body approves a drug that turns out to be harmful. In such cases, there are visible victims who can generate a significant backlash against supposedly clumsy regulators.

A "Type II" error, on the other hand, occurs when regulators fail to certify a beneficial drug. The victims in such cases are often invisible. Their illness continues or they die while the regulators delay or withhold certification.

Political pressures seem to dispose regulators toward overly conservative approval. There is usually a much greater problem dealing with the visible victims of Type I errors than the invisible victims of Type II errors. This is not purely theoretical. Bureaucrats will sometimes delay approval of new drugs—even when the evidence supports speedy approval (Miller, 2000). In some cases, these delays can be measured in thousands of total years of lost human lives. The United States and other countries have explored various regulatory initiatives to speed the approval process, but many critics worry that unless there is room for changing the process for certification, people will continue to suffer needlessly. One option is to reconsider who can offer certification, which is sketched in the next section.

Ending the state monopoly on drug certification

In any country with a drug industry, the state claims a monopoly on certifying drugs. There is then little competition for drug certification.

This can cause inconvenient delays for Westerners hoping for quicker access to the next erectile dysfunction medication. But it can also discourage or delay development of medications that can help relieve sicknesses endemic to the developing world.

There is some international competition in this sense: some countries approve medicines earlier than others, and so residents can have access to medical technologies sooner. This is common in the medical device market, where, for instance, US residents can find better access to medications or devices overseas (Rosenthal, 2013). How would this work for certifying medicines?

There are two good models for nonstate certification. One comes with the system for certifying kosher food. The other comes from the testing of electrical appliances.

There is a substantial market for kosher food in the United States. The market base is not simply observant Jews. Many people prefer kosher food because of taste or food safety concerns. Others who seek halal food can sometimes consume kosher. The market then is sizeable enough that food manufacturers have a strong reason to get their products certified. In the United States, over 300 independent certifiers maintain oversight at multiple levels of food production and distribution. These certifiers participate in friendly competition to provide reliable and efficient certification. They belong to a trade organization that oversees standards and monitors compliance. As Timothy Lyton writes, the providers "have developed a shared sense of mission that counteracts incentives to cut corners and promotes cooperation between competing certifiers" (Lytton, 2013, p. 26). Some such competition might be allowed for drug certification. This could decrease costs, speed approval time, and increase efficiency.

Another model takes a cue from a current nonstate process for certifying the safety of electrical appliances. Underwriters Laboratories is a nonprofit nonstate organization dedicated to testing new technologies. They establish standards and consult with companies preparing to market new products. They also provide important benchmarks in determining liability for product safety and defects.

Either model might point to possibilities for greater efficiency in pharmaceutical certification. We do not know what the institutions would look like because likely market actors are forbidden to create them. Time would tell whether such nonstate alternatives are less prone to devastating Type II errors or more prone to Type I errors. The incentives would seem to favor lowering the cost barriers for introducing new and potentially lifesaving drugs to the marketplace.

Even if such policy changes seemed overly bold, right now countries might have some sort of reciprocal acknowledgement of certification of other select countries. This could reduce unnecessary delays. Drugmakers might also have the option of introducing their product to market with the disclaimer that their product is not approved by some state certifying board.

Nonstate certifications are not necessarily better than state ones. Nonstate actors would face important quality control challenges. Much depends on empirical findings about what form of certification best satisfies goals for creation and distribution of needed medications. But ethical challenges shape the background by showing which healthcare goals should take priority.

Abolish requirements of effectiveness for drugs to be certified

Current drug tests involve several phases of testing. In early drug trials, a substance is tested for safety. Subsequent trials explore whether it is effective. Tests for effectiveness can sometimes delay the introduction of a drug for years. Some scholars propose allowing drugmakers to introduce a substance to the market before they have completed studies to determine its effectiveness. This could be especially valuable for drugs that promise help from lethal conditions, and it would leave the decision for taking a drug up to patients and their doctors. Some have suggested public policies that would tightly regulate prices during this initial release; the public policies would permit prices to rise to market levels after effectiveness tests were completed (Boldrin & Levine, 2012). Consumers might then have quicker access to drugs; meanwhile the diminished time to market might help hold down costs (Boldrin & Swamidass, 2011). Such changes might hasten health improvements for everyone, in the developed and developing world.

Changes such as allowing private certification boards, permitting market release short of proof of effectiveness, and permitting cross-country reciprocal recognition do not quite involve new policies; rather, they remove current barriers to people figuring out how to improve their lives and the lives of those they serve. And to be sure, weakening state oversight does not necessarily entail licensing private abuses. Consumers would still be in a position to claim tort protection from companies that misrepresent their products.

Prizes and advance market commitments

Even if the burdens of research and development for new medicines were to come down, research and development costs are still likely to be substantial. Patents are one device to reward the investment. Another might be by awarding a prize. Any person or company who can provide a medicine that meets certain technical specifications might earn a set prize amount. The prize might be funded by philanthropic organizations, by NGOs, or by government(s).

There are some drawbacks to some prize systems. If the prize is awarded purely for delivery of a medicine meeting certain specifications, there may be insufficient incentive to improve on the product after it is delivered. Moreover, there may be inadequate reason to be sure that the good can be delivered to likely consumers. The prize promotes new medicines only if the monetary reward exceeds that available from the open market. This last point is of course not a moral objection to a prize so much as an alert that it would need to be calibrated correctly.

A further challenge for any system of incentivizing pharmaceutical innovation is the "last mile" problem. This is the difficulty of getting the medicines into the hands of people who need them. This is sometimes a problem in Western countries, but it is often a devastating barrier in developing countries marred by poor roads, war, lack of refrigeration, and little medical infrastructure. One way to overcome the last mile problem is to compensate drugmakers not simply for creating a medicine but for providing concrete and measurable improvements in human well-being. Among the proposals for achieving this is the Health Impact Fund. Very briefly, the Health Impact Fund provides payments to drug companies in exchange for the health impact of any new medicine they can deliver (Pogge & Hollis, 2008). The fund is thus a type of "advance market commitment" where an agency agrees to buy certain medicines provided they meet certain technical specifications. The Health Impact Fund would give pharmaceutical companies special incentives to overcome the logistical obstacles to health improvements. Companies would have a reason to get the medicines to the people who need them because their compensation would depend on it. Pharmaceutical companies who commit a drug to the fund would need to show that they have made the appropriate health impacts and not merely that their medicines have the potential to provide improvements.

This fund may also help to get more pharmaceutical companies to target diseases that are the unique province of the poor, instead of, for instance, devoting their resources to the next erectile dysfunction drug. Since the fund would reward pharmaceutical makers with compensation based on a set formula for health impact, there would be less concern about the patients' abilities to pay and more with delivering measurable health improvements.

Some critics have questioned the plausibility of finding a reliable and consistent measurement of health improvements. Others worry that the public funds needed to support such a program might be better spent on causes that seem to promise greater public health gains. Creating such a program would require a new public policy and a new set of institutions. If theorists can deflect criticisms that the fund would misallocate scarce public health funding, the biggest challenge would then be finding the political will to support the budgets that would be needed.

Non-pharmaceutical improvements that diminish need for pharmaceutical interventions

When considering depressing public health statistics from the developing world, critics focus on pharmaceutical companies for their inattention to diseases of the poor and for their monopoly pricing. But pharmaceutical fixes are not necessarily the cheapest or fastest way of delivering the welfare improvements everyone hopes to see. In some cases, there might be more reliable gains by exploring improvements to infrastructure, education, or communication.

Some writers have noted that the developed world presents profound business opportunities that can work to the advantage of the poorest persons. Eric Bing and Mark Epstein describe the promise of wireless technology in their rousing book, *Pharmacy on a Bicycle* (Bing & Epstein, 2013). Mobile phone technology allows for delivery of medical interventions at a distance, with better control over inventory and diminished need for patients making wasteful and life-threatening trips. They describe the promise of medical franchises, which can deliver medical services specifically attuned to local needs, and thereby help overcome the last mile problem. With modest funding, various health microentrepreneurs can deliver some basic health services to their communities. Microclinics can bring medical services out to people in remote locations. This would be a considerable improvement over the current model in which ill persons must often travel great distances. When such patients are fortunate enough to survive the journey, they sometimes come to clinics lacking the medicines they need. The innovations Bing and Epstein describe might be quite a bit less expensive and much less disruptive than reconsidering policies governing pharmaceutical patents.

Resolving devastating and chronic public health problems is seldom simply a matter of adjusting pharmaceutical availability. Consider malaria, which in 2010 claimed over one million lives (Lozano *et al.*, 2012, p. 2105). One of the key vectors for transmission of malaria is the mosquito. Many people have proposed expanding the distribution of bed nets treated with insecticides as a way of controlling transmission. Another way to curtail malaria is to reduce the mosquito's opportunities to breed, which means reducing the extent that an area features standing bodies of water. Sometimes public authorities attempt to treat such wet areas. But we might also consider why there are not institutions in place for draining bodies of stagnant water. This is a function of infrastructure, which also depends significantly on levels of public funds. Amartya Sen and others have documented how rarely there are serious and sustained public health problems in countries with democratic accountability (Sen, 1982). And, unsurprisingly, nations with high rates of death from malaria tend to be nations with autocratic states. Many of those states are able to prop up their regimes with funds they access from the international banking system. They also acquire funds by selling off the nation's natural resources, and, combined with the funds they receive by borrowing, they can purchase the military hardware that secures their power, but which also makes their state an appealing target for military coups. The upshot is a state that has little reason to be accountable to its people by providing public health, infrastructure, or education. Thomas Pogge has documented these and other perverse features of current international policies (Pogge, 2008). The point here is not to deny that there is room for pharmaceutical reform, but to note that people may have desperate needs for medical intervention for chronic health problems because of reasons having less to do with pharmaceutical prices and more to do with the defective structure of global trade norms and inattentive state agencies.

Rather than tweaking pharmaceutical policies, economists can explore other means of promoting more lasting public health gains. Terminating Western support for autocrats might be a nice start. Other low-hanging fruit might be helping poor persons gain more reliable access to clean drinking water (Hoffman, 2011; Sobsey, Stauber, Casanova, Brown, & Elliott, 2008) or working to secure a rule of law in which poor persons might build the social institutions that create and transmit wealth across generations.

Conclusion

Current pharmaceutical policy provides monopolies for the parties who succeed in patenting important medications first. Those monopolies allow them pricing discretion for many years. The sickest persons in the developing world may seem to be disadvantaged by this system; it may avoidably deny them access to existing essential medication or prevent innovators from creating the medicines that might otherwise improve the lives of the sick. Still, patents may provide the reward needed to motivate the difficult research and development for new medicines.

Even within the current system, people can be better in a position to satisfy important interests in remaining disease-free. Reconsidering policies that confer state monopolies on certification may provide greater and earlier access to essential medicines. Removing the institutional impediments on economic growth in developing countries would permit public health advances that might postpone or weaken needs for essential medicines. Much hangs on the findings of social scientists who study alternative measures to promote public health. There is more to advancing public health than providing inexpensive medicines, but reducing barriers to getting such medicines is a sure start.

Our views about how and whether to pursue any public policy reform for pharmaceuticals are framed by ethical commitments. Current norms seem to reflect a blend of several ethical considerations, among which are respecting manufacturers' opportunities to maximize profit, ensuring reliable provision of pharmaceuticals and vital medical technologies, and protecting property rights in ideas. It is important to sort through the meaning and significance of such commitments, as this may guide us in understanding which pharmaceutical policy options deserve priority. But that would only be the start of a discussion of more fundamental moral considerations about health, disease, and public policy. What if anything is the proper place for the state in ensuring people have access to healthcare? Which sort of health, and whose health, deserves policy protection? Do national borders have any ethical significance in determining the shape of policy? Is health the sort of good that should allow institutions featuring profit-seeking? All of these and related questions hang partly on empirical findings. When we explore such ethical challenges, we might better appreciate what is at stake and how to frame policy priorities for controversies about pharmaceuticals.

Further reading

The literature on pharmaceutical policy is extensive. Of special note are any of the compelling accounts of the Health Impact Fund by Thomas Pogge and Aidan Hollis, such as their 2008 book, titled *The Health Impact Fund: Making New Medicines Accessible for All*, from Incentives for Global Health. Adam Jaffe and Josh Lerner discuss defects of current patent norms in their 2004 book with Princeton University Press, *Innovation and Its Discontents: How Our Broken Patent System Is Endangering Innovation and Progress, and What to Do about It*. Mentioned in the chapter's text above, but worth further study is the 2000 book from Hoover Institution Press by Henry I. Miller, MD, which features a disturbing narrative of perverse bureaucratic oversight, *To America's Health: A Proposal to Reform the Food and Drug Administration*. Readers curious for a more general critique of intellectual property norms might study some of Lawrence Lessig's work, such as *Free Culture: The Nature and Future of Creativity* (Penguin, 2005). To see how regulation of kosher dietary rules in the United States might be a model for nonstate regulation of significant market segments, see Timothy D. Lytton's full discussion in *Kosher* (Harvard, 2013). For those hungry for details about drug testing and the approval process, see, for instance, Rick Ng, *Drugs—From Discovery to Approval* (Wiley-Liss, 2004).

References

Amara, A. H., & Aljunid, S. M. (2012). Local pharmaceutical production as means to improve access to essential medicines in developing countries. *International Journal of Pharmacy & Pharmaceutical Sciences*, *4*, 233–40.

Bailey, R. (2003, May 21). This is Maine on drugs. *Reason.com*. Retrieved October 5, 2013, from http://reason.com/archives/2003/05/21/this-is-maine-on-drugs

Banerjee, A., Pogge, T., & Hollis, A. (2010). The Health Impact Fund. *The Lancet*, *375*(9727), 1693. doi:10.1016/S0140–6736(10)60736–2

Bing, E. G., & Epstein, M. J. (2013). *Pharmacy on a bicycle: Innovative solutions to global health and poverty*. San Francisco: Berrett-Koehler Publishers. Retrieved from http://search.ebscohost.com/login.aspx?direct=true&scope=site&db=nlebk&db=nlabk&an=562634

Boldrin, M., & Levine, D. K. (2008). *Against intellectual monopoly*. New York: Cambridge University Press.

Boldrin, M., & Levine, D. K. (2012). The case against patents. *Working Paper Series* (No. 2012–35). Retrieved from http://research.stlouisfed.org/wp/more/2012–35/

Boldrin, M., & Swamidass, S. J. (2011). A new bargain for drug approvals. *Wall Street Journal – Eastern Edition*, *258*(22), A15.

Chaudhuri, S., Goldberg, P. K., & Jia, P. (2006). Estimating the effects of global patent protection in pharmaceuticals: A case study of quinolones in India. *The American Economic Review*, *96*(5), 1477–1514. doi:10.2307/30034983

Clement, D. (2003, March 1). Creation myths. *Reason.com*. Retrieved October 7, 2013, from http://reason.com/archives/2003/03/01/creation-myths

DiMasi, J. A., Hansen, R. W., & Grabowski, H. G. (2003). The price of innovation: new estimates of drug development costs. *Journal of Health Economics*, *22*(2), 151–85. doi:10.1016/S0167–6296(02)00126–1

Flynn, S., Hollis, A., & Palmedo, M. (2009). An economic justification for open access to essential medicine patents in developing countries. *Journal of Law, Medicine & Ethics*, *37*(2), 184–208. doi:10.1111/j.1748–720X.2009.00365.x

Hoffman, J. (2011, September 26). LifeStraw saves those without access to clean drinking water. *The New York Times*. Retrieved June 2, 2014, from www.nytimes.com/2011/09/27/health/27straw.html

Jefferson, T. (1813, August 13). Letter to Isaac McPherson. *The Founders' Constitution*. Retrieved October 5, 2013, from http://press-pubs.uchicago.edu/founders/documents/a1_8_8s12.html

Kinsella, N. S. (2008). *Against intellectual property*. Auburn, AL: Ludwig von Mises Institute.

Locke, J. (1988). *Locke: Two Treatises of Government*. (P. Laslett, Ed.) (3rd ed.). New York: Cambridge University Press.

Lozano, R., Naghavi, M., Foreman, K., Lim, S., Shibuya, K., Aboyans, V., … Ahn, S. Y. (2012). Global and regional mortality from 235 causes of death for 20 age groups in 1990 and 2010: A systematic analysis for the Global Burden of Disease Study 2010. *The Lancet*, *380*(9859), 2095–2128. doi:10.1016/S0140–6736(12)61728–0

Lytton, T. D. (2013). Kosher certification as a model of private regulation. *Regulation*. Retrieved from www.cato.org/regulation/fall-2013

Maitland, I. (2002). Priceless goods: How should life-saving drugs be priced? *Business Ethics Quarterly*, *12*(4), 451–80.

Miller, H. I. (2000). *To America's health: a proposal to reform the Food and Drug Administration*. Stanford, CA: Hoover Institution Press.

Natz, A., Gerbsch, N., & Kennedy, J. (2011). *From challenges to opportunities: Towards a common strategic framework for EU research and innovation funding*. Brussels: European Confederation of Pharmaceutical Entrepreneurs. Retrieved from http://ec.europa.eu/research/horizon2020/pdf/contributions/post/european_organisations/european_confederation_of_pharmaceutical_entrepreneurs.pdf

Nozick, R. (1974). *Anarchy, state, and utopia*. New York: Basic Books.

OECD (2011). *Health at a glance 2011: OECD indicators*. OECD Publishing. Retrieved June 2, 2014, doi: 10.1787/health_glance-2011-en, Sec. 4.11

Pogge, T. (2008). *World poverty and human rights: cosmopolitan responsibilities and reforms*. Cambridge: Polity.

Pogge, T. W. (2005). Human Rights and Global Health: A Research Program. *Metaphilosophy*, *36*(1–2), 182–209.

Pogge, T. W., & Hollis, A. (2008). *The Health Impact Fund: Making new medicines accessible for all*. Incentives for Global Health. Retrieved from http://machif.com/wp-content/uploads/2012/11/hif_book.pdf

Rand, A., & Branden, N. (1986). *Capitalism: The unknown ideal*. New York: Penguin.

Ridley, M. (2010, June 14). Ideas having sex. *Reason.com*. Retrieved October 6, 2013, from http://reason.com/archives/2010/06/14/ideas-having-sex

Rosenthal, E. (2013, August 3). In need of a new hip, but priced out of the U.S. *The New York Times*. Retrieved from www.nytimes.com/2013/08/04/health/for-medical-tourists-simple-math.html

Sen, A. K. (1982). *Poverty and famines: an essay on entitlement and deprivation*. Oxford; New York: Clarendon Press; Oxford University Press.

Sobsey, M. D., Stauber, C. E., Casanova, L. M., Brown, J. M., & Elliott, M. A. (2008). Point of use household drinking water filtration: A practical, effective solution for providing sustained access to safe drinking water in the developing world. *Environmental Science & Technology*, *42*(12), 4261–7. doi:10.1021/es702746n

Stewart, D. J., Whitney, S. N., & Kurzrock, R. (2010). Equipoise lost: Ethics, costs, and the regulation of cancer clinical research. *Journal of Clinical Oncology*, *28*(17), 2925–35. doi:10.1200/JCO.2009.27.5404

Stiglitz, J. E. (2013, July 14). How intellectual property reinforces inequality. *The New York Times*. Retrieved from http://opinionator.blogs.nytimes.com/2013/07/14/how-intellectual-property-reinforces-inequality/

Trouiller, P., Olliaro, P., Torreele, E., Orbinski, J., Laing, R., & Ford, N. (2002). Drug development for neglected diseases: a deficient market and a public-health policy failure. *The Lancet*, *359*(9324), 2188–94.

United Nations Millennium Development Goals. (n.d.). Retrieved October 4, 2013, from www.un.org/millenniumgoals/poverty.shtml

World Health Organization. (2013). World Health Statistics 2013. Retrieved October 5, 2013, from www.who.int/gho/publications/world_health_statistics/2013/en/index.html

3 Immigration

Immigration policies have recently become increasingly controversial among and within industrialized countries. Economic concerns are part of the reason. People have misgivings about the impact of immigrants on the host country. They worry that immigrants exploit social welfare institutions without contributing offsetting tax revenues. But economics do not capture all of the controversy. Immigration policies also impact the freedoms of migrants and the persons who might wish to host or hire them. Furthermore, there are deep-seated disagreements about issues of group identity.

Immigration debates often revolve around what shape a national culture has and how it might and should evolve. Many writers also worry about the impact of immigration policies on home countries and, of course, on the prospective immigrants themselves. This is why immigration policy has important moral dimensions.

People wish to relocate for many reasons. Some hope for a better life, even if their current conditions are acceptable. Some hope to flee tyranny, oppression, or squalor. Others want to join communities of persons who have similar backgrounds, or they simply wish to take advantage of opportunities open to them or their families.

Immigration policies differ across countries, as do migration patterns. Substantial movements of peoples across borders have often inspired discussions about such policies. Recently, however, there has been renewed vigorous debate among political theorists about the various ethical stakes immigration engages. Here we will not pretend to resolve such theoretical disputes. But we can illuminate some of their features and how appreciating the relevant clashing principles and interpretations might help to sharpen policy debates and point a way toward some greater clarity on policy choices.

Background

Policies restricting movement of people into a country often vary by nation of origin. The policies also vary according to the prospective migrant's skills, educational level, age, employment status, family connections, military service, length of residence, and refugee status (among other factors). Some writers, however, advocate open borders. They insist that people should be free to move about as they please. But, as David Miller discusses (Miller, 2014, pp. 365–6), strictly speaking, no nation has such a policy. All nation states have some policies restricting who may legally reside in their territory and under what conditions. Indeed, all nation states have policies that prevent some people from moving about or going to some places, either because the *places* are of a certain type (such as private property, government property, environmentally sensitive areas, or areas under a curfew) or because the *people* are of a certain type (such as prisoners, severely mentally ill, children, or persons with highly contagious diseases). This suggests that we accept and perhaps rightly expect some rules that restrict who may go where (Miller, 2014). But few people would find it plausible to think that those rules may apply domestically but not to movement of persons across a border into a state. So immigration seems appropriate to restrict—at least sometimes. The question is when.

The national identities of some industrialized countries are deeply bound up with immigration. Australia, Canada, New Zealand, and the United States, for instance, were each significantly built by immigrants whose ingenuity, culture, and resources enriched the development of each country. Even today, substantial numbers of residents in industrialized nations are foreign born. Estimates of the proportion of foreign-born residents (legal or otherwise) vary, but they range from around 13 percent in the USA (United States Census Bureau – Foreign Born, n.d.), to over 12 percent in the UK (Migrants in the UK: An overview, n.d.), nearly 20 percent in Canada (Immigration in Canada: A portrait of the foreign-born population, n.d.), and 25 percent in Australia (Australian Visa Bureau, 2010).

Writers on immigration note that there are both "push" and "pull" factors that tend to foster the movement of peoples. The "push" side refers to the circumstances in the source country that encourage emigration to other lands. Among them are religious or political persecution, economic or political instability, and insufficient opportunities at home due to a poor job climate, overpopulation, or scarce land. On the "pull" side are all the factors that make the potential host country seem inviting, such as religious toleration, economic opportunities, and a more welcoming social and political climate.

While there are incomplete and sometimes conflicting data, economists generally agree that immigrants, on net, have a positive impact on the host economy. (See, for instance, Peri, 2010; Dixon & Rimmer, 2009; Simon, 1990.) However, there has been some concern that, in the short term, immigrants push down wages for low-skilled domestic workers (Borjas, Grogger, & Hanson, 2006), but other social scientists dispute this (Ottaviano & Peri, 2012). There is even some evidence that over the long term, immigrants might have no net depressive effect on wages (Borjas & Katz, 2007). Social scientists do know that the impact of immigrants varies by their skill level and their nation of origin. This might be no surprise. Those with a language or culture that is similar to the host nation, and those with skills in high demand, find fewer obstacles to becoming contributors to a new community. It is easier for them to find jobs, establish fruitful working relationships, and settle in a new community.

Even low-skilled or unskilled laborers with languages outside the mainstream of the host nation can provide important services. They often perform jobs that citizens of the host nation do not wish to do (or at wages that are unappealing to citizens). This is especially true of service sector jobs. In the United States in the mid 2000s, for instance, undocumented workers filled such jobs at rates far higher than authorized residents. They made up nearly one-quarter of agricultural workers and over one-third of workers who installed insulation (Passel, 2006).

Considering more educated and skilled immigrants, social scientists have also recently noticed the extent to which immigrants contribute to innovation and job growth. In the United States, for instance, immigrants are responsible for a significant portion of high-tech patents and company start-ups (Wadhwa, 2008). Given such trends, lawmakers and writers often defend policies intended to attract greater high-end talent to their shores.

Among key policy dimensions to the immigration controversy is how much newcomers exploit access to social welfare services from the state. The evidence here is also mixed, and it varies considerably depending upon the migrants' country of origin, age, and the skills and education they acquired in their home countries. Some studies suggest that immigrants (legal or otherwise) are net contributors to government coffers. However, in cases where a group of immigrants tends to take more from state services than they pay back in taxes, there can be immense strain on public services and long-standing residents (Beck, 1994).

Policymakers also often worry about the extent to which newcomers assimilate into an existing culture. All industrialized nations have policies and institutions designed to foster this process. Such policies govern issues such as access to education, tests to gauge familiarity with domestic language and social and political institutions before extending citizenship, expectations of employment, and waiting periods before access to various public benefits. Among the measures of assimilation are language use (including by children) of immigrants, residency patterns, and how immigrants' wages compare to those of longer term residents of the host country. The extent of assimilation varies considerably by nation of origin. Of special note is that on some measures in some industrialized countries, many immigrants are assimilating less than newcomers did in years past. They are sometimes more likely to live for extended periods in communities with a significant concentration of immigrants like them, and their wage levels are not keeping up with natives. This generates concerns about immigration as a locus of worrisome inequality and ghettoization.

What is the controversy?

Each industrialized nation has complex and evolving histories regarding immigration. Writers and public officials do not always speak with one voice within one nation at any one time (let alone through history). They might welcome some newcomers but express overt hostility to some other prospective immigrants.

Reaching as far back as to the eighteenth-century new world British colonies, some noted writers worried that recent waves of immigration brought in "the most ignorant, Stupid Sort" of peoples of a "swarthy Complexion" who would have difficulty assimilating (Franklin, 1751). Such sentiments are sometimes echoed in one way or another in many historical debates about immigration. In 1896, a writer worried about then recent waves of immigration to the United States; these immigrants had "revolting" habits and were unfit to be Americans: "They are beaten men from beaten races; representing the worst failures in the struggle for existence. Centuries are against them, as centuries were on the side of those who formerly came to us. They have none of the ideas and aptitudes which fit men to take up readily and easily the problem of self-care and self-government … " (Walker, 1896) Assimilation and racial concerns continue into current discussions in many industrialized nations. Recently, a New Zealand public official was criticized for worrying that there were too many Asians coming to the country (NZ First's Brown slammed for "racist" anti-Asian remarks, 2008).

Immigrants have made up the bulk of population growth in many industrialized nations for many years. Surprisingly, though, some immigration trends seem to be quite fluid. From 2005 to 2010, for instance, the number of Mexicans coming to the United States has been nearly completely offset by the number returning to Mexico. Social scientists attribute such trends to changing economic conditions, enforcement norms in the United States, and declining birth rates in Mexico (Passel, Cohn, & Gonzalez-Barrera, 2012).

Social scientists will continue to study the impacts of immigrants on host and source countries. But social science alone cannot resolve policy disputes about these issues. Even when people agree on the facts, they may still disagree about how best to move forward.

There are many dimensions to immigration policy. The specific policies turn on who gets allowed in, what they are allowed to do, and how many may come. Consider the moral issues involved. These often lie at the heart of disagreements about immigration policy. The controversies turn on many moral values. To simplify the discussion a bit, let us focus on some central ones. Stated quite generally, they concern distributive justice, freedom, and cultural identity. People disagree about how to understand each of these and their significance in fashioning acceptable immigration policies, but we can identify how the disagreements about immigration often turn on disagreements about the relevant moral values at stake. We might then point to how some policy approaches might begin to reduce some of the controversies where people disagree. Of course, any suggested policy remedies will not bring controversies to an end, but perhaps we can make progress in reducing the intensity of some disagreement and clarifying how to discuss remaining disputes.

Distributive justice

When philosophers discuss distributive justice, they consider a group of theories that each justify a way of assigning people various benefits and responsibilities. The benefits can come in many forms. They typically include important protected liberties such as property rights and voting rights, and they might include other central interests such as those regarding marriage, career, or religious practice. The responsibilities also vary from one theory to another. They might include various sorts of obligations individuals have to support persons or institutions or simply to stand out of their way.

Distributive justice is not the only moral dimension relevant to assigning responsibilities to residents of a political community. Criminal justice, restorative justice, and charity are among the other moral considerations that might determine what responsibilities and benefits different people ought to have. Let us focus, though, on distributive justice and consider how these benefits and burdens ought to be assigned among people who are living complete lives under shared institutions.

A tax code assigns responsibilities to many persons living together in a political community. Tax burdens are not the only responsibilities people face. There are many others that come from commitments to family, membership in a community, or being a citizen. Theories of distributive justice differ on which benefits and responsibilities people have, which people have them, and why. But nearly all theories trace the benefits and burdens on individuals to membership in some significant group.

Membership matters. As Michael Walzer argues (Walzer, 1983), distributive justice is meaningful only among a group of persons who belong to a group that shares a way of life. On his view, that group is a political community. A political community is the group that provides for deep shared meaning and for shared ways of building complete lives together. People live lives together in communities shaped by common institutions. These institutions determine who gets to do certain things, who may not do certain things, and why.

Membership is a crucial basis for figuring out who owes what to whom. Members of significant groups owe much if not all responsibilities to other members, but little if anything to outsiders. People who are not members are, Walzer says, "cut off from the communal provision of security and welfare" (Walzer, 1983, p. 32). So it is vital to figure out who is a member.

Imagine a time when people needed to figure out what they owed to one another or what they could demand of one another. Perhaps there is a controversy or disagreement. Perhaps people are in the process of figuring out how to structure or reform a government. There are nearly always social or political institutions for taking care of these cases. Ideally people get past the uncertainty without bloodshed. However, as they move past this controversy, they pay special attention to members of their group.

Consider, for instance, how people living near one another usually have institutions to protect themselves against violence or to provide other shared goods such as schools or roads. People who are not members of that community of people living near one another do not count for much, if at all, in how those institutions are designed. That is not because those people do not count for anything at all but because they do not share the special benefits and responsibilities that come from membership.

Suppose the people of a community called Springville were occasionally to observe intelligent life on Mars through a telescope. (See also Wellman & Cole, 2011, pp. 62–3.) Perhaps those Martians had a complex society of their own. If Springvillians were figuring out how to pay for their own police force and what the police force may or must do, the Martians would not count in that discussion. They would not count because the Springvillians are figuring out what they should do together and what they may expect of each other. The Martians are not Springvillians, and so Springvillians would not take themselves to owe anything to the Martians nor to be in a position to demand anything of them.

The point of this example is to show that membership matters. It commonly tracks our understanding of who owes what to whom and who may claim what from whom. Basically, membership matters because it tells us who counts in a particular discussion of who gets what. Of course, there are various sorts of groups, and different groups may generate different privileges and responsibilities for their members. On Walzer's view, membership in a political community is crucial because it is the main basis for determining what people owe to one another by justice.

Justice is that part of morality that justifies, among other things, the enforceable claims people have against others. What justice requires may need to be specified by a particular country's laws. For instance, what counts as trespassing varies across and often within nations. But shared membership in a political community helps to determine what we owe and to whom, and what we may demand and from whom.

Membership matters because it determines much if not all of the *scope* of distributive justice. The scope of distributive justice includes all and only those people (or perhaps other beings) who are sources of enforceable claims regarding shared benefits and responsibilities. Does the scope of distributive justice start and stop at state boundaries? If it does, knowing that might help shape the terms in which we discuss immigration policies. Such policies might not be matters of justice owed to prospective immigrants. Justice might say that the only persons that matter when shaping immigration policies are compatriots. "Outsiders" might at best be the beneficiaries of the performance of duties of justice owed only among fellow citizens.

Few people will accept a very strong reading of the sort of view that justice stops at state borders. On this sort of strong view, we only owe anything *by justice* to other persons in our political community. This is because we share a history with them, and, most importantly, we are all vulnerable to the same set of coercively maintained institutions (Blake, 2001). To be sure, what we owe by justice might still vary within that community in light of particular local memberships and affiliations. For instance, by justice parents owe special care to their children; others in the community do not have such extensive obligations to those children. The basic point on this sort of view is that justice tracks boundaries that are significant enough to divide insiders from outsiders, however understood.

But this sort of view strikes many people as implausible. Even if there is no shared culture or history between you and someone from a faraway place we might call Distantforeignland, that does not mean it would not be an injustice for you to steal from, assault, or murder the Distantforeignlander. So not all obligations of justice rigidly track state boundaries.

Many people will concede that everyone owes it to prospective immigrants not to steal from them or assault them. But they might argue that *theft* or *assault* typically make sense within a political community whose institutions define what these terms mean. And this is what is at stake: who is a part of the conversation, and who counts, when figuring out how institutions are structured to provide for common welfare? Who counts when determining what we may or may not do to each other? Immigrants, who are not here yet, may seem not to count yet.

But many people will reject this emphasis on membership for understanding what justice requires of us. These critics may say emphasizing membership above all else misses a key point. They might maintain that prospective immigrants are persons just as any other and that they do count now. Indeed, some writers argue at length that the proper scope of distributive justice is global. They insist that there are global institutions that significantly define a person's life prospects, liberties, and responsibilities. For instance, the situation of a Ghanaian cotton-farming family is affected not only by the structure of their government and the political and economic situation at home. Their prospects are also affected by, for instance, global rules regarding trade, various price and tariff policies by developed nations, various international policies regarding recognition of heads of state, transportation/trade of weapons of war and tools of policing, and norms regarding who may have access to capital on international markets and on what terms. (See related discussions in Pogge, 2008.) Immigration policies are but one facet of this system that has significant international dimensions.

These international dimensions are indisputable. Whether they furnish convincing proof that the interests of immigrants must count equally when setting immigration policy is another matter. If we are looking for some specific guidance on which policies to fashion, perhaps we need not first resolve the dispute about how much the interests of immigrants should figure in domestic policy.

One way (but hardly the only way) of framing some controversies about immigration and distributive justice is to note that at least the law-abiding citizens of a political community count now. Quite often they have legitimate interests in having more Distantforeignlanders enter the country, either as employees, family members, or members of a particular subculture. The citizens might, for instance, sponsor prospective immigrants and thereby pledge to fellow citizens that the prospective migrants will not impose financial or other burdens on unwilling others. Obviously, sorting through the relevant details is where much of the controversy lies. (Anyone who has dealt with long-term immigration for themselves, their families, or their employees can attest to the challenges.) Even if we are not sure (or are currently unable to agree) as to whether citizens by justice owe some foreigners an invitation to immigrate, people typically acknowledge the responsibilities they owe to fellow citizens. One's fellow citizens may have significant claims regarding permitting or denying immigration. These might be a platform for considering how best to fashion acceptable policies that respond to significant moral considerations. Among those are freedom.

Freedom

Among the key stakeholders in the immigration controversy are prospective hosts (such as employers or family members), the immigrants themselves, and interested third parties such as fellow citizens. For the sake of simplicity let us bracket the case of fellow citizens. Part of their interests concerns distributive justice, which we considered above and will return to shortly. Another part concerns issues of cultural identity, which we will discuss at the end of this chapter. Here we will consider mainly the key freedoms at stake for prospective hosts and for the immigrants themselves.

Freedom is a crucial political value for nearly everyone. Of course, people dispute what political freedom may mean and what sorts of things people should be free to do or to have. Some authors speak of freedom mainly in terms of absence of obstacles, especially those that other persons and state institutions might impose. Others speak of opportunities to live in certain ways, which might entail certain enabling conditions. And still others speak of capabilities to choose, which might also entail support for people to pursue various idealized interests or preferences. Once fully specified, some of these notions of freedom are incompatible. However theorists resolve these disputes, they seem to have in mind some notion of significant interests that political institutions ought to acknowledge, protect, or fulfill. People commonly regard four central interests as among important political freedoms worthy of social and political recognition and protection: the freedom of association, the freedom of contract, the freedom of movement, and the freedom from oppression. Each of these matters for understanding how to structure immigration policies in a way that acknowledges significant moral concerns.

Consider first the *freedom of association*. Being able to establish relationships with people is among the most central interests we have. We have interests in forming and sustaining romantic and family relationships. We also have important interests in being able to establish and sustain close friendships and other relationships with members of neighborhoods and religious communities. In many cases, these communities are crucial for giving us a sense of meaning and purpose. They provide a shared normative framework for understanding who we are and what is valuable. But limits on immigration restrict the associative freedoms of both immigrants and their prospective hosts. This is no small cost: sometimes families are kept apart. Often, immigrants are denied the opportunity to form close attachments as they see fit. This keeps them from realizing one of the most significant components of a good life, namely, what comes from fulfilling and rewarding relationships.

These restrictions affect immigrants as well as many current citizens. Often there are prospective hosts in a country that wish to have the immigrants join them in their families or communities. But immigration limits restrict their opportunities to do this.

The interest in building and expanding cultural communities is certainly more significant for some than for others. Some people feel at home in a country without craving the validation of others with similar backgrounds from abroad. However, we might note a special sort of interest that nearly everyone has: an interest in the opportunity to establish business relationships or employer/employee arrangements.

The *freedom of contract* is an important freedom, both as a basis for economic growth and as a platform for personal improvement. As Chandran Kukathas notes, often the only thing of value that persons in poor countries have is their labor (Kukathas, 2014). Their opportunity to exchange their labor for a wage sometimes represents their only hope for a decent life. And often, because of oppression, war, discrimination, or a horrible economy, they have no such hope in their homelands. On the flip side, employers may wish to hire persons from abroad. Restricting immigration may restrict their opportunities to employ people as they wish. This restriction on the freedom of contract, while perhaps not the most serious moral value at stake, is still a moral cost.

The *freedom of movement* is another important freedom. It is a protected opportunity to go from one place to another as one sees fit. As mentioned previously, this freedom is hardly unlimited, and we accept restrictions on this regularly. This freedom is still important as part of a commitment not to enable the world's worst regimes. As Kukathas notes, when citizens of a country lack some sort of protected opportunity to move elsewhere, this can embolden tyrants (or, minimally, remove incentives for them to reform) (Kukathas, 2014).

A *freedom from oppression* is perhaps one of the most serious freedoms at stake in the immigration controversies. While respect for human rights and standards of living have improved considerably since the industrial revolution, there are still disturbingly large numbers of people who languish in conditions where basic human rights are systematically violated. In many cases, whole peoples lack access to basic medical care or the minimum range of calories needed to sustain a decent life. The persons who fall into these categories are called "refugees," though in international law, this term is sometimes reserved for people fleeing religious, social, or political persecution. (See, for instance, the United Nations Convention Relating to the Status of Refugees.) Restrictions on immigration of refugees, however understood, restrict the opportunities of persons fleeing persecution, and they may even stop people who might wish to offer assistance to such persons. Proponents of more open immigration might then argue that human decency requires at least somewhat more open immigration. Certainly one is required not to persecute people, but, one might then add, people are also minimally required not to stop others who wish to help people suffering from various forms of persecution.

This may help to frame the controversy a bit, but it only goes a small part of the way. Not all prospective immigrants are refugees. And even for those who are, it is not obvious that one particular decent industrialized representative democracy is obligated to take any particular (let alone all possible) refugees seeking asylum. There is more than one possible country that might offer asylum. Critics of unrestricted immigration by refugees may insist that other decent societies should do their "fair share." This requires complex international agreements and difficult national policymaking about who counts as a refugee and how much any given nation should be expected to bear. If others are unwilling to do their fair share, it may seem churlish of a nation that has already done its fair share to deny further refugees admission. But before we jump to such a conclusion we should consider that refugees do impose some costs.

The Organization for Economic Co-operation and Development compiles data on many countries' costs for accepting or repatriating refugees. When refugees stayed for extended periods, the costs included those for programs such as housing and food subsidies, education, job and language training, and other forms of assistance. As of 2009, for instance, these first-year costs per refugee are sometimes modest, such as the equivalent of a few thousand US dollars in Spain, Austria, and the UK. Elsewhere, such as in the United States and Canada, the costs are over US$10,000 and sometimes more than double or triple such amounts in parts of northern Europe and New Zealand (OECD, 2012). This shows that helping out refugees imposes costs on third parties when governments oversee the programs.

The costs associated with assisting refugees might be an argument against unrestricted refugee admissions. Or, if people have misgivings with some or all levels of support for refugees, it might be the start of an argument against government-funded refugee assistance programs. Privately funded programs might reduce or eliminate some of the public costs here. Canada has programs that support private sponsorship of refugees, and these help integrate newcomers into the culture and reduce the public cost burdens. The United States has also seen several church groups sponsor refugee resettlements, though with some mixed success (Beck, 1994). Moreover, nations concerned about the morally significant interests of refugees can assist not merely by hosting refugees or granting them permanent asylum. As both Christopher Heath Wellman and David Miller have argued, developed world nations can assist potential refugees by working to improve conditions in developing countries (Miller, 2014, p. 368; Wellman & Cole, 2011, pp. 129–30). Regardless of the merits of specific programs domestically or abroad, it seems third-party domestic costs are not a clear reason to curtail or eliminate admission to refugees if alternatives are available to reduce or eliminate such costs.

Critics of immigration may be prepared to make exceptions for refugees, but they might still worry that an influx of immigrants will undermine the character of their culture. This brings up another crucial moral consideration common to immigration controversies, that of cultural identity.

Cultural identity

Immigration is such a flash point in public policy discussions because it engages many contentious disputes about social ideals. How a society is structured matters to residents because social structures affect their life prospects and what sort of world they can pass on to their children. Those social structures define the context in which people can pursue the various projects that give meaning to their lives. Immigration controversies may often turn on competing visions of a proper society. The presence of immigrants may alter some of the fundamental ways the society is organized. The immigrants' different ways of life may upset long-standing patterns of politics, public rituals, and the care and development of the environment. The immigrants may challenge how people conceive the character of their nation.

As Michael Walzer notes, people have a legitimate interest in the "closure" of communities at some level (Walzer, 1983, p. 39). In order for people to achieve the benefits that come from intimate association at any level, it is crucial that they can enjoy some restrictions, somewhere, over who gets to join the association. This is certainly true of marriages, for instance. If partners (or, in some cases, families) were not free to pick whom to marry and they were thus not free to restrict the benefits and burdens of marriage to some person of their choosing, then marriage would lose much of its significance. Similarly for larger and less intimate associations, people can achieve the benefits of close ties only if they are in a position to determine those with whom they will sustain such ties.

Christopher Heath Wellman stresses the significance of restricted association, especially when it comes to political communities. As he notes, "one's fellow citizens all play roles in charting the course that one's country takes" (Wellman & Cole, 2011, p. 40). This is why a freedom of association is vital: this freedom for a group of people is necessary for them to determine how they will organize their lives together. Unrestricted immigration threatens to undermine this freedom. It threatens to undermine, against current members' wishes, what their group will be like in years to come.

This emphasis on the significance of community attachments and fellow feeling is common among many writers in social theory. Yael

Tamir, for instance, stresses how a sense of connection and mutually shared identity root a significant part of our moral obligations (Tamir, 1993, p. 99). This sort of fellow feeling, Tamir argues, is crucial for making possible the projects that perpetuate the very social structures that give moral meaning to our lives (Tamir, 1993, p. 116). Following Tamir, we might say that these social structures are typically national in scope: they provide the locus for a sense of common identity and mutual identification with goals ranging over an entire life. Journalists frequently report versions of this view among laypersons. Many French complain that "France is over" because of the recent influx of immigrants (Smith, 2014). A recent movement to restrict immigration in Switzerland grew partly out of certain concerns about job availability and the preservation of a national identity (Hall, 2013).

Nations may provide the institutional framework by which people satisfy important moral interests such as security, fellow feeling, and a basis for meaningfulness. People may then have significant interests in sustaining and controlling their nation's identity. David Miller argues that we can understand nations by looking at how people inside them think about them (Miller, 1995). Those people take themselves to be part of a nation; they identify with it and with other members. They think of the nation as a shared project persisting through time and across generations. They think of their nation as a dynamic basis for collective deliberation and action. They think of their nation as territorially situated. Lastly, they think of their nation as resting on a "common public culture" determined partly by certain shared characteristics and commitments (Miller, 1995, p. 25).

In Miller's view (Miller, 2014), a sense of mutual identity is often necessary to sustain the national institutions that satisfy important moral interests. People cannot reliably provide mutual security and ensure basic welfare interests unless there is a common public culture. Regulating immigration, Miller argues, is then an appropriate way for a people to determine their shared fate. That shared fate need not be totalizing. As Miller notes, there is plenty of room for variation and subcultural affiliation. One's hobbies, dress, tastes, and sometimes one's specific religious practices need not be part of a national identity. Still, the basic shared public culture is a crucial part of the fabric that binds people together in morally significant projects. While that culture will be a forum for change, that culture is something that the people sharing it have an interest in sustaining and controlling. Control over immigration seems to be a natural implication of such moral interests.

When we consider the significance of an appeal to cultural identity for fashioning immigration policy, we must first be careful not to over-estimate the extent and implications of felt mutual identity. While more homogenous industrialized nation states such as Iceland and Japan may have a strong sense of shared identity, pluralist political communities such as those in Western Europe, North America, or Australia and New Zealand show robust and often intensely divisive disagreements. (Indeed, the same is true of many, if not most nations.) The people of each country manifest considerable differences in ways of life and fundamental views of what is valuable. Of course, they must all abide by certain basic legal requirements, but the extent to which they identify with national institutions and their reasons for supporting them (if they do) will significantly vary. This suggests that it is hardly obvious how deep and how strong people's sense of national identity is, nor is it at all clear that the identification is similarly significant and strong for all or most co-nationals. Once we say that a people have an interest in controlling their national character, we must ask precisely who those people are and whether institutions of control will be appropriately responsive to the deep disagreements among them. This is hardly to say that there should be no national institutions (let alone immigration policies). Sometimes some policy is needed to move forward and solve common problems. But those policies, particularly immigration policies, should be fashioned cautiously so as to acknowledge deep and perhaps permanent disagreements about what national policies should do and why.

A further reason for caution when considering the significance of cultural identity is that culture is fluid. Immigration would certainly affect culture, but so too do the choices people in a nation make, including the projects they pursue such as their careers, their art, their hobbies, their social theorizing, and, most notably, their families. We typically acknowledge a generous area of discretion in such domains, subject, of course, to the rights of others. For instance, a person may not create a work of art with someone else's property unless the owner gives permission. No one may make a hobby of beating up other people (unless it is consensual, such as with boxing or whatever else consenting adults might do). So if particular persons wish to invite others to live in the nation, we must ask whether this threatens the rights or significant interests of third parties. We must ask whether the potential change to national culture is a sufficient reason to restrict immigration.

Sometimes it seems to be. When there are clear threats to the legitimate interests of others—if, for instance, a person poses criminal threats or threats to public health—it seems reasonable for policy to restrict or forbid entry to prospective immigrants. It is not clear, however, that the reasons for restricting such immigrants stem from cultural identity considerations so much as from basic concerns for safety and health.

There are further concerns about appeals to an interest in sustaining a national culture. No doubt people may have strong preferences about what their world looks like. Sometimes those preferences are sources of reasons that we might even call "interests" in the sense David Miller might have in mind when he discusses the stakes people have in structuring their shared fate. But interests are not necessarily rights, even when they connect with important moral concerns. Even if they are rights, it is not clear that they might take precedence over the rights of prospective immigrants and their hosts. (We will soon discuss some rights of prospective immigrants.)

Many people will take certain prospective changes to the nation as unwelcomed costs. Careful policymakers might consider options that avoid contentious cultural identity considerations and focus on interests that all reasonable citizens share. Simply being unreceptive to change is not itself a morally significant cost worth attending to in policymaking, any more than disliking that certain subcultures tend to prefer different art forms, worship differently, or have very large families. The challenge is then to fashion policies that prevent people from imposing undue costs on others. When policies come with tradeoffs, they should be what people can justify to each other.

The rights of immigrants

Often lost in the discussion of immigration is the status of any moral claims by immigrants themselves. The vast majority of prospective immigrants are simply looking for a better life. There are often law-abiding citizens of the host nation who wish to let them come. When their co-nationals wish to use state institutions to stop people from inviting newcomers, they wish to restrict others' opportunities to live their lives as they wish.

Do immigrants have a right to enter other countries? Perhaps they do as an application of some strong moral claims they have for assistance by others. This idea is controversial. Many people wonder whether ethical principles can impose such seemingly strong demands. A less morally demanding requirement is that people simply stay out of others' way. As Michael Huemer notes (Huemer, 2010), drawing on such an idea, this is an argument available against most immigration restrictions. The argument turns on what, if anything, constrains a state's use of its coercive powers.

In many cases, the prospective immigrants are desperately poor and wish to improve themselves and their families by trading with a territory's residents. May someone restrict such relationships? Suppose Marvin is on the brink of a starvation that he might avoid by going into an area to exchange with willing others. It would seem inexcusable for Sam to use or threaten to use force to stop Marvin. Sam would then be responsible for Marvin's death (Huemer, 2010, pp. 431–4). This sort of violation against Sam is even worse than depriving residents of the opportunity to trade with Marvin, which might impose some losses on them. This is the start of an argument that immigration restrictions seem to violate the rights of prospective migrants. Those persons seeking entry to a country might have a right that others not stop them from interacting with willing trading partners and associates. And there are plenty such partners, such as employers, landlords, merchants, friends, and neighbors.

Much now hangs on whether there is indeed such a right to entry and how strong it is. Among the ethical challenges to such a right for people considering proper immigration public policy is any of the following considerations: (1) the weight of a government's responsibility to privilege the interests of its citizens and legal residents; (2) whether any potential adverse domestic economic impact gives a moral justification for restricting immigration; (3) whether states have a right to exclude foreigners—even if doing so is wrong. Let us consider each in turn.

1 People often maintain that a government has special responsibilities to its own citizens in how it allocates resources and exercises its powers. Immigrants represent potential drains on a nation's resources. They become eligible for social welfare benefits and upset social norms. Much here depends on empirical data about rates of assimilation and how much immigrants contribute to tax coffers versus what they draw out as publicly funded benefits. Social scientists dispute the data about these issues, but it seems there is rarely much cause for alarm (Caplan, 2012). And we must be mindful that there might be limits to a government's proper power to privilege its own. As Michael Huemer argues, few would think a country is justified in robbing the poor abroad or coercively extracting their organs if doing so would benefit its own citizens (Huemer, 2010, pp. 445–6). So we must consider what, if anything, limits such favoritism of one's own.

2 Sometimes immigrants impose burdens on citizens. Whether this might be a justification to deny immigrants entry depends on how extensive the costs immigrants impose are compared to the benefits they offer. Here too the data help. On some accounts, immigrants have at worst a modest and temporary depressive effect on wages for low-skilled domestic workers and over time no net adverse effect (Caplan, 2012, pp. 7–8). But we might ask when and whether such data should matter at all. May Smith coercively forbid Jones from applying for a job Smith wants because Jones is willing to work for less? (Huemer, 2010, p. 454) Presumably not. The question is whether things change when governments do the coercing.

3 Ultimately, some people considering the justification of immigration public policy might rest their case on the supposed rights of states to do as they please, even if it is unkind. A stranger might come to your door to ask for help in a storm. Even if he looks needy, many people

would argue you are within your rights to refuse to provide aid. You might be concerned about your safety or that of your family if you let him in. You might simply have other things to do. Even if those "other things" are less urgent than the stranger's needs, it might seem you should be free to decide how to spend your time and resources. Some people might go so far as to say you have a right to deny aid, even if doing so shows a despicable disregard for the needs of others. Perhaps this is a sort of "right to do wrong": the stranger has no right to your help, but since you are free to live your life as you see fit, you may (but should not) wrongfully refuse aid. Similarly, perhaps states have rights to refuse entry to needy prospective immigrants in just the way you have the right to refuse strangers the chance to enter your home. (Compare related arguments in Wellman, 2008.) States might have a similar sort of "right to do wrong." Among potential challenges to such an argument is that refusing entry might not merely be a refusal to lend aid. It might amount to the denial of someone's rights to help herself. It might also amount to the denial of the rights of association by citizens. What justifies these various competing rights, and determining their weights, is among the ethical challenges facing people attempting to resolve disputes over immigration public policy.

Some policy options

Nearly all developed nation states restrict immigration from developing countries. There are plenty of restrictions for prospective entrants from other developed countries, too. There are barriers even for those who arrive. In the United States, for instance, immigrants are ineligible for various state benefits during a waiting period lasting several years. Illegal immigrants are often ineligible for many state privileges, such as access to publicly funded education, political representation, and even the opportunity to open bank accounts.

While there might be costs for admitting immigrants, there are costs to residents and immigrants because of restrictions. When there are available alternatives that might reduce moral and economic costs, perhaps they are worth investigating. Among them are (1) lengthier (if not permanent) denial of access to state welfare benefits; (2) permitting access to state benefits only after exceeding a certain tax threshold; (3) allowing guest workers to stay only for a time in exchange for tax payments; (4) surtaxes or additional fees for entry; and (5) policies that offer longtime resident children more opportunities than adults. (See, for instance, Caplan, 2012; García-Peña, 2013; Davey, 2014; Young, 2014.)

There are moral costs to each of these. Refusing or delaying newcomers' access to state benefits may seem to marginalize them and entrench a second-class status. Granting access conditional on payment of taxes above a minimum seems to present state services as a commodity for sale rather than something due anyone legally in a territory. Permitting guest workers only temporary legal residence strikes some critics as exploitation of the desperate. These and similar such policies worry some people as denying all persons equal treatment before the law. Others believe that such policy options, while imperfect, offer an option to persons seeking opportunities for honest improvement. While any of these might seem politically challenging, the ethical stakes might be so high in the host country and for prospective migrants that alternative policy possibilities merit serious consideration.

Conclusion: some guidance from ethical reflections

The controversy over immigration policy rests partly in empirical issues. People are sometimes uncertain what the impacts of immigrants have been and might be, and people disagree on the significance of those impacts. Proponents of more open borders will argue that history and social science show that immigrants tend to improve themselves and those around them in their new homes. Those who are brave enough to leave their homelands to seek out better opportunities for themselves and their families are dynamic sources of innovation and energy in a political community. Immigrants typically do not draw out more in public resources than they contribute, and immigrants are a valuable resource since their very presence creates more jobs and more resources for everyone (Simon, 1999). Economists have frequently shown that everyone benefits from the products and services immigrants produce. Even those who face stiffer competition for jobs or living space will typically find that they do better over the course of a life because of the creativity and productivity of immigrant populations. Critics, however, can point to the significance of interests in sustaining or controlling current cultural norms, excluding entrants to wage markets, and the tangible and intangible challenges immigrants pose to host nations.

Immigration policy is and will surely remain complex and contentious. Among the ways of reducing the contention might be a greater appreciation of the morally significant interests at stake in terms of distributive justice, the freedoms of many stakeholders, and an understanding of cultural identity. Of course, looking to ethical values is no panacea. Ethics is hardly free of controversy. Disagreements about immigration might not lessen by, for instance, shifting the discussion to considering cultural identity.

Many of the moral values at stake in immigration highlight how people worry that others may keep them from doing what they have a legitimate interest in doing. People disagree about how to live, but reasonable people can agree that no one should inappropriately impose costs on others. One key challenge is then to sort out which policies might minimize how much trash people dump on unwilling others, literally or figuratively.

Carefully designed sponsorship policies may allow for people or companies to host newcomers and agree to bear the costs of assimilating immigrants. Perhaps immigrants might have restricted access to certain public benefits for a reasonable waiting period. Meanwhile, the immigrants could be adapting to the culture of their new home and contributing to the economy. In lieu of tying immigration policies to contentious issues of cultural identity, people might look for policies that allow others to live among those they choose while minimizing the costs they impose on others.

Further reading

The literature on immigration is extensive, both in social science and in social/political theory. Julian Simon's discussions of the beneficial effects of immigration are a touchstone for many social theorists. See, for instance, *Immigration: The Demographic and Economic Facts*, Cato Institute study, December 11, 1995, at www.cato.org/pubs/policy_report/pr-immig.html. Warnings about cultural identity are common. Among especially accessible treatments of this complex issue are David M. Kennedy, "Can We Still Afford to be a Nation of Immigrants?" *Atlantic Monthly*, November 1996, at www.theatlantic.com/magazine/archive/1996/11/can-we-still-afford-to-be-a-nation-of-immigrants/304835/. Worries about poorly executed sponsorship programs and failures to assimilate come from many quarters. Of note are the difficulties facing recent Burmese and Hmong immigrants. See, for instance, Roy Beck, "The Ordeal of Immigration in Wausau," *Atlantic Monthly,* April 1994, available at www.theatlantic. com/past/politics/immigrat/beckf.htm. Focusing particularly on the case of the United States, Alvaro Vargas Llosa discusses the role of migrants in shaping national identity and concludes that immigration is nearly always a moral, economic, and cultural benefit. See his *Global Crossings: Immigration, Civilization, and America* (Oakland, CA: Independent Institute, 2013). The debate between Christopher Wellman and Phillip Cole highlights many of the central moral and policy dimensions of the immigration dispute, including many not canvassed in the brief overview above. See Christopher Heath Wellman and Phillip Cole, *Debating the Ethics of Immigration* (Oxford: Oxford University Press, 2011). The more global and international dimensions of immigration policies are given a critical discussion in Gillian Brock, *Global Justice* (Oxford: Oxford University

Press, 2009). For a useful recent overview of the economic impacts of immigration on the host economy, see George Borjas, "Immigration," in *The Concise Encyclopedia of Economics*, available at www.econlib.org/library/Enc/Immigration.html. Ben Powell collected several essays exploring the benefits of reform in favor of greater international mobility of labor in *Making Poor Nations Rich: Entrepreneurship and the Process of Economic Development* (Oakland, CA: Independent Institute, 2007).

References

Australian Visa Bureau. (2010, July 30). *One in four Australians is foreign born, new figures show*. Retrieved November 11, 2013, from www.visabureau.com/australia/news/30-07-2010/one-in-four-australians-is-foreign-born-new-figures-show.aspx

Beck, R. (1994, April). The Ordeal of Immigration in Wausau. *Atlantic Monthly, 273*(4), pp. 84–97.

Blake, M. (2001). Distributive justice, state coercion and state autonomy. *Philosophy and Public Affairs, 30*, 257–96.

Borjas, G., & Katz, L. (2007). The evolution of the Mexican-born workforce in the United States. In G. J. Borjas (Ed.), *Mexican Immigration to the United States* (pp. 13–55). Chicago: University of Chicago Press.

Borjas, G., Grogger, J., & Hanson, G. (2006, September). *Immigration and African-American employment opportunities: The response of wages, employment, and incarceration to labor supply shocks* (Working Paper No. 12518). National Bureau of Economic Research. Retrieved June 3, 2014 from www.nber.org/papers/w12518

Caplan, B. (2012). Why should we restrict immigration? *Cato Journal, 32*(1), 5–24.

Davey, M. (2014, January 24). Immigrants seen as way to refill Detroit ranks. *The New York Times*, p. A12.

Dixon, P. B., & Rimmer, M. T. (2009). *Restriction or legalization? Measuring the economic benefits of immigration reform*. Washington, D.C.: Cato Institute.

Franklin, B. (1751). *Observations concerning the increase of mankind, peopling of countries, &c.* Retrieved June 2, 2014, from The History Carper: www.historycarper.com/1751/09/01/observations-concerning-the-increase-of-mankind-peopling-of-countries-c/

Garcîa-Peña, L. (2013, December 13). Suddenly, illegal at home. *The New York Times*, A39.

Hall, A. (2013, April 26). Switzerland says no to more foreign workers as it imposes new quota on immigrants amid fears of being swamped. *Daily Mail*. Retrieved July 3, 2014, from http://www.dailymail.co.uk/news/article-2315217/Switzerland-says-NO-foreign-workers-imposes-new-quota-immigrants-amid-fears-swamped.html

Huemer, M. (2010). Is there a right to immigrate? *Social Theory and Practice, 36*(3), 429–61.

Immigration in Canada: A portrait of the foreign-born population. (n.d.). Retrieved September 3, 2013, from Statistics Canada: www12.statcan.ca/census-recensement/2006/as-sa/97–557/p2-eng.cfm

Immigration: Almost four hundred years of American history – attitudes towards immigrants. (n.d.). Retrieved September 3, 2013, from Library Index: www.libraryindex.com/pages/2399/Immigration-Almost-Four-Hundred-Years-American-History-ATTITUDES-TOWARD-IMMIGRANTS.html

Kukathas, C. (2014). The case for open immigration. In A. I. Cohen, & C. H. Wellman (Eds.), *Contemporary debates in applied ethics* (2nd ed., pp. 376–88). Malden, MA: Wiley-Blackwell.

Migrants in the UK: An overview. (n.d.). Retrieved September 3, 2013, from The Migrant Observatory: www.migrationobservatory.ox.ac.uk/briefings/migrants-uk-overview

Miller, D. (1995). *On Nationality*. Oxford, Clarendon Press

Miller, D. (2014). Immigration: The case for limits. In A. I. Cohen, & C. H. Wellman (Eds.), *Contemporary debates in applied ethics* (2nd ed., pp. 363–75). Malden, MA: Wiley-Blackwell.

NZ First's Brown slammed for "racist" anti-Asian remarks. (2008, April 3). Retrieved September 3, 2013, from *The New Zealand Herald*: www.nzherald.co.nz/politics/news/article.cfm?c_id=280&objectid=10501783

OECD (2012). *ODA reporting of in-donor country refugee costs*. Retrieved June 3, 2014 from www.oecd.org/dac/stats/RefugeeCostsMethodologicalNote.pdf.

Ottaviano, G., & Peri, G. (2012). Rethinking the effect of immigration on wages. *Journal of the European Economic Association, 10*(1), 152–97.

Passel, J. S. (2006). *The size and characteristics of the unauthorized migrant population in the U.S. – estimates based on the March 2005 current population*. Pew Hispanic Center. Retrieved June 3, 2014 from www.pewhispanic.org/files/reports/61.pdf

Passel, J. S., Cohn, D., & Gonzalez-Barrera, A. (2012). *Net migration from Mexico falls to zero – and perhaps less*. Pew Hispanic Center.

Peri, G. (2010, August 30). The effect of immigrants on U.S. employment and productivity. *FRBSF Economic Letter, 2010*(26), 1–5.

Pogge, T. (2008). *World poverty and human rights*. Malden, MA: Polity.

Simon, J. L. (1990). *Population matters: People, resources, environment, & immigration*. New Brunswick, NJ: Transaction Publishers.

Simon, J. L. (1999). *The economic consequences of immigration* (2nd ed.). Ann Arbor: University of Michigan Press.

Smith, J. H. (2014, January 5). Does immigration mean "France is over"? *The New York Times*. Retrieved June 3, 2014, from http://opinionator.blogs.nytimes.com/2014/01/05/does-immigration-mean-france-is-over/

Tamir, Y. (1993). *Liberal nationalism*. Princeton, NJ: Princeton University Press.

United States Census Bureau – Foreign Born. (n.d.). Retrieved September 3, 2013, from United States Census Bureau: http://usgovinfo.about.com/gi/o.htm?zi=1/XJ&zTi=1&sdn=usgovinfo&cdn=newsissues&tm=46&f=00&su=p284.13.342.

ip_&tt=2&bt=0&bts=0&zu=http%3A//www.census.gov/population/www/soc demo/foreign/index.html

Wadhwa, V. (2008, July/August). *America's other immigration crisis.* Retrieved September 3, 2013, from *The American*: www.american.com/archive/2008/july-august-magazine-contents/america2019s-other-immigration-crisis

Walker, F. A. (1896, June). *Restriction of immigration.* Retrieved September 3, 2013, from *The Atlantic Magazine*: www.theatlantic.com/magazine/archive/1896/06/restriction-of-immigration/306011/

Walzer, M. (1983). *Spheres of justice.* New York: Basic Books.

Wellman, C. H. (2008). Immigration and freedom of association. *Ethics, 119*, 141–58.

Wellman, C. H., & Cole, P. (Eds.). (2011). *Debating the ethics of immigration.* Oxford: Oxford University Press.

Young, C. E. (2014). *Global poverty, migration, and guest worker programs.* Thesis, Georgia State University, Atlanta. Retrieved July 3, 2014, from Georgia State University: http://scholarworks.gsu.edu/philosophy_theses/148

4   Same-sex marriage

Writers on marriage often speak of what they call a "traditional" marriage as a permanent union between a man and a woman. This notion is captured by the laws of many nations, leading many people to think that heterosexual monogamous marriage is simply what marriage *is*. It turns out, however, that marriage has a complex history. Marriage sometimes is not and was not monogamous. There is a long history of polygamous marriage in many cultures. We need only read religious texts to learn that. Historians have written that in various cultures reaching back to antiquity, same-sex partners married—and sometimes in religious ceremonies. (See the selections in Sullivan, 2004, ch. 1; and Coontz, 2005.)

Marriage norms are evolving. Previously, marriage was often a union that families arranged privately, especially to coordinate property holdings and manage kin networks. Today, however, marriage is often for romantic love, and many regard the state licensing of marriage as essential. Moreover, legal systems increasingly allow gays or lesbians to marry. In early 2014, for instance, couples of the same sex were legally permitted to marry anywhere in a dozen nations and in many parts of several others. Writers also point to various polling data to show growing public acceptance throughout the world for gays, lesbians, bisexuals, and for same-sex marriage.

The debate over same-sex marriage engages deep emotions, perhaps partly because people recognize the special significance of marital union. *Marriage* may be difficult or impossible to define; it may lack any essential characteristics (Corvino, 2012, pp. 21–44; Brake, 2012, ch. 6). But as an institution, marriage often involves some from a group of features such as emotional commitment, exclusivity, a promise to provide support and care, a signal to others to treat the parties as committed partners, the agreement to share many things (such as property, sex, children, and a life together), and a legal status. Even if people dispute what should be in a definition of marriage, what is uncontroversial is this: marriage is central to the lives of many of us—even if we are unmarried and plan to stay that way. Marriage is among the fundamental social and political structures that determine how people live together in a political society.

Proponents of same-sex marriage argue that their views rest significantly in a commitment to moral and legal equality. Critics worry that same-sex unions undermine the meaning of marriage, jeopardize child welfare, and wrongfully impose unwelcome forms of life. Recent legal trends have further inflamed the dispute. This chapter presents some background to frame the controversy. It considers how reducing the involvement of states in marriage might be an alternative to consider in public policy debates. When the political stakes are reduced, the controversy might decrease as well.

Some background

Much is at stake in disputes about same-sex marriage. Opponents of same-sex marriage point to the sanctity of marital unions and the welfare of children. Proponents point to equality before the law and the chance for gays and lesbians to enjoy all the benefits of life as loving and committed couples.

Many legal privileges, powers, and rights attach to marriage. The rules vary among and sometimes within jurisdictions. Often, however, married couples enjoy opportunities unavailable to unmarried couples. Among such opportunities are special tax statuses, access to many state and private benefits (such as retirement, education, healthcare), tax-free sharing of property, surrogacy powers, inheritance rights, and the privilege in courts not to testify against spouses (see, for instance, Sunstein & Thaler, 2008, pp. 380–81). In the United States, there are over 1100 federal benefits, rights, and privileges that depend on marital status (General Accounting Office, 2004). The question is whether this status may only be available to couples consisting of one male and one female.

Reasons to marry

Marriage is controversial, even in its "traditional" heterosexual monogamous form. Historically, marriage has been linked to the subjugation of women. It often gave men powers over their wives that effectively erased women's status as civil persons, denied women the right to refuse sexual access, and consigned women to a life of miserable domestic servitude. Indeed, many activists challenge whether gays and lesbians ought to want the chance to be married. They argue, for instance, that allowing same-sex marriage gives greater scope to an illegitimate institution. Even if marriage no longer involves (as much) oppression as it once did, critics sometimes complain that marriage as such disrespects the distinctive identities of gays and lesbians. (See, for instance, Card, 1996; Ettelbrick, 1989; and the selections in Sullivan, 2004: ch. 4.) Whatever its history, marriage involves many constraints. Why then might any rational persons want to marry?

Marriage is a type of commitment. What it specifically involves may vary from one marriage to another, but as a commitment, it involves at least some opportunity costs. As with any commitment, married partners give up some benefits in order to acquire some other greater ones. Spouses commit to one another in order to get the social, legal, economic, and personal benefits of spousal partnering. They accept the costs of not sharing certain goods with outsiders (such as sex, property, and intimacy) in order that the couple may enjoy them together.

Marriage invokes a host of institutions to secure a commitment. Legally, married couples increase their "exit costs." Unlike roommates, who can usually readily dissolve their relationship, spouses bind themselves together in a way that makes dissolution of the union more complicated. Spouses are legally entitled to much of each other's property and are socially and legally privileged to do things for and to one another that outsiders cannot. A marriage also signals to others in their community that the partners have accepted a mutual commitment that excludes outsiders in many ways. This gives added meaning to spousal commitment and provides reason to sustain it. Personally, marriage expresses spouses' mutual commitment and allows them to build a life together by knowing they can rely on one another.

Of course, not all marriages involve the same specific commitments and the same shared understandings. By marrying, however, partners typically signal to one another and to their community a commitment to some enduring form of mutual care. People seek such relationships as a unique source of special value for themselves and their partners. The controversy here is about whether to restrict such benefits to male/female couples.

Context matters. History is marked with institutionalized oppression and violence against gays and lesbians. Indeed, in many countries, being gay is still an offense punishable with imprisonment or death (Human Rights Council, 2011). For many gays and lesbians, protecting the opportunity to marry is important as an expression of their equal legal, civic, social, and moral status.

The definitional approach

Many discussions of same-sex marriage start by exploring definitions of marriage. After all, it seems we should know what we are talking about before tackling the hard work of exploring appropriate applications of a concept. Perhaps the very idea of marriage can shed some light on whether there can be such a thing as same-sex marriage.

Some writers argue that marriage has a fixed meaning that cannot be changed by wishing or legislation. As Maggie Gallagher writes, "Politicians can pass a bill saying a chicken is a duck and that doesn't make it true. Truth matters" (Gallagher, 2009). Critics of same-sex marriage argue that marriage simply is a certain union between a male and a female.

This is what John Corvino calls a "definitional objection" (Corvino, 2012). This objection basically runs as follows. Marriage is a relationship that is valuable for what it brings about (such as improving the partners and contributing to children's welfare). Marriage is also good in itself: it involves a special unity of two persons, ordered to a shared biological goal, namely, procreation. The only sort of union that can be directed toward that end is one including only a male and a female; only a male and female pair is capable of becoming a special whole whose activity together can solidify and express their union. (See, for instance, Girgis, 2014.) "Same-sex marriage" is on this view an oxymoron, just as "harmless poison" or "cold-blooded mammal" is. Given the meanings of terms, these sorts of combinations are impossible.

Unfortunately, this definitional approach has not helped reduce the controversy. The proper application of the term is precisely what is at issue. It may seem question-begging to insist that marriage simply means a union of a man and a woman. As Evan Wolfson writes, "ending the exclusion of gay people from marriage does not change the 'definition' of marriage any more than allowing women to vote changed the 'definition' of voting" (Wolfson, 2011) What makes the definitional approach more problematic is that marriage does not have a fixed definition. Marriage is a social institution, but people understand it in many different ways. Unlike terms whose meaning is set, the shape (and so the meaning) of the institution of marriage evolves (Brake, 2012, ch. 6). The meaning of the term itself might not preclude gays and lesbians from being eligible to marry.

Marriage does not seem to be linked by definition to procreation. Throughout the developed world, a growing proportion of children are born out of wedlock (Harris, 2009); a substantial number are in single-parent homes (Rampel, 2010). This is not to commend these trends; it simply challenges the idea that procreation is inextricably tied to marriage. Increasingly, it is not.

Who counts within certain social categories is often open to revision, at least sometimes because of previous unjust exclusion. Millions of persons of African descent were enslaved in many nations dominated by persons of European descent. It would have been circular for whites to say that former slaves could not become citizens because part of the definition of citizen is *free white person*. Who should be a citizen was precisely the issue. We can respond similarly to the definitional objection to same-sex marriage. Denying gays and lesbians the chance to marry is not justified simply by reading the exclusion from the supposed definition of marriage. If marriage is restricted to heterosexuals, appeals to the meaning of terms might not be the best justification.

Civil union and analogies to racist public policy

Same-sex marriage is available in over a dozen developed countries. Some additional countries restrict marriage to heterosexual couples but grant same-sex couples many of the rights and privileges of marriage through civil unions or some other officially recognized intimate partnership that is not called "marriage." Some writers defend alternative labeling for same-sex unions as a viable political compromise (Hull, 2006, pp. 205–11). Other proponents of same-sex marriage, however, reject alternative terms (such as "civil union") as a half-hearted gesture that wrongly reinforces the politically subordinate status of gays and lesbians (Corvino, 2012, pp. 31–32).

In the United States, early attempts at "separate but equal" public accommodations for whites and blacks proved both politically and morally unsustainable (Cottrol, Diamond, & Ware, 2003). Often the separate was inherently unequal. Suppose, then, there were separate institutions with exactly equivalent rights and powers such that "marriage" was the label for opposite-sex couples and some other term was designated for same-sex unions. But the name matters. As the Massachusetts Supreme Judicial Court stated in 2004, "The dissimilitude between the terms 'civil marriage' and 'civil union' is not innocuous; it is a considered choice of language that reflects a demonstrable assigning of same-sex, largely homosexual, couples to second-class status" (Neilan, 2004). John Corvino concurs. He writes that using different labels suggests "a difference that isn't present, and in turn creates a legal hierarchy" (Corvino, 2012, p. 31).

US legal history provides much ammunition for proponents of same-sex marriage. Among leading notable precedents are those acknowledging the special significance of marriage. The 1920 US Supreme Court case *Meyer v. Nebraska* acknowledged that a legal commitment to protecting liberty includes protecting certain basic opportunities for a person such as that to "marry, establish a home and bring up children, to worship God according to the dictates of his own conscience, and generally to enjoy those privileges long recognized at common law as essential to the orderly pursuit of happiness by free men" (*Meyer v. State of Nebraska*, 1923). Starting with the 1964 case *Griswold v. Connecticut*, the Court found that a right to privacy protects people in making intimate decisions. Most notably, the 1967 case *Loving v. Virginia* invalidated anti-miscegenation statutes. The Court affirmed that marriage is among the "basic civil rights of man" and found race was an inadequate basis to deny access to this institution (*Loving* v. *Virginia*, 1967). Proponents of same-sex marriage thus argue that sex is just as arbitrary a basis for restricting marriage as race is.

Recently, various parts of the United States have allowed gays or lesbians to marry. Some states litigated their way into extending marriage to same-sex couples. *Goodridge* v. *Department of Public Health* (2003) required Massachusetts to offer marriage licenses to same-sex couples. Other states, such as New York and Vermont, instead legislated such marriage rights.

Thea Spyer and Edith Windsor were same-sex spouses married in Canada. They later moved to New York. Spyer died and left her estate to her wife, but the US Internal Revenue Service refused Windsor's claim for federal estate tax exemption for spouses. The agency pointed to the Defense of Marriage Act, a 1996 federal law that restricted such a status to heterosexual couples. This mattered for Windsor: since the federal government did not recognize her marriage, she owed it over US$300,000 in estate taxes (*United States* v. *Windsor*, 2013).

It seemed difficult for opponents of same-sex marriage to explain why someone such as Edith Windsor should owe the US government over US$300,000 simply because her spouse happened to be a woman. In a June 2013 ruling, the US Supreme Court found that, in certain cases, states that denied full marriage benefits to same-sex couples were behaving arbitrarily and denying gays and lesbians the due process of law. Refusing to recognize same-sex marriage, the Court also ruled, can be an offense against "personhood and dignity" and unjustifiably impose a second-class status on gays and lesbians.

Of course, legal rulings do not settle the issue. They might make salient certain ways of thinking about the controversy. And as we know, legal rulings can be mistaken. So let us consider some of the ethical considerations that frame the controversy.

Ethical considerations at stake

Equal protection of the law

Proponents of same-sex marriage point to equality before the law. Just as race provides no legitimate basis for exclusion from the privileges and immunities available to citizens, it seems that sexual orientation fares no better. If state benefits are available to heterosexual spouses, it seems arbitrary to deny them to same-sex spouses. Respecting the right of same-sex couples to marry would then be an application of principles of equal citizenship. Imagine, for instance, gays were forbidden to vote. This would be an unjustified denial of a key right. Given how central marriage is for defining a life for oneself and making a family, proponents believe it is arbitrary and unjustified to deny gays and lesbians the right to marry.

US courts distinguish among laws impacting various groups of persons. Racial classifications must survive "strict scrutiny" by courts in the United States. This means that laws drawing racial distinctions must have especially powerful reasons on their side. Sexual orientation, however, does not inspire such strict scrutiny by courts. So, in the United States currently, the two sorts of classifications are not legally analogous. The analogy of restrictions on same-sex marriage to racial segregation might, however, still be powerful as part of an ethical argument.

Opponents of same-sex marriage might argue that equal protection under the law is not at stake. What matters here is whether the state may use its power to uphold a sensible view of a democratic majority about how a crucial social and legal institution may be structured. For the state to overrule such a majority, opponents might argue, is judicial overreach.

Here as in other areas of social public policy, the controversy engages fundamental disagreements about state power. We must consider the proper justification and role for state power in shaping social institutions. We must also consider what if anything justifies and constrains what courts may do. These are not merely legal theoretic disputes. They turn on ethical and political issues about what states may or must do.

The welfare of children

Historically, marriage has been the key forum for procreation. Some writers speculate that marriage evolved partly to allow and accommodate a sort of division of sexual labor. As the story goes, both bearing and raising children are costly in many ways. Women would devote themselves to it only with the promise of secure support from the men who would make them mothers. Men agree to provide such support only when there are practices or institutions in place to ensure that the children are their own. Marriage evolved to satisfy these interests.

This story is oversimplified and deeply controversial. (See Coontz, 2005, ch. 3.) Alternative accounts include the views that marriage evolved as a tool of oppression or as a way of deepening kin networks. Some writers insist that any plausible account of marriage expresses the important connection of sex to procreation. To paraphrase Maggie Gallagher, marriage is a universal institution that accommodates three truths: (1) people like sex; (2) sex makes babies; and (3) children need a father and a mother (Gallagher, 2012, pp. 108–9). Marriage is a way of ensuring responsible procreation. It protects women and children by tying fathers to the results of sexual intercourse.

Opponents of same-sex marriage point to the ethical significance of advancing the welfare of children. Allowing gays or lesbians to marry, on this view, deepens a troubling trend toward separating marriage from procreation. Maggie Gallagher writes, "If marriage is no longer the social institution which incarnates the ideal that children should have a mother and father, there will no longer be any social institution that represents or institutionalizes that ideal" (Gallagher, 2012, p. 126). Now, without further evidence to show the special significance of two different-sexed parents, Gallagher's point is at best in favor of stable homes with two loving parents.

It is easy to find social scientific data about the drawbacks of growing up in a single-parent home. According to common measures of well-being and material success, children who grow up in stable two-parent households typically do better in school and do better in life. Proponents of same-sex marriage do not dispute this data. They simply argue that it is not essential that one parent be male and the other female.

There are now plenty of children growing up in households with same-sex partners. Extending their caregivers opportunities to marry might improve children's well-being and express a commitment to the significance of stable families (Corvino, 2012, p. 20). Excluding gays and lesbians from marriage in order to protect children might then be a poor means to a worthy end.

People can search for data about how caretakers' sexual orientation affects children. The data are currently not conclusive. Some scholars argue that the social science does not show that children in households with same-sex caretakers do any worse than peers in "traditional" homes. The data might even suggest that children with two same-sex caretakers tend to do quite well when compared to similar peers. Others question whether there is any good evidence on this issue one way or the other (Pawleski *et al.*, 2006; Eckholm, 2014; Marks, 2012).

Were there to emerge conclusive social scientific evidence that children of same-sex parents are measurably disadvantaged compared to peers in comparable homes with heterosexual parents, that might be a reason to restrict some of the rights of same-sex couples (such as rights to adopt). But even such data might not settle the issue. After all, we can recognize that some factor about family circumstances links with some cost to a child's well-being. But we might still argue that restricting rights to be parents in such circumstances would entail unacceptable costs or involve misplaced policy priorities. Imagine, as seems likely in many developed nations, that the children in some demographic tend to have lower levels of educational achievement and higher incidence of criminal activity later in life. These would not be decisive reasons for a public policy restricting the rights of persons in such a demographic from having children. Much more ethical reflection and policy analysis would be required before justifying such measures.

In any case, there now seems to be insufficient justification for ruling out same-sex marriage on behalf of children. Given the large number of children that are wards of various states, the shortage of competent heterosexual parents, and the eagerness of many same-sex couples to adopt, a concern with children's welfare is insufficient for ruling out same-sex marriage.

Critics may reply that the lack of evidence the same-sex marriage harms children cuts both ways: there is also insufficient evidence for altering what is now a fundamental social and political institution. Absence of evidence is not evidence of absence. Here, people may wish to consider how and whether (lack of) evidence of effects figures in justifying public policies. May states only permit that for which there is conclusive evidence of little or no harm? Or is good evidence good enough? Or is lack of evidence of harm—even when we looked for it—good enough for the state to stand back? This matters not just for same-sex marriage public policy. It matters for figuring out what if anything constrains or justifies state regulation of the lives of its citizens.

Religious freedom

Some critics worry that legally permitting same-sex marriage will crimp the religious liberties of the clergy and members of their congregations. Clergy may be required to perform marriages they find pernicious. Congregants may be forced to accept same-sex couples into their group. This may threaten their freedom to determine how and with whom they practice their religion.

Same-sex marriage does not pose this sort of threat. Typically, legal changes that permit same-sex couples to marry do not require that some member of clergy officiate at any given ceremony. For example, Canada's 2005 Civil Marriage Act, which permitted same-sex marriages throughout the country, states that "religious groups are free to refuse to perform marriages that are not in accordance with their religious beliefs" (Government of Canada, 2005). This seems typical of many judicial rulings or legislation: the state will recognize the marriages, but religious officials need not perform the ceremony. Furthermore, members of the clergy are not legally required to officiate at any ceremony. They can refuse to perform marriages for congregants from elsewhere. Catholic priests can refuse to marry persons whose prior marriages have not been properly annulled. Indeed, clergypersons can (legally) refuse to perform marriages for any reason they wish. They might, however, face informal reprisals from their community for their actions or inactions.

If a religious group changes its rules to allow same-sex couples to marry in its sacred spaces and to attend religious services, this might not be a restriction on dissenters' religious freedom. That might be a case of a group doing something despite some members' disagreement. The fact that it is a religious group is beside the point. If dissenters object to the change, they are free to persuade their members to reconsider, or they can go find (or found) another religious group.

Intimacy

Another moral value that marriage norms engage is that of intimacy. Intimacy means different things and can be expressed in many ways, but it typically seems to involve at least some level of shared privileged knowledge. What defines special relationships of any sort is uniquely privileged and shared access to some things, such as physical spaces, human bodies, facts, viewpoints, or experiences. The privilege defines who is inside the relationship and who is outside. Intimacy is a marker and condition of the sorts of significant relationships that give special meaning to our lives. This is especially true of marriages, where *privileged* conversation, shared history, sexual access, and honesty define the relationship. When others outside the marital union have the same sorts of access to one's spouse, we typically wonder what is wrong with the marriage.

Same-sex marriage does not seem to threaten this. Indeed, it seems to deepen the significance of same-sex unions by acknowledging the equal possibilities for meaningful privileged intimacy. That Larry and Steve can be intimate in the context of legally recognized marriage does not jeopardize the intimate possibilities for Abdul and Corrine's heterosexual union. In one narrow sort of case, however, there may seem to be a threat. It concerns what it called the "spousal privilege."

The spousal privilege is a special immunity against being required to provide testimony in certain court cases. To a limited extent in the UK, but more so in the United States, spouses sometimes cannot be compelled to testify against one another in legal proceedings. The spousal privilege is controversial in itself, as it basically protects people against the state gathering incriminating testimony from knowing witnesses. A witness spouse can waive the privilege, but an accused cannot (at least, not any more) exercise the waiver so as to exclude incriminating testimony from a willing spouse.

The justification for this privilege seems to be rooted in the special intimacy that marks marital unions. Allowing the state to compel adverse testimony between spouses may disrupt marital harmony. Granting the state such powers, the argument runs, is not simply a problem for the particular marital union where one spouse may have knowledge that incriminates another. It is a threat to the institution of marriage itself. Recognizing the privilege then preserves family intimacy, even if at the occasional cost of criminal convictions. (See the discussions at Sulzberger, Jr., 1961; Lewis, 1983.)

The reason same-sex marriage might pose a problem here is that it widens the possible scope of cases where the spousal privilege might apply. Previously, only heterosexual couples were eligible for this privilege; they were the only ones who were candidates for the immunity from compelled testimony. Same-sex marriage enlarges the group of persons who can enjoy this privilege. The same-sex marriage opponent might complain that there would then be a larger potential class of persons who would be immune to compulsory testimony against defendants. The objection is that allowing same-sex marriage unjustifiably decreases the number of persons who could be compelled to provide incriminating testimony in courts of law. Once gays and lesbians can marry their partners, the argument goes, there are fewer witnesses available to convict persons for nefarious deeds. This is especially a problem given that partners often have the privileged knowledge that can convict a malefactor.

This argument, however, is not an objection to same-sex marriage. It is an argument against the spousal privilege. Or, it may be an argument that there are important legal costs to marriage, and so we should not extend the class of persons eligible to marry without very careful thought. If we push such arguments, they would not seem to be challenges to *same-sex* marriage but would be challenges to *marriage*. Indeed, critics who raise this objection would do well to consider recent trends in marriage. Marriage is on the decline in many developed countries. If we try to reverse this trend, there would be more married people. But, the more married people there are, the fewer good eligible witnesses the state can compel to testify. It does not matter whether the partners are gay or lesbian. The problem here, if there is one, is with the spousal privilege.

Freedom of association, inheritance, and an interlude on adopting pets

Proponents of same-sex marriage see opportunities to marry as natural extensions of their freedom to associate. Interestingly, this freedom cuts both ways. As this section discusses, even opponents of same-sex marriage might argue that they should be free to set the terms of their relationships without undue intrusion by others. And, one such intrusion, they argue, comes from permitting same-sex marriage.

First, consider the real-life challenges of same-sex couples who cannot live together because of immigration restrictions. In the United States, for instance, spouses of citizens have special privileges in obtaining "green card" residency rights. But, prior to the US Supreme Court ruling in June 2013, same-sex spouses had no more opportunities to live together in the United States than strangers of different nationalities. This led to heartbreaking difficulties for many gay and lesbian couples (Preston, 2013).

Critics of same-sex marriage, however, can point to the freedom of association. They might argue that they should not be compelled to associate with same-sex couples as married. This need not be so shallow a claim as saying, in effect, "Do not compel me to suffer gays in my midst!" After all, same-sex marriage involves no such compulsion. One need neither marry a gay person nor have one as a friend. But a subtler version of the argument goes as follows.

Being married invokes a host of social and legal privileges. If the law allows same-sex couples to marry, then participants in various institutions are required to treat such couples on a par with heterosexual spouses. Ordinarily, this is no burden. That one's community hospital allows same-sex spouses to make surrogate decisions when one partner is incapacitated can hardly be costly to third parties. (If anything, it would relieve hospitals of the uncertainty of what to do in such cases.) But other cases might have critics crying foul.

Consider inheritance rules. While specific intestacy norms vary from one jurisdiction to another, in many cases a person inherits a substantial portion of the estate of a spouse who dies without a valid will. Any children are still entitled to some of the estate.

Suppose Pat has a child, Chris, from a previous heterosexual marriage. The spouse with whom Pat raised Chris has died. Pat recently married another person, Lee, of the same sex, but Pat has died intestate. Without same-sex marriage, Chris would have been entitled to a larger portion of Pat's estate.

Of course, Chris has a legitimate complaint about reduced inheritance rights only if same-sex marriage is suspect. That Chris stands to lose in this case is not itself an argument against same-sex marriage. This might simply be a case where a child complains about evolving applications of intestacy norms that fail to extend previously available advantages. Chris is in no more position to complain than a male child whose father died intestate centuries ago during a shift away from primogeniture. If he were the only male heir when his father died intestate, under primogeniture he might get nearly all the estate. But without primogeniture, his mother and eight sisters might be entitled to a significant portion of the estate. If he complains, we could reply: those previous default norms were unjust or inappropriately applied.

Consider another example on behalf of the opponent of same-sex marriage. Imagine a world close to our own but featuring a growing movement to permit the legal adoption of pet animals in the way people can legally adopt human children. Proponents of nonhuman companion-animal adoption argue for all the legal, social, and economic advantages available to persons who adopt human children. Such parity, they say, would recognize and affirm the deep significance of the relationships they have with their nonhuman dependent companions (NDCs, for short). Relations with NDCs, they argue, are sources of deep meaning because of the reciprocal affection involved and the special opportunities to provide sensitive care for voiceless living beings who cannot live well on their own.

We can elaborate on this example as follows. Proponents of NDC adoption wish for the same tax advantages, family leave opportunities, and insurance benefits available to humans who adopt other human beings. Restricting these benefits to cases of human dependents unfairly privileges one type of caring relationship over others. Raising and caring for NDCs can often be expensive. Insofar as the state helps to reduce the relevant burdens, it should not privilege one type of adoption.

In this imagined case, critics might say that it is impossible to "adopt" a nonhuman animal except in some metaphorical or secondary sense, as in "adopting" a cat from the local animal shelter. Humans and pets cannot have the same sort of relationship as that involving human parents and adopted children. The relationship cannot feature the same level of emotional intensity and the same sort of moral significance. More sharply, the critics would say that any such proposed change undermines the unique value of human relationships.

To these likely objections, proponents of our imagined NDC adoption policy might reply:

> All of that is pernicious speciesism! Why is a human's relationship with an adopted human child necessarily of greater moral significance than what I might have with my nonhuman dependent companion? If you can get tax benefits for having adopted human children, so should I for my NDC. If you are guaranteed family medical leave to care for your tragically and chronically ill adopted human child, I should have the same privileges when my cat develops debilitating feline leukemia. If you get special discounts for paying for your human child's medical care, I should have the same opportunity for my NDC. Don't discount the significance of my relationship with my nonhuman dependent companion; to do so shows us great disrespect.

Some NDC adoption proponents might even inflame the controversy further by pointing to "marginal cases." They ask why caregivers who adopt profoundly mentally disabled human children are entitled to the social, economic, and legal advantages of adoption, but those who adopt NDCs with comparatively greater cognitive capacities are denied such advantages.

Critics of permitting NDC adoption might point to various costs the policy might impose on unwilling others. Once NDC adoption becomes the legal equivalent of "traditional" human adoptions, taxpayers are compelled to subsidize a lifestyle that bears a status they reject. They have no problem with taking care of pets the way people have been doing it for thousands of years. They do not deny that pets can be a source of great meaning and value in a family. They also do not deny that taking care of pets can be an emotional and financial drain. They simply reject the legal equivalence of NDC adoption with that of current adoption of human beings. They also object that taxes and insurance will treat pet ownership on a par with caring for children. They will have to pay for this, even if only with somewhat higher rates.

Critics of NDC adoption might also complain that changing adoption norms is misguided. People are still able to have pets; they simply cannot and should not be able to adopt them as if they were human children. After all, pets are animals. Now, NDC adoption proponents might say, "if you do not like the idea of adopting a nonhuman animal, with the same rights and privileges that human parents have regarding their adoptive children, then do not adopt one!" But this would miss the critics' point. They insist that shifting norms in this way is pernicious: it wrongly elevates a less valuable relationship at the expense of other more genuinely valuable ones, namely, human parent/child relations. Once pets count as much as children do for the purposes of taxes and family leave, that cheapens the genuine value of the relationships human beings have with their human children. This is no small cost. And this can be a reason to oppose changing some of the ways we structure institutions. The proposed change denies people the rights to associate with others in a way that acknowledges the unique value of human relationships.

To be clear, there are some important differences between this and the same-sex marriage case. First, human/pet relations are not historically a target of unjust oppression. Second, there is no serious movement afoot to push for adoption parity like this. People who currently cannot enjoy this legal status with their nonhuman dependent companions do not complain about moral, economic, or political marginalization because of the scope and application of current adoption rules. Third, there may seem to be good reasons to privilege adoptions of humans over those of pets. The state needs children to persist; it does not need pets. And (human) family relations may be a core social institution in a way that relations with pets never can be. Of course, NDC adoption proponents might reply that all this just begs the question against the significance of the relationships they support.

The point of the adoption thought-experiment is to notice how expanding the class of beings who are eligible for certain state benefits may impose costs on others. Policy changes also involve transforming institutions and altering normative frameworks. There can be unintended consequences that cut against the fundamental values of dissenters. No doubt, some dissenters might be misguided and intolerant persons. But the law is a blunt instrument to help them see the error of their ways.

Some opponents of same-sex marriage might simply dislike gay or lesbian sexual orientations. Perhaps that is their problem. They may not wish social institutions to lend gays and lesbians any (more) credibility. Perhaps such a view simply expresses what Ronald Dworkin calls an "external preference." These are not preferences about what happens to oneself but are preferences about what happens to others (Dworkin, 1978, p. 234). Perhaps such preferences simply should not count in determining public policy. But given the structure of social and legal institutions, extending marriage rights to same-sex couples sometimes imposes real monetary costs on unwilling others. Their preferences not to incur such costs need not be entirely "external"; they may be personal preferences about their world and the costs they pay. Even if we find such preferences misguided or objectionable, the question is whether people may impose such costs on others.

Disestablishing marriage

Privatizing marriage to reduce the controversy

Critics of same-sex marriage may have preferences others find objectionable. One of the marks of a fair society is that people are not asked to incur costs they can reasonably reject. Having married gays in one's midst may strike some persons as objectionable, perhaps even costly in some intangible way. Taking this as a cost may simply be someone's tough luck. We would not take the "discomfort" some feel because there are interracial spouses in their community as a good reason to forbid "miscegenation." Sometimes people do things we dislike. In a society that respects each person's equal freedom to live his or her own life, this is a cost we have to accept.

At other times, however, political, legal, and social institutions impose financial or other opportunity costs on people who do not obviously have unreasonable complaints. They may object to extending tax and other privileges to persons whose lives and values they find deeply objectionable. The tax laws vary depending upon jurisdiction and income. So, the accounting does not tell a single story. Sometimes letting same-sex partners marry may not decrease tax receipts but actually impose a greater tax burden on the couple. Let us nevertheless suppose for argument's sake that the critic can plausibly show she suffers some marginally greater tax burden traceable to same-sex marriages.

The critic may also complain that letting same-sex partners marry gives them access to certain immigration rules that favor spouses. This, the critic may say, unfairly privileges same-sex couples. There are other equally deserving unmarried heterosexual couples or even close Platonic friends who do not have access to such privileges.

The critic may further complain that health insurance pools may suffer greater burdens once same-sex partners are allowed in as spouses. This can cost the critic money. Here too, let us suppose the critic can somehow show greater financial burdens to heterosexual couples. (Note that it might be quite the opposite. Indeed, letting same-sex partners marry may foster the long-term health of partners.)

Allowing same-sex partners to marry, the same-sex marriage critic might add, cheapens the significance of traditional marriage. Marriage, she might argue, loses part of its special purpose and significance if it is available to same-sex couples. This impedes her opportunities to enter a relationship with the restrictions she seeks, and so, she says, it diminishes the value of any heterosexual marriage she may ultimately enter.

These sorts of objections appeal to undue costs. The costs seem to be of at least three sorts. First, some costs appeal to discomforts. If those come from others living their lives in peace, then those costs might simply be something the supposed victim must endure as with any peaceful differences. Second, there are costs secondary to the voluntary choices of others that impact institutions and groups. If one's insurance company or religious congregation, for instance, accepts same-sex couples and that somehow imposes financial costs or inconvenience on same-sex marriage critics, then the critics need only find a new church or join another insurance company. Exit options reduce the sting of such costs. We must consider whether public policy may permit the imposition of such costs. A third sort of cost, however, is harder to avoid. The state creates or imposes such costs. States impose immigration restrictions that favor spouses, same-sex or otherwise. States impose tax codes that privilege spouses, same-sex or otherwise. States enforce family leave and antidiscrimination laws that require private employers to acknowledge same-sex unions on a par with heterosexual marriages. States extend social security and veterans benefits to spouses.

Perhaps there is an argument that these state norms impose costs that some people might reasonably reject. If the critic were to provide such an argument, it would not be an argument against same-sex marriage. It might be the start of an argument against the state provision of certain costly privileges, entitlements, and immunities.

One way to avoid continuing disagreement might then be to reduce the stakes. Perhaps the state should get out of the business of saying who can be married and what marriage is. If the state distributed fewer privileges, there might be less reason to complain about who can get married.

No one can reasonably complain about the decisions competent adults make when dating. Nothing much of public consequence depends on such choices. As long as parties can enter and exit on terms they find mutually acceptable, no one beyond friendly third parties should care one way or the other about what the couple does.

Of course, we treat marriage as more significant and lasting than mere dating relationships. We acknowledge that married couples *share a life together*, so we respect their authority to make surrogate decisions on behalf of incapacitated partners. We accept that they can and should share property without the tax consequences of similar exchanges among unrelated others. We accept that the estate of a spouse who dies intestate should go in large part to the surviving spouse. And so forth. The state acknowledges these norms and captures them in certain state regulations. But they need not be norms because the state acknowledges them. The state acknowledges them because they are norms. In other words, we might argue that the state need only *recognize* the norms people acknowledge regarding the significance of lasting marital unions.

This is but a sketch of a more complicated argument about the binding force of social norms. A fuller argument would discuss the origin of such norms and how state action affects their content, structure, and force. The important point here, however, is that when states only recognize those marital privileges and immunities that people accept independently of state action, there might then be less of a chance that people will come to an impasse about who counts as married.

State involvement in licensing marriage is a relatively recent development in human history. Previously, people would partner according to the enduring traditions of their community, and their neighbors would regard them as spouses (Coontz, 2007). On such a model, a relationship can still be quite significant but does not need the imprimatur of the state to count as a marriage. Of course, those earlier marital unions were often a forum for deeply problematic roles for women who had nearly no exit options. But the law need not guarantee oppression. It might still protect women from marital rape and loss of community property upon divorce or widowhood.

More interestingly, to the extent that the law accepts or acknowledges any norms about marriage, it is not essential that all such norms be the same everywhere. In the United States, for instance, after the June 2013 US Supreme Court decision, it was up to each state whether to allow residents of the same sex to marry. (The federal government was forbidden to deny federal marital benefits, privileges, immunities, and rights to any legally married same-sex spouses.) Allowing different jurisdictions to experiment with different legal norms gives local residents some opportunities for democratic self-determination and allows people opportunities to choose from among competing legal regimes.

Critics may worry that the right to marry is a basic human right that democratic majorities should not be able to deny competent unrelated adults. This worry poses a challenge to any public policy (non)resolution. It is unclear whether the right to marry is such a basic human right, but supposing that it is, it might be satisfied as long as couples have opportunities to wed *somewhere* without incurring draconian costs. They would then be able to enjoy their rights to live their lives together as they see fit while others could still reject the significance of their marriage. Allowing different legal norms to flourish might help lower the volume of the dispute. It might also demonstrate that same-sex marital unions need not jeopardize the civilization that permits them. People would still need to consider, however, the ethical challenge about the proper scope of democratic authority.

Disestablishing the state from marriage need not mean the state may have no laws about marriage. It might still have rules that exclude certain persons from marrying, perhaps because of public health or independent moral reasons. For instance, the state might refuse to acknowledge any supposed marriage involving minor children, siblings, or nonhuman animals. But it can have still have "default rules" regarding inheritance, property, taxation, and surrogacy (Sunstein & Thaler, 2008). It might even have various rules protecting a "spousal privilege." The state can leave the task of specifying terms of marriage to the partners and the institutions whose approval they seek. Marriage need not be the same single package for all parties. It might involve a menu of rights, privileges, and immunities from which parties can choose as part of defining their lives together. (See the illuminating related discussion of "minimal marriage" in Brake, 2012, ch. 7.)

This account of reducing the state's role in defining a single view of what marriage is or entails does not escape without facing several important worries. Among these are challenges about children, oppression, and uncompensated state burdens. The next final section briefly considers these challenges.

Challenges to privatizing marriage

Getting the state significantly if not entirely out of the marriage business might help to reduce some of the controversy about whether same-sex couples can marry. It nevertheless invites many concerns. Among them, and most notably, is the welfare of children. If states have little or nothing to say about who is married, it seems parents might easily skip out on obligations to support children's well-being.

One possible solution is simple to name but perhaps challenging to implement: separate marriage from parenting. While historically these are often linked, they increasingly are distinct. Responsibilities of parenthood, to the extent they are legally enforced, need only attach to *parents*, not spouses. As Elizabeth Brake writes, "Marriage allows partners to signal the importance of their relationship, to gain access to legal entitlements, and to invoke legal and social safeguards of commitment" (Brake, 2012, p. 151). Even if the extent of legal entitlements were reduced, Brake's point is that marriage can be separated from norms establishing a "parenting framework" to ensure children's welfare. She advocates openness to alternatives to traditional heterosexual parent pairs, including extended care networks that amplify the opportunities for people to love and support children. What shape these alternatives take might vary considerably. But the key point here is that parenting and support responsibilities can be upheld and enforced legally regardless of marital status.

A further worry is about oppression. Getting states out of the marriage business may retreat on the advances made for various women's rights, including those against violence, to property, and to civic participation. Disestablishing marriage may seem to be a retreat by leaving women vulnerable to oppressive marriage norms.

In reply, we should be clear that getting the state out of the marriage business need not mean getting the state out of the business of protecting against assault, theft, and freedom of movement and association. States can and should still protect women (or anyone) from being victims. States should uphold ordinary rules forbidding battery, rape, and extortion. These acts do not become permissible when the parties are spouses.

A final worry is something same-sex partners know well. They can cobble together many agreements (after great expense and time) that specify many of the rights currently available to heterosexual spouses. There are some privileges and rights, however, that they cannot arrange by contract. Among these are immigration privileges, residency privileges, tax benefits, legally mandated caretaker leave programs, and various state entitlements such as veterans, disability, and social security benefits. But as Elizabeth Brake notes, these rights and privileges depend on how the state structures its institutions. In these and related cases, those state institutions are inherently "relationship-threatening" (Brake, 2012, p. 183). Geographical borders are an example: they are obstacles that keep partners apart. But such borders are state creations. Disestablishing the state from marriage might then consign it to the private marketplace. But this might leave people without adequate opportunities to enjoy a central good—one that must by justice must be available to them (Brake, 2012, p. 183).

This is not a worry that couples might not find anyone to officiate at a wedding. With significantly disestablished marital norms, couples can simply marry themselves. (Perhaps they can then simply register their marriage at a state office.) The bigger worry rests on whether market providers would deliver third-party marital benefits in a fashion that respects what people are due by justice. This is partly an empirical question and partly a moral one. Social scientists would need to furnish some data. And we would need to sort out what married couples are due. In the meantime, there might be many reasons to remove legal barriers to same-sex marriage. And people may then consider whether there are good moral reasons for the state to allocate various benefits and opportunities according to marital status.

Closing thoughts

Proponents of same-sex marriage appeal to significant moral and policy considerations such as equal citizenship, freedom of association, and the special value of intimacy. Opponents might believe heterosexual marriage is a crucial social institution best left alone. Allowing same-sex couples to marry might impose costs on such critics.

Not all costs that public policies impose are easy to discount. One way to reduce some of the controversy is by reducing the state's role in determining who gets to marry and what sorts of privileges and rights attach to the status. Social scientists and moral philosophers will need to sort out what rights partners have against others and the state, and whether reducing state involvement in marriage licensing would threaten couples' opportunities to enjoy their rights.

Even if we are not professional policymakers, we still confront important challenges of whether to support shifts to public policy norms. As we consider the proper role, if any, of the state in this policy domain, we need to reflect on the enduring moral principles that shape people's concerns about such a fundamental social institution. We might sharpen our understanding of what is at stake by exploring and testing key ethical considerations. Among them are the freedom to live our lives as we see fit and the proper extent of state power. These may justify reconsidering public policies about intimate relationships.

Further reading

Linda J. Waite and Maggie Gallagher discuss some of the many advantages of marriage in *The Case for Marriage: Why Married People are Happier,*

Healthier, and Better Off Financially (New York: Doubleday, 2000). David Friedman discusses the benefits of marriage as a precommitment strategy and how family norms evolved to protect spouses' interests in chapter 13 of his *Law's Order: An Economic Account* (Princeton, NJ: Princeton University Press, 2000). An excellent overview of many features of the debate, including history, religion, and disputed legal developments, is available in Andrew Sullivan, ed., *Same-Sex Marriage: Pro and Con* (New York: Random House, 2004). A discussion of how to shape social policy with a focus on preventing harm (including on children) comes in Eric M. Cave, "Harm Prevention and the Benefits of Marriage," *Journal of Social Philosophy*, 35 (2004): 233–43. A survey of some of the recent social science regarding various impacts of legalizing same-sex unions is available from Ronald Bailey, "The Science on Same-sex Marriage," reason.com, April 5, 2013, http://reason.com/archives/2013/04/05/the-science-on-same-sex-marriage, accessed November 9, 2013. A helpful survey of some of the studies of same-sex marriage, which seems to show no ill effects, is available in William Meezan and Jonathan Rauch, "Gay Marriage, Same-Sex Parenting, and America's Children," *Marriage and Child Wellbeing* 15 (2005), 97–115.

References

Brake, E. (2012). *Minimizing marriage*. Cambridge: Cambridge University Press.

Card, C. (1996). Against marriage and motherhood. *Hypatia, 11*(3), 1–23.

Coontz, S. (2005). *Marriage, a history: From obedience to intimacy, or how love conquered marriage*. New York: Viking.

Coontz, S. (2007, November 26). Taking marriage private. *The New York Times*. Retrieved July 3, 2013, from www.nytimes.com/2007/11/26/opinion/26coontz.html

Corvino, J. (2012). The case for same-sex marriage. In J. Corvino, & M. Gallagher, *Debating Same-Sex Marriage* (pp. 4–90). Oxford: Oxford University Press.

Corvino, J. (2014). Same-sex marriage and the definitional objection. In A. I. Cohen, & C. H. Wellman (Eds.), *Contemporary debates in applied ethics* (2 ed., pp. 277–89). Malden, MA: Wiley-Blackwell.

Cottrol, R. J., Diamond, R. T., & Ware, L. B. (2003). *Brown v. Board of Education: Caste, culture, and the constitution*. Lawrence: University of Kansas Press.

Dworkin, R. (1978). *Taking rights seriously*. Cambridge, MA: Harvard University Press.

Eckholm, E. (2014). "Opponents of same-sex marriage take bad-for-children argument to court." *The New York Times*, February 22. Retrieved June 3 2014, from www.nytimes.com/2014/02/23/us/opponents-of-same-sex-marriage-take-bad-for-children-argument-to-court.html

Ettelbrick, P. (1989). Since when is marriage a path to liberation? *Out/look: National Lesbian and Gay Quarterly, 6*(9), 14–17.

Gallagher, M. (2009, November 5). *The Maine vote for marriage*. Retrieved July 1, 2013, from *Real Clear Politics*: www.realclearpolitics.com/articles/2009/11/05/the_maine_vote_for_marriage_99020.html

Gallagher, M. (2012). *The case against same-sex marriage*. In J. Corvino, & M. Gallgher, *Debating Same-Sex Marriage* (pp. 91–178). Oxford: Oxford University Press.

General Accounting Office. (2004, February 24). *Defense of Marriage Act: update to prior report*. Retrieved July 1, 2013, from gao.gov: www.gao.gov/assets/100/92442.html

Girgis, S. (2014). Making sense of marriage. In A. I. Cohen, & C. H. Wellman (Eds.), *Contemporary debates in applied ethics* (2 ed., pp. 290–303). Malden, MA: Wiley-Blackwell.

Government of Canada. (2005). *Civil Marriage Act*. Retrieved July 2, 2013, from Justice Laws Website: http://laws-lois.justice.gc.ca/eng/acts/C-31.5/page-1.html

Harris, G. (2009, May 13). Out-of-wedlock birthrates are soaring, U.S. reports. *The New York Times*. Retrieved July 2, 2013, from www.nytimes.com/2009/05/13/health/13mothers.html#

Hull, K. E. (2006). *Same-sex marriage: The cultural politics of love and law*. Cambridge: Cambridge University Press.

Human Rights Council. (2011). *Discriminatory laws and practices and acts of violence against individuals based on their sexual orientation and gender identity*. United Nations General Assembly. Retrieved July 2, 2013, from www2.ohchr.org/english/bodies/hrcouncil/docs/19session/A.HRC.19.41_English.pdf

Lewis, G. S. (1983). Evidence – privilege against adverse spousal testimony. *Villanova Law Review, 28*, 820–34.

Loving v. Virginia, 388 U.S. 1 (U.S. Supreme Court 1967). Retrieved July 2, 2013, from http://caselaw.lp.findlaw.com/scripts/getcase.pl?court=US&vol=388&invol=1

Marks, L. (2012). "Same-sex parenting and children's outcomes: A closer examination of the American Psychological Association's brief on lesbian and gay parenting." *Social Science Research, 41*(4): 735–51. doi:10.1016/j.ssresearch.2012.03.006

Meyer v. State of Nebraska, 262 U.S. 390 (U.S. Supreme Court 1923). Retrieved July 2, 2013, from http://caselaw.lp.findlaw.com/scripts/getcase.pl?navby=CASE&court=US&vol=262&page=390

Neilan, T. (2004, February 4). Gays have full marriage rights, Massachusetts court says. *The New York Times*. Retrieved July 3, 2013, from www.nytimes.com/2004/02/04/national/04CND-MASS.html

Pawleski, J. *et al.* (2006). The effects of marriage, civil union, and domestic partnership laws on the health and well-being of children. *Pediatrics, 118*(1), 349–64.

Preston, J. (2013, July 1). Gay married man in Florida is approved for green card. *The New York Times*, A11.

Rampel, C. (2010, March 10). Single parents, around the world. *The New York Times*. Retrieved July 2, 2013, from http://economix.blogs.nytimes.com/2010/03/10/single-parents-around-the-world/

Sullivan, A. (2004). *Same-sex marriage: pro and con*. New York: Random House.

Sulzberger, Jr., E. (1961). Privilege against compelled adverse testimony by a spouse. *Washington and Lee Law Review, 18*, 98–103.

Sunstein, C. R., & Thaler, R. H. (2008). Privatizing marriage. *The Monist, 91*, 377–87.

United States v. Windsor, 12–307 (U.S. Supreme Court 2013). Retrieved July 2, 2013, from www.law.cornell.edu/supct/pdf/12–307.pdf

Wolfson, E. (2011, January 25). *Economist debates*. Retrieved July 1, 2013, from *The Economist*: www.economist.com/debate/days/view/634

5 Women and the family

Women's status in what is now the developed world has changed significantly in the past two hundred years. It was once difficult if not impossible for women to own property, acquire a formal education, or participate in public life by voting or holding office. Social and political institutions treated the typical woman as a wife and mother. Women's rights and opportunities were severely restricted compared to those available to men.

There have been improvements in all these respects. Women are in the paid workforce in greater numbers. There are more women in management and professional positions. Property and inheritance laws now typically acknowledge women as the legal equals of men. Women may now own businesses. Marriage and divorce laws have changed in a way that gives women greater exit rights from bad relationships and some better protections from economic disadvantage should they exercise such rights.

However, women still tend to face considerable challenges. Women make up the vast bulk of victims of sexual violence, which still tragically persists. There is still considerable inequality between men and women on many measures. Here, however, we consider how public policies impact the opportunities a woman has to succeed in a career or even to keep a job. These opportunities might be in tension with the demands of family life.

Public policies governing taxation, childcare, and the opportunities available in workplaces still seem to reflect an antiquated view of the proper place for women. These policies often seem to presuppose that women's main and proper task is tending to the home. When they reflect such a view, these policies often represent barriers to the economic advancement of women. This is a problem not just for women hoping to improve themselves, but also for their dependents. There may then be room for improvement in such policies.

This chapter considers some of the challenges of framing policy that targets women's opportunities, especially given their frequent role as caregivers. Two points need to be made clear from the start. First, the chapter dwells on issues in the developed world. Of course, there are plenty of opportunities for improvement in poorer countries, and not simply with their domestic policies. However, many of the laws and norms richer countries sustain have significant effects on the status of women and families abroad. For example, rules regarding immigration, patents and copyrights, international trade, and foreign aid have both policy and moral impacts. They make a difference for how and whether women can feed their children, keep them healthy, and get themselves and their children an education. However, controversies about family and workplace policies in the developed world also turn on ethical disputes. We might then explore opportunities for progress in this area.

Second, policies concerning issues such as family leave, taxation, and childcare are not merely *women's* issues. They are important for anyone who hopes to improve human welfare and establish institutions that treat everyone with equal concern and respect. Perhaps these issues seem to be women's issues because of persistent gender norms regarding who cares for dependents. Nevertheless, because of those norms, the relevant policies have a distinct impact on women. These impacts vary in important ways depending upon women's class position.

This chapter begins by noting variations in conceptions of family and the role of work. It discusses why family life in general and work/family balance in particular may be legitimate targets of public policy. It discusses just a few of the many policies regarding family and the workplace. It considers whether there might be important reasons in this area to be leery of the power of public policy to improve things.

Some preliminaries

Policy controversies about the family often dwell on how to improve the health and well-being of family members—or, at least, how to stop harmful practices. But any discussion of the family first needs to be clear about what its subject is. Otherwise, people who disagree may talk past one another. The first task is then to be clear on the meaning(s) of various key terms.

Once we have some sense of what we are talking about, we can consider why the family and work/life balance are proper subjects of *policy* disputes at all. Some people may argue that the family is in a special private sphere and so should be immune from significant public scrutiny or regulation. If so, maybe there should not be any public policies about the family at all. The second task is then to be clear why the family belongs in public policy discussions. Addressing this might help focus the policy terrain that people consider controversial.

Once we have a sense of why the family is a legitimate target for policy regulation, we need to isolate which issues to consider. Any discussion of policies regarding the family will necessarily have to be selective. There are many relevant candidates, such as tax structures and laws regarding marriage, divorce, and inheritance. But other policies have less obvious but still significant impacts on women's caretaking roles and family structures, including drug laws, prison sentencing guidelines, and licensing regulations for daycare providers. The third task is then to consider specific policy controversies.

What is the family?

We sometimes read that the family is in crisis. People may cite statistics about rising rates of divorce and unmarried cohabitation, declining fertility rates, and rising numbers of children born to unwed mothers. Should these and similar trends be alarming? Much depends on what is at stake. To know whether there is a crisis for the family, we should first understand what the family is.

Aristotle described the basic unit of society as a household consisting of a male and female pair, their children, and slaves (Aristotle, 1998, book I, sec. 2). Some sacred texts portrayed women submitting themselves to husbands who had considerable power advantages in the home. (See e.g. 1 Timothy 2:11–15; and Ephesians 5:22–24.) These earlier notions of family structure should give us pause as we sort out what family means. That they might strike us as antiquated suggests that what counts as a proper family evolves.

Anthropologists and social historians document the many forms households have taken through history. Of note is how families in the developed world now often begin with a couple who share a loving commitment to each other. Historically, this was not the rule (Coontz, 2005). As Stephanie Coontz notes, "For most of history, marriage was more about getting the right in-laws than picking the right partner to love and live with" (Coontz, 2008). Marriage was arranged among male-dominated families to secure and exchange ties to property. The prospective brides were often little more than spectators to the process. Securing male dominion in the family through force was officially tolerated. It was often legally impossible for men to rape or assault their wives. The family was also the prime locus of economic production. Families in preindustrial cultures were typically tied to the land on which they depended for their sustenance. The husband, the wife, and the children all participated in what by today's standards was often grueling toil. Nobody, let alone wives and mothers, had the chance to consider a "career" outside the home. The home was how and where they lived.

Historians dispute how congenial we should find families of the past. (For a glimpse, see the somewhat gloomy portrait by Shorter, 1976; for a more optimistic account, see e.g. Ozment 2001.) However we assess the trends, it seems that many of the norms common to premodern families have changed. Women now have greater freedom to decline to marry. People often marry for love (and can exit more easily now if they choose). Women have opportunities for careers outside the home. It is against the law for men to assault their wives. As we know, increasing numbers of families are led by same-sex couples. There are of course significant variations in the rules and trends regarding marriage, divorce, domestic violence, and careers. A once common view that the family is a forum for production has been replaced by the notion of the family as a private space for shared consumption. There are variations among and within countries and across time. But the point is this: what families can be has changed and changes still.

Furthermore, we should be careful to note, as many writers do, that there might be no single "function" to a family. The modern idea of family might be "fragmented" in a way the idea of marriage is. (See Chapter 4, on same-sex marriage, in this book.) Indeed, there might be no single meaning for *family*. It might be difficult if not impossible to identify necessary and sufficient conditions for something to count as a family. Unlike "oxygen" and perhaps "oak tree," the "family" is not what philosophers call a "natural kind"; it is not a set of things whose properties are features of nature and not mainly a function of human conventions. At best there may be some cluster of shared features among groupings we call families.

In case our task of defining terms were not hard enough, we should note that reasonable people disagree about whether something can count as a family. (Compare Brake, 2012, ch. 6 for a discussion of fragmented notions of marriage.) This matters because policies often target family structures and dynamics. When they do, they privilege a particular range of conceptions of family and women's roles.

Perhaps there is no single notion of family. But the term is not infinitely elastic. Among the assorted clusters of features that mark out families often seem to be the following: (1) a multigenerational unit of persons, who (2) share a life, and (3) raise children (Hursthouse, 2008, pp. 60–61; and Archard, 2003, pp. 68–9). There is much room for variation and specification here. There can be one parent or multiple parents with different levels of responsibility for children. The extent to which the group shares a life may vary considerably. Parents and their adult children may constitute a family even if they do not live together. And so forth. This broad list of features should be sufficiently inclusive to help us begin to sort out how and whether policies should target family structures.

Why policy?

Earlier it may have been common for a woman's job to be the home. Of course, *much* earlier, a family's job was the home. With the advance of industrial society in the eighteenth and nineteenth centuries, however, wage labor became common. In that era, men, women, and children went into cities in increasing numbers to work in factories. Wages for many families eventually increased so that families could afford *not* to have everyone working. Mothers could stay home while fathers went to work. Children could get an education. But the trend toward wage labor for all parents changed again. Throughout the developed world since the 1950s, an increasing number of women work outside the home. The literature describing these various trends is extensive but it confirms the decline of the model of the household where a man works outside the home and the woman is in charge of domestic life.

Despite the increasing number of professionally educated women, men still dominate leadership positions (Rosin, 2012). As of 2013, 46 women are CEOs of Fortune 1000 companies (Catalyst, 2013). In many professions, women earn degrees and get jobs at rates comparable to men, but, as Kay S. Hymowitz notes, women tend to disappear the higher up the career ladder you look (Hymowitz, 2012). Perhaps this is because, in some respects, career advancement is modeled on a sort of "ideal worker" who is capable of the single-minded dedication to a job that is incompatible with any sustained caretaking role at home (Williams, 2000).

In recent history, regardless of which parent(s) worked outside the home and what level jobs they had, someone still needed to prepare meals, clean the house, and change soiled diapers. Among heterosexual couples, this task typically fell to the woman, and it still does. In many Western nation states, both men and women note that women do the bulk of domestic tasks. Reported domestic hourly work by women is sometimes between 1.9 and 4.7 times the amount men perform (Crompton, 2006, pp. 139–50). These trends confirm certain normative assumptions. In many people's views, family work just is women's work (Okin, 1989).

We can recite many other trends. Throughout the Western world, women are marrying later (or often not at all) and having fewer babies. Increasing numbers of households are led by single women; increasing numbers of children grow up in single-parent homes. Indeed, fewer people in many Western nation states are marrying (Organization for Economic Cooperation and Development, 2012a). And while women's wages are creeping toward men's in many fields, men typically tend to earn more than women.

Some writers find many of these trends alarming and suggest policy remedies to redirect them. But some critics may ask why these and other features of the workplace or the family merit policy scrutiny. After all, the argument might run, these trends are none of the policymakers' business. These are purely private matters that should be immune to public regulation.

The idea that the family is part of some protected private realm touches on the controversial distinction between the public and private spheres. (For a glimpse of the controversy, see e.g. Okin, 1989, ch. 4, who is very critical of this distinction; and the essays in Weintraub and Kumar, 1997.) One application of this sort of position is to say the principles of justice do not apply to the family. There are various possible accounts of why this might be the case. One is to say that justice should govern relations among equals, but the family is by nature a hierarchical group. Another is to say that the family has a special value that is corrupted by subjecting it to principles of justice. Those principles might seem more suited to regulating entire societies. And a third may be to say that the family is a source of affective connections that are incompatible with principles of justice (Archard, 2003, pp. 103–15).

Saying that the family excludes talk of justice is, however, importantly misguided. For one thing, justice clearly does apply to the family at least in some ways. It is unjust for someone to murder a spouse or for parents to torture their child. Clearly, then, justice may at least *constrain* family structure and the conduct of persons within families. This is something expressed in various public policies such as laws and institutions regarding domestic violence, child custody, marriage, divorce, and compulsory education. (See, however, Chapter 4 in this volume for a discussion of whether as a matter of justice public policies ought to determine who can marry whom.) Several writers, however, want to take this position further. They offer compelling arguments that justice does not merely constrain the family but ought to play a role in shaping it in the first place.

John Rawls, for instance, provided an influential account of the political significance and relevance of the family. The family is part of what he calls the "basic structure" of society. That basic structure consists of a group of institutions that extend various benefits and burdens to citizens (Rawls, 1971; 1993). The family is perhaps the most important forum for inculcating moral habits in citizens. It is also the place where people extend privileged care and other resources to each other. This is partly why Rawls had some misgivings about the family's role in promoting justice; the partiality characteristic of family connections may clash with realizing justice on a wider scale. He nevertheless thought that principles of justice applied to and could regulate the family.

The state and its policies have a fundamental influence on the shape of families (Eichner, 2010). As Maxine Eichner notes, besides determining what may count as a family (and thereby specifying who might be eligible for assorted privileges, immunities, and rights), the state claims the authority to determine or regulate many institutions that crucially shape family life, including the conditions of employment; the availability of health insurance; standards of parental care; and whether, when, and which employers must allow employees to take extended leave to care for dependents (Eichner, 2010, pp. 53–63). Public policies fundamentally affect family structures and dynamics. They can, do, and at least sometimes ought to structure basic social institutions.

Isolating some representative policies

Many institutions and the norms they embody shape family structures and women's opportunities to make work/life balance decisions. How might policy approach these complex questions? Here, as in many other policy domains, causes and cures are as much in dispute as are what ethical principles constrain or require action of policymakers. One potential way to focus the discussions is by considering some of the lesser controversial principles that might shape policy. Such principles might not only shape policy but also limit its reach.

Public policy, as noted in this book's introduction, is any institution, norm, or rule a state upholds *to guide people's behavior*. For a state justifiably to create institutions, enact rules, or enforce norms, it must be in a position to justify those acts, rules, and institutions to the people to whom they apply. The state often uses (or threatens) coercion to do what it does, and in any case its various policies provide advantages to some persons and disadvantages to others. In short, the state should be able to offer justifications for what it does (or for what it does not do) that those persons could not reasonably reject.

What all this means is the subject of much recent debate among social and political philosophers. What is important here is that the state is not foisting policies on an unwilling populace. This does not require actual stated or signed agreement among anyone and everyone. It seems to demand minimally that the use of political measures *not* be something a person who is affected by them could reasonably resist. What makes for "reasonable" is also subject to dispute. Simply suffering a loss compared to some alternative is not necessarily the basis for some reasonable disagreement. The principles justifying what a state does must be the sort of thing that no reasonable person could reject. Thinking in these terms might help us generate specific policies, but that would require a lot of work. Instead, we can narrow the field a bit by first considering which sorts of policies are *ruled out*. This can help focus the policy debate.

So, to be clear, what follows is not an exhaustive consideration of possible justifications of public policies. There are plenty such justifications, including welfare, justice, solving coordination problems, and many others. Instead, by considering what people might reasonably reject, we might remove certain items from the policy agenda—or at least adjust the discussion so that apparently reasonable concerns would need to be met before enacting new policies or continuing old ones. Furthermore, this discussion will not specifically consider how and whether a person might reasonably object to some policies. Instead it will point the way to considering what this would mean or involve.

A glimpse at some policy controversies

Social scientists document improvements in the status of women in the developed world. They can point to decreasing wage gaps, increasing education rates, and increased labor force participation—especially among educated professionals. However, women, and particularly women with children, still face many challenges. They must still confront persistent gender norms for caretaking. The bulk of domestic work falls to them, even when both parents have careers outside the home. Taking care of children is expensive and time-consuming. To the extent that a parent spends time with children, that parent's career may stall. This can jeopardize the parent's prospects for advancement or raises. Moreover, managing schedules for children, including their school, activities, and doctor's appointments, is hard enough without having a full-time job. It is nearly impossible for a parent to *parent* while dedicating herself to her job in the way many employers demand of their "ideal workers" (Williams, 2000). Many high-profile women have thus argued recently that they cannot "have it all" and so must make hard choices (Spar, 2012; Slaughter, 2012).

The challenges of parenthood increase when someone faces them alone, and typically solo parents are mothers. Rates of single motherhood vary considerably by country, as do rates of employment among single parents (Rampell, 2010). Poorer women often simply cannot *afford* to leave work to tend to their children and so they lack meaningful opportunities to parent. Some government assistance is available in many countries, though such welfare supports vary in strength and structure. However, even with such supports, opportunities for career advancement often clash with family demands. Navigating such demands is often more daunting for women on the lower end of the economic ladder. In the United States, far more families led by single women are poor than are families led by married couples (Ludden, 2012). Poor women are more likely to be single and more likely to have children out of wedlock; indeed, the majority of their babies do not come home to married parents (Shattuck & Kreider, 2013).

Over the past 40 years, marriage rates have declined in each of the developed countries of the Organization for Economic Cooperation and Development (Organization for Economic Cooperation and Development, 2012a). Rates of cohabitation have correspondingly increased, but so have rates of children born out of wedlock (Organization for Economic Cooperation and Development, 2012b). Policy might attempt to address these trends, but, as Stephanie Coontz notes, marriage is not necessarily a "panacea" (Coontz, 2008b). Marriage is but one indicator of the opportunities available to a mother. Other more important factors affecting her opportunities might be persistent poverty, access to education or healthcare, and the safety of her community.

Complicating matters further is the persistent gender pay gap within developed countries. This gap captures the wage differences between men and women. Across a lifetime, the typical man earns more than the typical woman does. Policy theorists dispute what contributes to this gap and why it varies. And the data suggest that marriage and children damage women's wages more than men's (Loughran & Zissimopoulos, 2009). Some writers point to different career paths: males tend to dominate in high-paying jobs; women tend to dominate in low-paying ones (Rosenbloom, Ash, Dupont, & Coder, 2008). But even within a particular field, men often tend to earn more than women. Some scholars wonder whether there are systematic social biases at work that discourage girls from pursuing careers in high-paying fields in the first place and which, later in life, explicitly or implicitly crimp their prospects for advancement. This may point to underlying discriminatory factors.

Taxes

The tax code is not simply a way to finance government operations. It is a device to inspire or discourage behavior. In many developed nation states, the tax code is progressive in a way that higher brackets of incomes are taxed at higher rates. In such progressive structures, some married couples pay more taxes than they would were they single. Married couples are sometimes less in a position to take advantage of deductions for healthcare, business, or childcare expenses. On the other side, there are tax benefits for married couples where one person earns significantly less than the other (or nothing at all) (Urban Institute and Brookings Institution, 2008).

Many adverse tax consequences from marriage particularly hit the wealthy. But there are offsets. Married couples may transfer property without paying taxes and, up to a generous level, pass on estates without tax. This might help some but not all couples. In the United States, married couples in lower income ranks can lose access to considerable funds because of how the Earned Income Tax Credit works. A husband and wife who each earn $20,000 face a marriage tax penalty of over $3000—funds that they would have had were they filing taxes separately as unmarried persons (Urban Institute and Brookings Institution, 2008). There are similar such penalties in several European countries for lower-income earners (Immervoll, Kleven, Kleiner, & Verdelin, 2009; Tall, 2013).

More two-parent households are two-earner households nowadays than in the mid twentieth century. Women are earning a greater share of family income, and, in many cases, more women out earn their husbands (especially in lower income quintiles) (Glynn, 2012). In light of these trends, the effect of any "marriage tax" is equivocal. Some analysts say it discourages women from working because of higher marginal tax rates (Fichtner & Feldman, 2012). Others claim it encourages women to work *more* than they might otherwise in order to offset the effect of these marginal impacts (de Rugy, 2012). The impact, if there is any, likely depends partly on income levels. Poorer women may be less able to adapt to marginal increases in tax burdens by abandoning work or cutting back. But at the margin, the effect may be to discourage single low-income mothers from marrying.

Tax codes that privilege families with a single breadwinner strike many critics as a relic of a bygone era, and one that hits the poor particularly hard since they are more likely to have comparable income couples (Murray & Ventry, 2013). Ultimately, this tax penalty, though hardly the most pernicious policy affecting women today, shapes decisions in a way that cuts against widely shared values. First, it might discourage poorer women from marrying, and so might remove incentives for them to find or retain some stable breadwinning companion to assist with running a household. Social scientists still study whether such women compensate by cohabiting instead of marrying, and whether this is neutral for their long-term career prospects and well-being (Goodman & Greaves, 2010; Beaujouan & Ní Bhrolcháin, 2011). Second, for richer women, the higher marginal tax rates privilege single-earner families and so foster precisely the gender norms that many people strive to overcome. (For related discussion, see McCaffery, 2013.)

One possible alternative proposal is to explore taxing people independently of marital status. This might help reduce the extent public policy shifts tax burdens from one group to another. A policy that encourages marriage may seem to put more burdens on cohabiting or single persons, and in doing so may have the state privileging one way of life over entirely reasonable alternatives. This is not to say that such policies are not justified, but any tax regime that favors marriage would need to be something that persons uninterested in marriage can find justifiable according to reasons they could not reasonably reject. At first glance, it may seem that single persons might have reasonable misgivings about such cost shifting. Now, they might be mistaken to have such misgivings. This is something that would need to be shown.

What might seem a bit less controversial to all would be a tax policy that is neutral on people's marital status. Reducing the state's involvement in marriage (see Chapter 4 of this volume) might then correspondingly help reduce some of the controversy about tax structures. But there is still much room for discussion here. Single persons might have reason to support some state policies that encourage marriage because of the support the institution lends to social stability. Here, as elsewhere, the details matter. What social scientists tell us about the impacts of alternative policies matters for determining what reasons people have when considering policy possibilities. Even if ethics cannot point the way, it can sometimes constrain which possibilities to consider.

Some writers will argue that the state does have a stake in marriage since it is a key institution for the production of future citizens. However, this is increasingly not the case; people make lots of babies out of wedlock. Whether tax policy is the best way to ensure future citizens is disputable and, in any case, hangs on whether the state has any business fostering (or not) the production of children in the first place. This brings us to the next issue, that of childcare.

Childcare

As more mothers enter or return to the workforce, more young children spend their days—and longer portions of them—with caretakers outside the home. Maxine Eichner cites studies showing that, in the United States, over 75 percent of preschool-aged children of working mothers receive some care by nonparents, and approximately half such children are enrolled for over 35 hours each week. Over one-third of the children are in a facility or center; relatives assist with nearly half of the children (Eichner, 2010, p. 40).

Subsidies or tax credits are available in the United States and elsewhere. France, for instance, offers access to subsidized crèches and a universal preschool program staffed by trained and educated workers (Lundberg, 2012). This contrasts with many US daycare facilities, where staff members are often poorly educated and paid little, leading to high staff turnover. Many other European countries offer generous subsidies or credits for childcare (Crompton, 2006, pp. 122–9). Many writers call for increasing access to daycare in order to improve women's opportunities to work.

Plenty of studies explore the impact of daycare on children's long-term development. As one would expect, children enrolled at the higher quality (and hence more expensive) providers tend to do better over time. One important challenge, though, is a continuing dispute about the function of daycare. Some are happy to think of it mainly as a place to keep children safe. Others think of it as fulfilling an important educative role. If it has such a role, different mothers will have different views about its proper direction.

Reducing the cost of quality daycare might improve some children's educational attainments and women's job opportunities. Public subsidies might be one mechanism for achieving this. But they can be controversial, at least partly because they would require expanding the state's role in determining what counts as acceptable daycare. The state's limited involvement has already had mixed results. Regulation has in some cases constrained the variety and convenience of daycare options. For instance, in the United States, state regulations such as those governing zoning, staffing ratios, and facilities have increased the cost of daycare without necessarily increasing its quality or availability. Zoning rules restrict neighbors from operating childcare services in their homes. Those facilities might otherwise be perfectly acceptable to all involved parties. Staffing ratio and facility regulations, though intended to set minimum thresholds, might price certain families out of the market or drive down the quality of care by forcing cutbacks on other facility expenses (such as for staff salaries). Such regulations might then reduce access by the most disadvantaged women to daycare for their children (National Center for Policy Analysis, 2011).

There are a variety of proposals and tools available to address the cost of daycare. The state might attempt to reduce the burden of childcare by removing regulatory obstacles. Parents and communities might then find it easier to discover how best to provide daycare services given local circumstances and needs. But critics may suggest the state needs to take a more active and supporting role. Perhaps the state might (as it often does!) subsidize daycare through direct payments or tax credits for parents. Such assistance might be need-based. The state might also fund facilities directly, in part or as a whole. Well-intentioned policymakers have explored different proposals; actual policies vary among and often within jurisdictions.

Direct state support might produce overall welfare gains by improving early childhood education, especially for children from the poorest families (Heckman, 2013). Others might question these benefits, noting that there seems to be little evidence of lasting gains to children who had state-funded early preschool (Dalmia & Snell, 2013; U.S. Department of Health and Human Services, 2010). As the social scientists sort out the comparative benefits of alternative approaches, consider now whether any publicly funded program can be supported by principles that no reasonable person could reject.

When the state funds daycare, it does so partly by increasing the tax burden on those who do not take advantage of daycare services. This is not a burden merely on the childless. It is also a burden on those who choose to arrange for preschool care by using the services of a family member or trusted neighbor. Part of what makes state subsidies of daycare controversial is that such policies may seem to some people to privilege one way of life—and one approach to that way of life—over others. This might be justifiable to those who do not pursue such ways of life. Fuller consideration of this would assess what reasons people have to support policies that privilege others' choices. Among alternative possibilities is having the state abstain from providing or subsidizing day care. This is no easy alternative given the expectations and plans people have reasonably developed in light of current public policies. The failure to subsidize daycare would leave a great expense for families hoping to find such services, and this can pose great difficulties for single women—especially the poor. There are continuing concerns about poor bargaining power for low-skilled women.

All this might be the start of an argument for public policies that provide some basic childcare benefits to the poor. But more fundamentally, this is an opportunity for thinking creatively about how to foster the creativity people show when satisfying central human needs. Perhaps allowing people the flexibility to determine what works in their circumstances might justify a tax credit and thereby encourage experimentation and discovery. Perhaps states can allow for limited experimentation or themselves try out different policy options.

The steep cost of quality childcare makes it difficult for parents to pursue careers demanding "ideal workers" who seem to have no domestic responsibilities. Should the state fail to subsidize or provide childcare services, it may then seem to perpetuate gender norms in which women provide the bulk of childcare. We should note two points here. First, social scientists and policy theorists must determine which among rival policy approaches (including policy abstinence) would best undo the effects of previous state privileging of pernicious gender norms. But, second, such findings would not settle the matter. Reasonable persons may disagree about how best to avoid and undo the impact of arbitrary gender norms. Families who prefer a stay-at-home mother might object to principles and policies that would reduce the cost advantage of family-provided care. Of course, their objections might not be reasonable, but this is something that would need to be shown. As people sort through the continuing controversy, they can consider ways of allowing parents to discover what works for them while acknowledging that we might not know once and for all what is good for everyone. And more fundamentally, people need to consider how and whether ethical principles might constrain what states can require and what employers may demand regarding terms of employment.

Scheduling and leave policies

Setting schedules is a daunting challenge in modern lives increasingly marked by time deficits. Workplaces often expect employees to be available in a way that clashes with the need to feed children, tend to them when they are sick, and provide the emotional support appropriate to attentive parenting. As Susan Moller Okin writes, "We can no longer cling to the by now largely mythical assumption that every worker has 'someone else at home to raise "his" children'" (Okin, 1989, p. 176). Without access to paid leave for high-profile jobs, many parents, especially many mothers, have little choice but to enter the more flexible "mommy track" (Slaughter, 2012). Or, if they have prestigious jobs, they might abandon them in case of protracted family need.

Maternity leaves in Europe vary in length and terms. In some cases, such as in Germany, parents may receive paid leave for many months with a significant portion of their salary. Finland and other countries arrange for parents to share paid leave after a certain period and then allow unpaid leave for several years. The United States is among the few developed countries that does not mandate paid parental leave.

Since many of the policies are young, the long-term impact may be uncertain. Some trends are clear now. Employees in countries that require paid leave sometimes report lower levels of perceived work/family conflict than in countries with comparably less generous policies. But there are some notable outliers to this trend. As Rosemary Crompton reports, in the case of France, the state benefits that subsidize childcare and provide paid leave freed males to indulge gender norms that might have otherwise never been expressed (Crompton, 2006, pp. 139–62). The generous paid leave may have opened the door for them to demand that wives take on "traditional" roles. Nordic countries' reported low perceived work/family conflict may be a function not so much of generous legally mandated leave policies but other norms about the appropriate role for women and the place of work in life.

Social scientists will help us to understand the sources of any noteworthy differences in various policies and the variable impacts on employment and wages. What is clear is that many workers want scheduling flexibility. In the United States, for instance, increasing numbers of polled workers report that scheduling flexibility is nearly as important to them as wages and more important than available benefits (Boushey, 2011, p. 167). This sort of flexibility tends to be more available to workers among the higher income echelons or those with greater education (Boushey, 2011).

It may be tempting to respond to perceived shortfalls in flexibility by imposing a single policy that determines what must be available for all. Many European countries have policies providing greater paid time off; perhaps other countries could take a cue? This may also provide better opportunities for lower-paid employees, especially the lower-income women of color who are often struggling with work–family balance decisions on their own.

Would requiring paid leave or lengthier unpaid leave improve women's opportunities to make work/family decisions? It might for some, such as for those who already have jobs. But critics warn that such policies might restrict overall hiring, and they might have a special impact on women in particular. Some economists and policy analysts warn that increasing the cost of having a female employee makes an employer more reluctant to hire one (Henrekson & Stenkula, 2009). Moreover, if we are concerned with promoting women's labor force participation, we might take a lesson from Germany's experience. A lengthy paid leave rule in Germany left no room to experiment. It lowered women's post-birth labor force participation. Once the policy was adjusted to reduce the amount of paid leave available, women's post-birth labor force participation increased (Ghei, 2009).

The example of Germany might be the start not of an argument against paid leave, but of an argument against overly long paid leave and against state policies that offer few opportunities to explore alternatives. Critics, though, worry that any such state-mandated measures will privilege only full-time workers and typically those in higher income brackets. As some critics might point out, these measures cost money. They may depress women's wages, or they might depress hiring. Economists will need to explore long-term wage and labor force participation impacts. Meantime, we would certainly see women taking advantage of such leave policies. What might be harder to see, however, are the women and other persons who are never hired because there are fewer resources available to employers to create jobs. Measuring the extent of such a counterfactual is a challenge for social scientists to unravel.

Suppose there is much reasonable dispute about whether continuing or creating a public policy will bring about consensus improvements. (This is true for nearly every public policy!) Should the state then not enact or continue the controversial policy? It is tempting to think that policy inaction is the better course: reasonable people might find less that is objectionable, and there might be less of a chance that the state will make a mistake. On the other side, though, is the idea that some policies should proceed when there is at least some reason to believe there may be consensus improvements. And besides, people's resistance to change is not always rational. Social scientists have repeatedly documented numerous biases, including the "status quo" bias and the "endowment effect" (Ariely, 2010; Gilovich, Griffin, & Kahneman, 2002). There is then room for much more fruitful discussion about what the default should be in setting public policy (Thaler & Sunstein, 2008).

Many theorists wonder how to fashion leave policies in a way that does not perpetuate pernicious gender norms. Among various proposals are those by Janet Gornick and Marcia Meyers (Gornick & Meyers, 2008), who defend giving each parent six months of paid leave, which each parent can use—or not. This poses some fairness concerns about whether single mothers would be unduly deprived of the chance to provide their children twelve months total coverage by a parent figure. Erik Olin Wright and Harry Brighouse (Brighouse & Wright, 2008) suggest allowing parents up to six months of leave, in some cases on the condition that both parents take the leave. Each would get the same amount. This may encourage fathers to become more involved in domestic duties. Anca Gheaus and Ingrid Robeyns warn, however, that this proposal would leave one parent at the mercy of the "arbitrary will" of another, which could constrain a parent's autonomy (Gheaus & Robeyns, 2011). They propose a policy that all parents would be provided a certain amount of nonsimultaneous paid leave. Parents could opt out of such leave, but the leave would become a policy-based "default option" with normative significance: it might produce "long-term egalitarian effects on the gender division of labor within the family" (Gheaus & Robeyns, 2011, p. 184). They admit this policy would restrict individual choice a bit, since it imposes costs on certain sorts of choices for family structures and child-rearing, but they think it is worth it for promoting gender fairness and parental care (Gheaus & Robeyns, 2011, p. 185).

These or other policies might "work" in promoting certain social goals. But they would not be without cost. They impose costs, minimally, on employers (so then on some actual or potential employees as well). Whether those costs are justifiable by principles no reasonable person could reject is something that must be shown. One possibility worth considering is whether the burden of justification might be less if there were less to justify. If the state were simply not to privilege any particular leave policy through requirements or subsidies, parents and their employers could discover which arrangements work better for their particular circum-stances. We would need to consider, however, which if any state policies might foster such fruitful discoveries.

Without public policies for paid time off to care for dependents, where would that leave women? They might eagerly seek out jobs featuring flexible scheduling because of their concern with striking a certain work/family balance. They may want opportunities for leave (paid or unpaid). And, to borrow from economists' ways of thinking, if the women provide sufficient value, employers will offer paid leave opportunities to them. This is already underway in the United States, which does not require paid leave. The Society for Human Resource Management found that in 2011, 16 percent of employers offered paid maternity leave exceeding disability requirements. One-quarter offered paid family leave, and even 16 percent offered paid adoption leave (Society for Human Resource Management, 2011). They offered these programs as a way of recruiting and retaining talented employees.

Critics will worry that leaving it to employers' discretion is not enough; they might argue that single low-income working mothers would not be offered such benefits unless a state required their employers to do so or unless the state funded it. Others will make moral appeals and argue that it is not appropriate to leave such an important dimension of one's life to the vagaries of market negotiations. (See, for instance, Crompton, 2006; Boushey, 2011; and Alstott, 2004.) They might very well be right. The problem is that we might not know yet what sorts of institutions are best since employers and employees have not finished discovering them. And even when we find out what produces certain results, people will still vigorously disagree about policy priorities. Even if some measures might crimp hiring to some extent, we might think something more important is at stake. Perhaps a fundamental value that we can all accept requires that the state protect working women's opportunities to make certain choices about their families.

Critics of state policies may warn that women's moral, political, and economic statuses are too important to impose a uniform policy on everyone about terms of employment. They might argue that women figuring out how to strike a work/life balance might have a better chance at hitting the target they want when they are able to sort out what arrangements will work for them. Perhaps we might consider further the significance of employees' opportunities to explore with employers what arrangements might prove fruitful. This flexibility—this plurality of arrangements and policies—might help even the poorest of women if they were more likely to be offered jobs in the first place. Those jobs might not have generous paid leave, but they would be jobs. So a challenge again is to sort out whether paid leave policies preclude hiring. Of course, much here hangs on the findings of social science. Allowing the field to study and compare the results of different regimes across different countries should be illuminating in the coming years.

Closing thoughts

Persistent gender norms about work and sex roles may suffocate women's opportunities to live the lives they want. Policy may offer some opportunities for improvement, at least by reducing the barriers women face. There is continuing controversy about what counts as a *barrier* appropriate to policy reform. Some may argue that lack of economic opportunity is itself a barrier meriting state intervention. Some might then advocate robust policies to reduce the opportunity costs women face when making choices.

Sometimes, establishing a uniform set of institutions is required by justice, especially when doing so is a way of preventing or remedying violence. Social theorists may defend such uniformity in other cases as well, especially as a way of remedying unfair disadvantages stemming from pernicious gender hierarchies. An important challenge with imposing a single resolution is the danger that it might restrict opportunities for people to discover how best to live their lives in cooperation with willing others. Perhaps less ambitious public policies would reduce the extent to which the state privileges a particular way of taking care of families. There might then be less of a chance of running up against the reasonable disagreement of persons who are affected by public policies. When rethinking the proper role of public policy here, we must also acknowledge that people deeply disagree not just about empirical matters. They disagree about what the role of the state should be in fostering certain social institutions, what form of family is best, and what are appropriate (if any) gender norms.

Allowing people to experiment with different sets of norms might give them the flexibility and opportunity to learn what works for them. One size need not fit all. Indeed, fashioning policies with an eye to improving women's workforce participation may unduly foist what Stephanie Coontz calls a "middle-class 'life script'" on the poor (Coontz, 2008b). That script might not work for them. It may be best to let them figure out which one does. There might be more than one acceptable life script.

Further reading

Diemut Bubeck, *Care, Justice, Gender* (Oxford: Oxford University Press, 1995) offers a compelling account of how the care of dependents typically rests on oppressive arrangements at women's expense. For comments on the Swedish welfare state and recent changes toward increased flexibility in programs, see Karin Svanborg-Sjövall, *Private Choice in the Public Sector: The New Swedish Welfare Model* (Stockholm: Timbro, 2012). For a historical overview of how industrialization may have undermined the integrity of the American family, see Allan C. Carlson, *The Family in America: Searching for Harmony in the Industrial Age* (Piscataway, NJ: Transaction), 2003. Arlie Hochschild offers an insightful overview of the challenges of two-parent wage-earner households in *The Second Shift* (New York: Viking, 1989). An account of early-twentieth-century gender norms, and their surprising reversal, comes in Dorothy Canfield's 1924 novel, *The Home-maker* (Chicago: Academy Chicago Publishers, 2005). Edward J. McCaffery discusses how tax laws in the United States are systematically designed to privilege single-earner families (and so disadvantage dual-earner couples) in *Taxing Women* (Chicago: University of Chicago, 1999). A seminal and searing criticism of gender norms and their suffocating effects on women is in Betty Friedan's 1963 book, *The Feminine Mystique* (New York: Norton, 2013). For a sense of changes in women's roles in the workplace through American History, see Barbara J. Harris, *Beyond Her Sphere: Women and the Professions in American History* (Santa Barbara, CA: Praeger, 1978). For a critical view of impacts on women, children, and the poor of many recent changes in American marital laws and norms, see Kay S. Hymowitz, *Marriage and Caste in America: Separate and Unequal Families in a Post-Marital Age* (Chicago: Ivan R. Dee, 2006); and, from a very different perspective, Martha Albertson Fineman, *The Neutered Mother, the Sexual Family, and Other Twentieth-Century Tragedies* (New York and London: Routledge, 1995). An intriguing account of how lower income women assess the relative significance of motherhood and employment is in Kathryn Edin and Maria Deflas's *Promises I Can Keep: Why Poor Women Put Motherhood before Marriage* (Berkeley and Los Angeles: University of California Press, 2005). An accessible overview of various economic, cultural, and medical developments that transformed women's labor in the twentieth century is available in Claudia Goldin, "The Quiet Revolution That Transformed Women's Employment, Education, and Family," *AEA Papers and Proceedings* 96 (2006), pp. 1–21. Some people attribute wage differences to how women and men negotiate. See, for instance, many of the works by Linda Babcock and Sara Laschever, such as *Women Don't Ask: Negotiation and the Gender Divide* (Princeton, NJ: Princeton University Press, 2003). This chapter briefly mentioned the possibility that cognitive biases may impact openness to policy possibilities. In addition to the other citations, Thomas Gilovitch offers an overview of our tendencies to be less than fully rational in *How We Know What Isn't So: The Fallibility of Human Reason in Everyday Life* (New York: Free Press, 1993).

References

Alstott, A. L. (2004, April/May). Alstott replies. *Boston Review*. Retrieved July 27, 2013, from http://new.bostonreview.net/BR29.2/reply.html

Archard, D. W. (2003). *Children, family and the state*. Burlington, VT: Ashgate.

Ariely, Dan. 2010. *Predictably irrational: The hidden forces that shape our decisions*. New York: Harper Perennial.

Aristotle (1998). *Politics*. (C. D. C. Reeve, Trans.). Indianapolis, IN: Hackett Publishing Company.

Beaujouan, É., & Ní Bhrolcháin, M. (2011). Cohabitation and marriage in Britain since the 1970s. *Population Trends, 145*, 35–59. Retrieved June 3, 2014, from www.ons.gov.uk/ons/rel/population-trends-rd/population-trends/no–145–autumn-2011/ard-pt145-cohab-marriage-trends.pdf

Boushey, H. (2011). The role of the government in work-family conflict. *The Future of Children, 21*(2), 163–89.

Brake, E. (2012). *Minimizing marriage*. Cambridge: Cambridge University Press.

Brighouse, H., & Wright, E. O. (2008). Strong gender egalitarianism. *Politics and Society, 36*(3), 360–72.

Catalyst. (2013, July 1). *Women CEOs of the Fortune 1000*. Retrieved July 25, 2013, from Catalyst.org: www.catalyst.org/knowledge/women-ceos-fortune-1000

Coontz, S. (2005). *Marriage, a History: From obedience to intimacy, or how love conquered marriage*. New York: Viking.

Coontz, S. (2008a, January 14). The future of marriage. *Cato Unbound*. Retrieved July 24, 2013, from www.cato-unbound.org/2008/01/14/stephanie-coontz/future-marriage

Coontz, S. (2008b, January 23). Minding the marriage gap. *Cato Unbound*. Retrieved July 26, 2013, from www.cato-unbound.org/2008/01/23/stephanie-coontz/minding-marriage-gap

Crompton, R. (2006). *Employment and the family*. Cambridge: Cambridge University Press.

Dalmia, S., & Snell, L. (2013, March 1). The dispiriting evidence on preschool. *Wall Street Journal*, A13.

de Rugy, V. (2012, April). Women vs. the state. *Reason*. Retrieved July 26, 2013, from http://reason.com/archives/2012/03/08/women-vs-the-state

Eichner, M. (2010). *The supportive state: Families, government, and Amerca's political ideals*. New York: Oxford University Press.

Fichtner, J. J., & Feldman, J. (September 2012). Taxing marriage: Microeconomic behavioral responses to the marriage penalty and reforms for the 21st century. Mercatus Center. Retrieved July 26, 2013, from http://mercatus.org/sites/default/files/FichtnerFeldman_MarriageTax_1.pdf

Gheaus, A., & Robeyns, I. (2011). Equality-promoting parental leave. *Journal of Social Philosophy, 42*(2), 173–91.

Ghei, N. (2009, August 4). The argument against paid family leave. *Newsweek*. Retrieved July 27, 2013, from www.thedailybeast.com/newsweek/2009/08/04/the-argument-against-paid-family-leave.html

Gilovich, T., Griffin, D. W., & Kahneman, D. 2002. *Heuristics and biases: The psychology of intuitive judgement*. Cambridge and New York: Cambridge University Press.

Glynn, S. J. (2012, April 16). *The new breadwinners: 2010 update.* Retrieved July 26, 2013, from Center for American Progress: www.americanprogress.org/issues/labor/report/2012/04/16/11377/the-new-breadwinners-2010-update/

Goodman, A., & Greaves, E. (2010). *Cohabitation, marriage, and child outcome.* London: The Institute for Fiscal Studies. Retrieved September 15, 2013, from www.ifs.org.uk/publications/6599

Gornick, J., & Meyers, M. (2008). Creating gender egalitarian societies: An agenda for reform. *Politics and Society, 36*(3), 313–49.

Heckman, J. J. (2013, September 15). Lifelines for poor children. *The New York Times*, SR5.

Henrekson, M., & Stenkula, M. (2009). Why are there so few female top executives in egalitarian welfare states? *Independent Review, 14*(2), 239–70.

Hursthouse, R. (2008). The good and bad family. In L. Thomas (Ed.), *Contemporary debates in social philosophy* (pp. 57–68). Malden, MA: Blackwell.

Hymowitz, K. S. (2012, Autumn). The plight of the Alpha female. *City Journal, 22*(4). Retrieved July 25, 2013, from www.city-journal.org/2012/22_4_alpha-female.html

Immervoll, H., Kleven, H. J., Kleiner, C. T., & Verdelin, N. (2009). *An evaluation of the tax-transfer treatment of married couples in European countries.* Bonn, Germany: Institute for the Study of Labor. Retrieved September 13, 2013, from http://ftp.iza.org/dp3965.pdf

Loughran, D. S., & Zissimopoulos, J. M. 2009. "Why wait?" *Journal of Human Resources 44* (2), 326–49.

Ludden, J. (2012, September 13). *Can marriage save single mothers from poverty?* Retrieved July 26, 2013, from npr.org: www.npr.org/2012/09/13/161017580/can-marriage-save-single-mothers-from-poverty

Lundberg, C. (2012, November 2). *Trapped by European-style socialism—And I love it!* Retrieved July 27, 2013, from Slate.com: www.slate.com/articles/life/family/2012/11/socialist_child_care_in_europe_creche_ecole_maternelle_and_french_child.single.html

McCaffery, E. J. (2013, April 14). The law was never fair, and is now just silly. *The New York Times.* Retrieved July 27, 2013, from www.nytimes.com/roomfordebate/2013/04/14/improving-on-the-tax-codes-marriage-penalty/the-marriage-penalty-was-never-fair-and-is-now-just-silly

Murray, M., & Ventry, D. J. (2013, April 24). Get rid of the penalty. *The New York Times.* Retrieved July 26, 2013, from www.nytimes.com/roomfordebate/2013/04/14/improving-on-the-tax-codes-marriage-penalty/eliminate-the-marriage-penalty

National Center for Policy Analysis. (2011). *Enterprise programs: Freeing entrepreneurs to provide essential services for the poor.* Dallas, TX: National Center for Policy Analysis. Retrieved July 27, 2013, from www.ncpa.org/pdfs/Enterprise-Programs-Freeing-Entrepreneurs-to-Provide-Essential-Services-for-the-Poor.pdf

Okin, S. M. (1989). *Justice, gender, and the family.* New York: Basic Books.

Organization for Economic Cooperation and Development. (2012a). *Marriage and divorce rates*. Social Policy Division – Directorate of Employment, Labour and Social Affairs. OECD. Retrieved September 14, 2013, from www.oecd.org/els/family/SF3.1%20Marriage%20and%20divorce%20rate%20-%20updated%20240212.pdf

Organization for Economic Cooperation and Development. (2012b). *Share of births out of wedlock and teenage births*. Social Policy Division – Directorate of Employment, Labour and Social Affairs. OECD. Retrieved September 15, 2013, from www.oecd.org/els/family/SF2.4_Births%20outside%20marriage%20and%20teenage%20births%20-%20updated%20240212.pdf

Ozment, S. (2001). *Ancestors: The loving family in old Europe*. Cambridge, MA: Harvard University Press.

Rampell, C. (2010, March 10). Single parents, around the world. *The New York Times*. Retrieved July 26, 2013, from http://economix.blogs.nytimes.com/2010/03/10/single-parents-around-the-world/

Rawls, J. (1971). *A theory of justice*. Cambridge, MA: Harvard University Press.

Rawls, J. (1993). *Political liberalism*. New York: Columbia University Press.

Rosenbloom, J. L., Ash, R. A, Dupont, B., & and Coder, L. 2008. Why are there so few women in information technology? Assessing the role of personality in career choices. *Journal of Economic Psychology* 29(4), 543–54. doi:10.1016/j.joep.2007.09.005

Rosin, H. (2012). *The end of men*. New York: Penguin.

Shattuck, R. M., & Kreider, R. M. (2013, May). *Social and economic characteristics of currently unmarried women with a recent birth: 2011*. Retrieved July 26, 2013, from census.gov: www.census.gov/prod/2013pubs/acs-21.pdf?.

Shorter, E. (1976). *The making of the modern family*. New York: Basic Books.

Slaughter, A.-M. (2012, July/August). Why women still can't have it all. *The Atlantic*, 85–102.

Society for Human Resource Management. (2011). *2011 employee benefits*. Retrieved July 27, 2013, from www.shrm.org/research/surveyfindings/articles/documents/2011_emp_benefits_report.pdf

Spar, D. (2012, October 1 and 8). American women have it wrong. *Newsweek*, 38–48.

Tall, S. (2013, July 3). *Two-thirds of married couples excluded from Tories' marriage allowance*. Retrieved September 15, 2013, from Liberal Democrat Voice: www.libdemvoice.org/twothirds-of-married-couples-excluded-from-tories-35165.html

Thaler, R. H., & Sunstein, C. R. 2008. *Improving decisions about health, wealth and happiness*. New Haven, CT: Yale University Press.

U.S. Department of Health and Human Services. (2010). *Head Start impact study final report*. Washington, D.C.: Administration for Children and Families. Retrieved September 15, 2013, from www.acf.hhs.gov/sites/default/files/opre/hs_impact_study_final.pdf

Urban Institute and Brookings Institution. (2008, April 4). *Taxation and the family: What are marriage penalties and bonuses?* Retrieved July 26, 2013, from The Tax Policy Briefing Book: www.taxpolicycenter.org/briefing-book/key-elements/family/marriage-penalties.cfm

Weintraub, J., & Kumar, K. (Eds.). (1997). *Public and private in thought and practice: Perspectives on a grand dichotomy*. Chicago: University of Chicago Press.

Williams, J. (2000). *Unbending gender: Why family and work conflict and what to do about it*. New York: Oxford University Press.

6 Education and "intelligent design"

Charles Darwin published *On the Origin of Species* in 1859. His work was one example of the nineteenth century's growing scientific interest in explaining the diversity and ancestry of life forms. Scientists were particularly interested in how traits may be passed on or changed through various generations. Speaking broadly, theoretical approaches in the tradition of Darwin hold that many of a population's characteristics determine the features of its descendants. Those traits that allow organisms to survive in a way to reproduce successfully and give descendants similar survival advantages will tend to be "selected" and privileged across the generations.

Since Darwin's work, writers have described how generations within and across species might change. For instance, primitive life forms did not have lungs, but those that developed structures that could function as proto-lungs (such as air bladders that might assist in controlling buoyancy underwater) would have been able to explore land outside of water. This gave them access to new food sources and living space. The ability to navigate on land became a trait that offered a survival advantage. Over time (and, to be clear, often over a *very long time*), populations changed in such a way that their lungs became essential and, eventually, beings with such features could only reproduce among themselves. Entirely new species emerged (Orr, 1997).

The sciences related to evolutionary biology are rich and complex. They embrace many disciplines such as molecular biology, paleontology, anthropology, organic chemistry, genetics, game theory, ecology, and many other fields and subfields. Though important debates rage within these various disciplines, scholars generally concur that the traits in a population have an immense impact on its ability to survive and reproduce successfully. Those traits that help a population to survive and reproduce can be passed on to successive generations. Sometimes those traits change or new ones emerge. If traits help a population to survive and reproduce, they will tend to proliferate throughout a population.

Some writers worry that these many developing sciences tacitly suppose a worldview in which the sorts of things that scientists study are the only sources we need for formulating an adequate account of the origin and diversification of life. They worry that science crowds out a spiritual or supernatural understanding of life and living things. Some writers offer another framework, sometimes instead of or in addition to that which is common among active scientists. They suggest that we best understand life on earth partly by appealing to the work of some intelligent agent. Appeals to some such intelligent force, they argue, help to explain how certain features of life are so complex but so effective in allowing generations to flourish. Indeed, according to writers in this "intelligent design" (ID) tradition, the work of some such agent is crucial for understanding life and for making possible life as we know it.

Whether ID is crucial for an account of life might seem to be the sort of dispute belonging to scientists or philosophers. But it becomes an important flash point for policy because of controversies over the content of primary and secondary school curricula. The central controversy revolves around what children should learn about evolutionary theory and its rivals in their schools. This is a window into more basic controversies, which include, in part, what counts as science, whether and how disputes among scholars should affect school curricula, what control parents should have over their children's education, and how much religion belongs in the classroom.

Some writers suggest that we can separate out religious and scientific domains so that there is no tension between science and religion. The Catholic Church, for instance, holds that science and religion are compatible. The Church endorses many features of the theory of evolution (Catholic Church, 1997, esp. secs. 159, 283–4). So the teaching of science might not generate any threats to religious beliefs or practices. This chapter does not dwell on religious doctrine. It takes on a challenge to the dominant model of teaching science as a forum for considering how public policy may address disagreement about curricular objectives.

This chapter briefly considers the challenge of "intelligent design" arguments. It discusses the merits of such arguments and how their success matters for justifying teaching intelligent design accounts in schools. The chapter approaches this controversy as a platform for beginning to reflect on several more basic issues, including parental authority over children, what a child's proper claims are for education, and the state's interest in fostering education.

The chapter approaches the issue of ID from the standpoint of and for a layperson who is not an expert on the science. The proper judges of good science are scientists themselves, who, through experimentation and presentation of their findings to their peers, can determine what is settled and what is controversial. While there seems to be a strong consensus among scientists that ID is a poor account of our world, some critics will warn against hasty deference to their agreement. Independently of how we might approach these important questions of what counts as scientific knowledge, ID proponents advocate for policy changes to accommodate their views and criticisms. Their views raise important challenges about what latitude public policy ought to allow for the pluralism of deeply held views about fundamental values.

The chapter will argue that this controversy might best be left without a single policy solution. More precisely: there are often insufficient reasons for the state, through the government, to dictate how and whether all students should learn about ID in the same way, if at all. Allowing families and the communities they form to address the controversy will generate many different approaches. Such plurality of approaches might best help to satisfy many of the important moral values at stake. The discussion might illustrate how sometimes we can avoid some controversy in public policy by having fewer ambitions for policy to resolve our disputes.

Background

Design arguments' objections to evolutionary accounts

Most scientists treat evolutionary theory as presenting a compelling explanatory framework for the development of life and living populations on earth. This is not to ignore significant disputes among the scientists about the precise mechanisms and paths of evolution. The theories falling under the general evolutionary approach, however, are scientifically accepted as the best bases for understanding and predicting observable phenomena such as the emergence of new species in the fossil record and the development and spread of new traits among populations. The various fundamental evolutionary theories (especially those involving natural selection and adaptation) are among the best confirmed accounts of our world.

Some twentieth-century writers objected to such scientific approaches as incompatible with religious accounts of the origins and significance of life. They often worried about making room for religious understandings of the world. Some young earth creationist writers, for instance, argue that the earth's age is as stated in the Bible: a few thousand years old. (This clashes with the scientific consensus that the earth is several billion years older than that.) Other writers, on the other hand, have taken biblical verses about the days of God's creation as more of a metaphor, thereby making room for accepted science as to the age of the universe.

Recent attacks on evolutionary theory have taken a different turn by coming from scientists with some scholarly credentials. These ID advocates do not always speak with one voice. Some "progressive creationists," for instance, accept scientific findings about the age of the earth but argue that some intelligent designer sometimes created new forms of life. These occasional supernatural interventions left room for pockets of naturalistic evolution among and within those living kinds. Other writers accept the notion of evolution from common ancestors but argue divine action inspired the changes producing new species (Hasker, 2009, p. 591).

This section will not offer a comprehensive overview of the disputes among the significant writers. We should nevertheless glimpse part of what motivates the objections to evolution by advocates of ID. One common objection starts by pointing to the apparent complexity of biological phenomena. The idea is something like this: the organization of some biological systems involves vast numbers of crucially interconnected parts and functions. The system as a whole cannot have emerged by accident or by a series of randomly developing parts. It must have been deliberately designed by some intelligent being.

This sort of design argument is not new. Among the more famous examples of the argument was that by the early-nineteenth-century English writer William Paley. In his 1802 book *Natural Theology*, he asked readers to imagine discovering a timepiece on the ground. He argued that one could apprehend its complexity and conclude that the watch could not have come to be by accident. The springs in the timepiece and the various carefully calibrated gears had to be put together by some intelligence in order for the device to do what it does. There must be a watch*maker*.

The watchmaker argument is important for demonstrating the plausibility of ID arguments. The timepiece is supposedly an analogue for the complexity of some or all biological phenomena. The human eye, for instance, consists of numerous tissues that perform various interconnected functions. On some critical accounts, the eye cannot have emerged by "accident." Nor, such critics continue, could the eye have developed in small steps; incremental changes would not have conferred any evolutionary advantage. The same is supposedly true of the simple (but hardly simple!) flagellum. The flagellum is a device small organisms use to propel themselves through, and sometimes sense aspects of, their environment. As noted advocate of ID Michael J. Behe writes, the flagellum requires such spectacular coordination among parts as to amount to an "irreducibly complex" system that "cannot have arisen gradually" (Behe, 1997). It seems to show the influence of some designing intelligence.

A favorite example of the ID argument is that of a mousetrap. The mousetrap consists of several parts such that removing any one of them leaves you with a useless set of individually useless things. The mousetrap's parts exhibit a sort of interconnected complexity, ordered to a single end, such that the parts could not have come together (let alone come to be individually) unless they all performed their interconnected functions at once. Behe argues that the trap had to be made as an "intact system" (Behe, 1996, p. 47). Similarly, design advocates argue, many organs, organ systems, and biological processes are such that they could not have emerged from primitive beings through gradual changes that conferred marginal advantages across generations. The steps along the way would have conferred no advantage at all.

Scientists and philosophers have objected to these and related design arguments. For instance, some scientists have argued that what Behe calls "irreducible complexity" could gradually emerge over time (Orr, 1997). Incremental steps might very well have conferred some evolutionary advantage. Or, they might not have provided any disadvantage and so, through chance, they were eventually selected when a fortuitous combination with another trait did provide an advantage. Among the philosophical complaints are arguments questioning the notion of "complexity" and concerns about what properly counts as sound theorizing in a science (Forrest, 2011; Hume, 1779/1994). David Hume, for instance, suggested that order might spontaneously emerge based on unknown causes—and without any intelligence directing the process. As Hume and others suggest, our conclusions about how things operate should not outrun our understanding of the world.

Is ID science?

Part of the dispute about the status of the various ID claims is whether ID counts as a science at all. Consider first, very broadly, what science is. Science is a family of fields of inquiry that take empirical investigation and testing as ways of expanding our understanding of our world. The various sciences are united, not so much by specific beliefs, but by a commitment to a method, namely, the formulation and testing of hypotheses intended to explain and predict our observations.

Many proponents of ID portray the view as scientific. They argue that intelligent agency best explains certain features of our world. Some writers speak of ID as a scientific theory that helps to understand the *information* contained in and flowing through nature (Dembski, 2002, pp. 106–7). Both evolution and ID, many ID proponents say, equally suppose testable views about observable data. Each approach can also be buttressed by competing views about what can count as true and what sorts of things might qualify as real. The two views strike some writers as "symmetrical positions": ultimately, they are both either science or nonscience. (See e.g. Nagel, 2008, p. 197; and Nord, 1995.)

Even if ID is a scientific hypothesis or set of hypotheses, that does not mean it is valid. It might be *bad* science. Its hypotheses might have little predictive power. They might offer an insufficiently rich account of observable data. They might involve importantly incomplete, inadequate, or incoherent definitions. Indeed, much critical discussion of ID over the past 25 or so years attempts to argue that ID is bad science. The critics of ID attempt to refute each of its hypotheses.

Several scientific writers note that ID arguments have never been published in peer-reviewed science journals. They instead appear in philosophy journals, education theory journals, or in outlets intended for lay audiences. If we take the science classroom as a platform for instructing children on the methods of established science, there might then seem to be a reason to omit ID from science curricula.

ID proponents resist this conclusion. They insist that it is hardly settled that ID is mistaken and so, they argue, students should at least be exposed to the controversy. This "teach the controversy" approach urges allowing students to consider seeming gaps and challenges to the competing theoretical accounts of life's origins. ID opponents strenuously resist, however, the idea that ID and evolution are on the same theoretical playing field. They say there are no serious debates among scientists as to whether intelligent design may explain and predict our world and its history. Including ID in the science classroom, according to such critics, would then falsely portray it as a viable theory. As such, these critics continue, we may just as well include in biology classes the view that AIDS is divine retribution for the supposed immorality of gays, or in earth science that the Haitian earthquake is divine retribution for an earlier Haitian pact with the devil, or in history that Nostradamus foretold the September 11 attacks in New York City and Washington, D.C. Critics worry that the floodgates to irrationality will open once any unsubstantiated appeals to the supernatural achieve supposed parity with science (Forrest, 2011, pp. 373–4; Sloan-Lynch, 2010, pp. 22–3; Dworkin, 2006; Beckwith, 2006).

The consensus among scientists is that ID is not a serious contender for verifiably explaining and predicting our world. It does not seem, however, that there is a deep consensus as to whether it counts as science at all. Discussions of this question are often marred by *ad hominem* attacks on ID proponents. Critics frequently go to great lengths to question the motives and credentials of ID proponents. Among the frequent charges are any or all of the following. They speak on topics outside their area of expertise. They have unsavory friends and unpalatable political views. They maliciously misrepresent the work of advocates of evolutionary theory. They have ulterior religious motives for advocating ID, often inspired by a specifically Christian agenda. They hope to challenge the dominant materialist worldview and leave room for supernatural understandings of the world. All of these charges might be true but they seem irrelevant to the question of whether ID belongs in children's classrooms in some capacity. It might matter, however, that ID hangs on religious views.

Is ID religion?

If ID is ultimately a religious view, it may run up against legal provisions forbidding the mixing of the church and state in publicly run schools in certain Western democracies. In the United States, for instance, there are constitutional prohibitions against the state establishing any religion. Courts have often interpreted this to mean that state-funded institutions may not require the observation of any particular religious practice nor may such institutions unduly privilege one religious denomination over others. The meaning of these provisions is still subject to vigorous scholarly dispute. Among the frequently cited cases from the United States are the following. In 1962, in *Engle vs. Vitale*, the US Supreme Court ruled that a public school may not establish and promote an official school prayer. In *Lemon vs. Kurtzman* (1971), the US Supreme Court ruled that laws and state actions must have secular purposes, they must neither advance nor hinder religion, and must avoid "excessive government entanglement" with religion. In *Wisconsin vs. Yoder* (1972), the US Supreme Court held that the state may not compel parents to educate their children beyond the eighth grade given the weight of parents' religious liberties. More recently, in the 2005 case of *Kitzmiller vs. Dover Area School District*, a US district court ruled that intelligent design is a form of creationist religion that may not be included in public schools.

In other countries, the boundaries between religion and state are fuzzier. Religious instruction is often part of a compulsory curriculum. Different countries have different provisions because of different histories. Some states provide some funds toward the salaries of the clergy, the maintenance of religious institutions, or the support of education tailored to promote a specific denomination.

Some critics of ID insist that the position must inevitably appeal to some form of supernatural (and hence unknowable) explanation. (See e.g. Forrest, 2011; Sober, 2007.) Proponents of ID, however, have been careful to distance their public views from specifically religious accounts of the origin of the universe. While many critics are quick to point out that ID advocates have such views, this seems irrelevant. Their religious views can be a detachable module from any ID hypothesis. They are separable just as the view that it is always wrong to take a human life is separable from the view that capital punishment is unjustified, or in the way the view that animals are morally considerable might be detached from any defense of vegetarianism. There might be many justifications for any given position. That someone has a reason for holding a view does not mean it is the only reason for holding it. Accordingly, it would not even matter that every proponent of ID happens to be a young earth creationist (which they are typically not). What matters are the reasons they offer in defense of their views. The reasons must be publicly accessible. If the reasons are to support a public policy that determines the direction or allocation of state resources, they need to be of a sort that reasonable persons from different backgrounds cannot find objectionable. Appeals to personal revelation are not of that sort. Appeals to competing accounts of explanatory adequacy are.

It remains disputable how to classify ID hypotheses. ID might include misguided and unfounded scientific hypotheses, but it is not obviously and essentially a religious doctrine. In any case, resolving disputes about how to classify the doctrine would not be entirely fruitful. If it is a religious hypothesis in whole or in part, it may still be appropriate to include in classroom instruction in some way, either because religious instruction is sometimes permitted in the schools or because instruction about ID serves some independently valuable function. To consider whether there needs to be a *policy* to govern whether it should be in the schools, we must first consider competing accounts of the proper task of primary and secondary education.

What is school for?

The history of modern education for any given nation links industrial, economic, political, and social developments to changes in curricula, the structure of schools, and the shape of institutions determining how schools are organized. Some primary education and secondary education is now compulsory in most countries. Though historically such education may sometimes have been intended to promote religious devotion or to serve the ends of those holding the reins of economic or political power, over time children's education has come to serve important purposes for the improvement of the child and to promote fundamental social goals.

To speak very generally, there are several possible goals for education. These are not mutually exclusive. They are sometimes in tension with one another. Among the leading goals education theorists mention are:

1 cultivate competence as a consumer and contributor to a post-industrial market economy;
2 cultivate individual autonomy or self-governance;
3 promote the possibility of some form of human flourishing;

4 promote the development of democratic citizens in a stable political community;
5 respect parents' and communities' opportunities to live their lives according to deeply held values. (See e.g. Brighouse, 2005; Galston, 2002, ch. 8.)

There is considerable discussion about the merits of these different models of education. Which model(s) one accepts importantly determines how to structure curricula and the institutions that govern schooling. Fortunately, we do not need to resolve this complicated matter. (But for a glimpse of the discussion, see Brighouse, 2005; Brighouse, Howe, & Haydon, 2010; Macedo, 2000; Guttman, 1999.) What matters here is this: on any of the leading models of education, including ID in science (or *any*) curricula is neither forbidden nor required. Once we see that our leading models do not resolve the dispute for us, then we must consider how best to handle continuing disputes regarding the content of curricula. What follows is a brief consideration of each model and why the models, taken singly or together, are agnostic on the place of ID in curricula.

None of the models of education requires ID or rules it out

On the first model of education, which might be called a market model, the task of education is to prepare children to be good consumers and producers in an economy. What this requires might be quite disputable. Some may argue that schooling should prepare children to learn skills so that they can hold a job and be critical consumers of media. Others may defend the idea that children should learn how to be constructive (perhaps cooperative) participants in an increasingly globalized economy. However we might fill in the details of this model, being exposed to ID—or not—is neither forbidden nor required. Having learned about ID, or even having been taught to be receptive to it as a potentially adequate account of our world, would not obviously hinder a person's ability to function in a post-industrial market economy. Of course here we must assume that ID would not be taught (or that an alternative would not be taught) in such a way that the child's critical capacities for understanding the world are stunted. Learning about ID, furthermore, hardly seems *necessary* for consumer competence.

Similarly, on the second model, introducing (or not introducing) ID would not obviously hinder or promote a person's capacity to live autonomously. What autonomy means is subject to continued debate. We might consider autonomy as a capacity to respond appropriately to reasons. Learning about intelligent design—or not—would not seem to hinder that capacity. Here again we must assume that educators are not using ID (or some alternative) as a platform for suffocating a child's critical capacities.

The argument would be much the same for the third model of education that stresses human flourishing. We should note, though, that there are many different models of flourishing. They often vary according to which or how many fixtures of a good life they include. On most reasonable accounts of flourishing, the capacities, opportunities, and commitments that are part of a flourishing life do not preclude or require some specific exposure to (or shielding from) ID in the schools. Clearly it would also be question-begging to say that any good life must include (or exclude) some specific view about ID.

Of course, these are mainly arguments in broad strokes about the commitments and possibilities open to educators and parents under different models of education. It may be possible that there are some unforeseen adverse impacts on children or communities when they learn about (or do not learn about) ID, or learn about it (or do not learn about it) in some specific way or context. This is something we cannot know in advance. There does not seem to be any reliable social science on this. But the lack of evidence might suggest we should be open to various possibilities regarding ID, including one that does not require a single policy solution. More on that shortly.

The next two models of education call for a bit more discussion. They each touch on more fundamental controversies about the proper reach of public policy. They also help to illustrate how the controversy about ID is not simply about ID; it is also about the proper role of the state regarding people's liberties and opportunities to live their lives.

Consider the view that education's task is to mold democratic citizens in a stable political community. Proponents of this model do not reject the goals of other models. However, they often see education as ultimately intended to cultivate liberal citizens. Liberal citizens are persons capable of leading their own lives. They inhabit a community where they share the task of building and maintaining the institutions that distribute the benefits and burdens of citizenship. To perform this task at all (let alone to do it well), a person must be able to understand different ways of thinking and to be willing to accommodate herself to others. In matters that involve others' interests, she must be disposed to offer and accept reasons that are publicly justifiable. In other words, she must be open to considering the reasons others offer regarding certain actions or policies. She must also be prepared to justify her acts and suggestions to others in terms they can reasonably be expected to understand and accept (Dworkin, 2006; Guttman, 1999; Macedo, 2000; Costa, 2010; Callan, 2004).

This model of education is an expression of a more fundamental politically liberal philosophy. However, it still seems consistent with widely shared visions of political society and self-understandings among many persons and communities in the developed world. Political philosophers have argued that this notion of citizenship need not be totalizing. Citizens need not have any specific fundamental view of the world in order to be good citizens (Rawls, 1993). They can be orthodox Jews, Quakers, Anglicans, socialists, technophobes, polygamists, or accept nearly any specific comprehensive view of the world. As long as they are receptive to reasonable arguments and are prepared to offer their own arguments to others in terms that can be understood and not found objectionable, then they can fill the role of good citizens while living according to whatever deep commitments they might otherwise have. They can foster a political community that endures across generations amidst diversity.

As with other models of education, presenting ID hypotheses in classrooms—or not—seems compatible with the civic virtues required for being a good citizen. Of course, what specifically counts as a good citizen is disputable. But, on most plausible notions of liberal citizenship for nations featuring rich diversity of views, a person can be readily disposed to accommodate herself to others while accepting, rejecting, or having no particular view about the possible merits of ID hypotheses. A person who believes that appeals to intelligent agency are required for adequate accounts of the world need not be automatically inclined to use the resources at her disposal to foist a way of life on others. She might be just as disposed as an ID critic to tolerate different ways of life and to offer reasons for any of her particular views that affect the interests of others. She can be just as committed to fostering a stable political society through time as her ID-critical neighbor.

The last model of education we will consider is not so much a model of education as it is a view about the proper function of the state in education or in any domain. On this view, the state should acknowledge and respect citizens' liberties to define and live their own lives according to their fundamental values. William Galston defends this sort of model of "expressive liberty," which he takes to be an absence of restrictions that would impede persons from living in ways that express and cultivate their deepest understandings of what makes life meaningful (Galston, 2002, p. 101). Galston notes that this sort of liberty is crucial for fostering "civic unity" amidst diversity (Galston, 2002, p. 101). While parents still have enforceable responsibilities to provide children with education that meets certain minimum standards, that is compatible with much parental latitude about the content or method of education.

Parents and the communities they form shape their lives and institutions according to their values and views about a good life. One application of that freedom is an opportunity to decide on curricular issues that do not jeopardize any rights to which children are independently entitled. This is why the freedom to direct education is, as Galston notes, "rebuttable" (Galston, 2002, p. 100). Introducing children to ID (or not) would not seem to jeopardize any of a child's basic competencies. Given how central the issue is for parents and their communities, there may yet be good reason for public policy to acknowledge some space to express fundamental value commitments in the design of curricula.

There may yet be a good argument that some instruction in *evolution* is required for a person to realize the goals in any of the models of education. But the various models of education seem not to require or forbid including ID in science curricula. What we have is then a sketch of one alternative view about teaching ID. It passes no judgment on the ultimate merits of ID. It holds that teaching ID—or not—is permissible. This does not help us to sort out whether it *should* be included in curricula. Perhaps we need not resolve this at all. The next section considers how policy can remain partly silent on this controversy.

Models of policies and models of policy silence

A court has ruled that intelligent design may not be taught in classrooms in the middle district of Pennsylvania in the United States. In England, instruction in ID is covered by the "Guidance on the Place of Creationism and Intelligent Design in Science Lessons," which determines, in part, the national curriculum requirements for science instruction in the country. The guidance excludes ID from accepted science but allows that students may be instructed "about" a topic without being taught the topic. The guidance proposes framing discussions of ID as opportunities to help children understand the differences between scientific and non-scientific hypotheses.

England has a national curriculum on science and prescribes one approach to ID. But the national curriculum on some subjects allows some latitude to parents. In particular, parents have the option of withdrawing their children, in whole or in part, from some aspects of sex and relationship education. The same is often true for such topics in many communities in the United States. In some European countries (such as Germany, the Netherlands and Sweden), however, sex education is compulsory.

When there is robust consensus in a community about how to structure a curriculum, perhaps there need not be any special provisions to accommodate alternative views on how or whether to include discussion of ID. The problem arises when some reasonable persons object to exposing their children to any particular account of the origin of life. A conscientious person who is open to hearing alternative views and offering reasons to others seems to qualify as reasonable. (There might be more to be being "reasonable" than that, of course.) But such a person might very well think ID should be included in curricula. Or not. Given that there seem to be reasonable differences on the competing views, this may be an opportunity to consider not having a policy dictating what must happen for everyone. Perhaps, in short, parents (or sometimes portions of communities) might decide what to do on their own. On this approach, parents would have the opportunity to choose a path instead of one being set for them. This would give them the space to figure out what might work given their other commitments. Moreover, it would offer a laboratory of possibilities for exploring what seems to work in promoting any particular aim in educating the young.

This does not specify what to do except to sketch an approach of allowing people to explore what to do. No doubt, how the choice is structured matters. If the default view is to teach evolution and relegate discussions of ID to classroom presentations about pseudoscience, that will be what students typically get, and most parents will not bother to opt-out or explore other options. If the default view is instead to teach ID as a viable theory, many parents may exercise the option to exempt their children from attending instruction on such a controversial topic. One possibility is to treat it like sex education and give parents the right to exempt their children from instruction on the topic. Or, the default can be that no student receives instruction on the topic unless parents opt-in.

Many writers worry that policy regimes allowing such flexibility would be objectionable. Eamon Callan and Stephen Macedo, for instance, warn that the institutions required to sustain a free society demand certain civic virtues (Macedo, 2000; Callan, 2004). Callan notes that the willingness to accommodate oneself to others "would be severely compromised by selective compliance and free-riding if the institutions were widely valued only as means of advancing private ends" (Callan, 2004, p. 74). Randall Curren similarly writes that parents' discretion over their children's education must be constrained by the children's "right to an education that will enable them to contribute politically to their own future well-being" (Curren, 2009, p. 50). Curren goes on to discuss how a right to an education comes out of the fair equality of opportunity that all persons would enjoy in a just society. Perhaps most starkly, the Council of Europe's Parliamentary Assembly passed a resolution in 2007 that stipulated the importance of religious tolerance but warned "creationism could become a threat to human rights" (Parliamentary Assembly of the Council of Europe, 2007). Similarly, the American Association for the Advancement of Science (AAAS) claimed that instruction in evolution is crucial to being a functioning citizen. AAAS warned against legislation and policies that would "deprive students of the education they need to be informed and productive citizens in an increasingly technological, global community" (American Association for the Advancement of Science, 2006).

Absent definitive evidence that introducing ID into science will undermine the basis of free civilization, these sorts of concerns seem a bit overblown. While ID seems deeply scientifically suspect and may at best be very bad science, including it alongside evolution (or not) does not undermine any minimal threshold for what children should learn in order to lead at least minimally adequate lives in a peaceful political community marked by deep diversity of views. Critics sometimes warn that education institutions should express and guarantee a commitment to fair educational opportunity. But, the choice to include ID—or not—does not necessarily crimp the virtues or knowledge base called for by a commitment to fair educational opportunity. While exposure to the theory of evolution might be necessary on such accounts in a post-industrial twenty-first-century representative democracy, exposure to ID—or not—seems to be neither required nor forbidden.

As the science unfolds (and as the evidence against ID grows), allowing parents and communities the opportunity to explore alternative ways of addressing this issue may give people a better chance to abide by deeply held values. Embracing the possibility of intelligent design is not an unreasonable position—even if the preponderance of science seems to be aligned against it. Allowing these different approaches across and within communities may allow people better to understand what works for helping children to become successful adults, all while sustaining deeply held values about community and meaning.

Conclusion

Science has built an impressive case in favor of evolution as an account of the development of life on earth. Many scholars still believe that ID is a scientifically plausible hypothesis. It is not conclusively settled whether ID counts as science, though there seems to be a growing and robust consensus that if it is science, it is very bad science.

Intelligent and reasonable laypersons might be unsure about the merits of ID or the merits of including it in a primary or secondary curriculum. Some reasonable persons might not want to include it at all, or only to include it as an example of junk science. Others might reasonably want it to be portrayed as a viable alternative to evolution.

The various models of education neither require nor forbid ID from science curricula. Because of this reasonable disagreement, and because ID seems not to threaten a child's chance to realize the values driving any of the various models of education, public policy might allow parents and their communities to choose to include ID in their curricula. Or to choose

not to include it. Or to include it in a way that is guided by the suggestions of scientific authorities. Allowing them to explore alternative
approaches may foster greater understanding of what helps children and
communities to realize deeply held and widely shared values.

This discussion hardly settles the matter. It is vulnerable to findings in
social sciences that teaching ID in some way (or in any way) undermines a
child's later ability to be a productive member of society, or to be a critically
thinking adult, or to live a flourishing life. Empirical social science may also
produce evidence that allowing ID into schools in some or any way might
jeopardize democratic values, undermine political stability, or threaten a
child's fundamental interests. Were such evidence available, there might
then be excellent reason for public policy to forbid it.

Some critics of ID might still have lingering worries. They may fear
that allowing ID into the schools is too *dangerous* a threat to key political
and moral values. They would need to offer an argument for this position
since so far, it does not seem to be warranted.

The controversy here does not simply revolve around the merits of ID.
It turns on more fundamental issues, to which the ID controversy is only
a window. We must continuously consider and discuss what the proper
role of public policy is in fostering views about the content and methods
of education. Given concerns about the danger to liberty and children's
interests, we must also consider how far the state may intrude into
parents' and communities' discretion to live their lives according to their
deeply held values. And we need to reflect on what role if any the state
should have given the inconclusive findings of empirical science. These all
revolve around important ethical disputes and commitments. Making
those explicit might help us to understand the controversy and make
some progress on it.

Further reading

Amy Guttman offers a helpful overview of educational controversies in
multicultural societies in "Education," in R. G. Frey and C. H. Wellman,
eds., *A Companion to Applied Ethics* (Malden, MA: Blackwell, 2005),
pp. 498–511. Among philosophers who argue that intelligent design is
bad or dead science, see Barbara Forrest and Paul R. Gross, *Creationism's
Trojan Horse: The Wedge of Intelligent Design* (New York: Oxford University
Press, 2007). See also Philip Kitcher, *Living with Darwin: Evolution,
Design, and the Future of Faith* (New York: Oxford University Press, 2009)
and *Abusing Science: The Case against Creationism* (Boston: MIT Press,
1983). A frequently mentioned controversial textbook that advocates
intelligent design as an explanation for life is Percival Davis and Dean H.
Kenyon, *Of Pandas and People: The Central Question of Biological Origins*

(Dallas, TX: Haughton Publishing, 1989). Phillip E. Johnson has written frequently against evolutionary theory. See for instance his *Darwin on Trial* (Downers Grove, IL: Inter-Varsity Press, 2010). The Discovery Institute is a Seattle-based organization dedicated to critiquing scientific materialism with an eye to making room for religious explanations and accounts of human knowledge and cultural institutions. See www.discovery.org. A helpful overview of some debates about evolution comes in Andrew J. Petto and Laurie R. Godfrey, eds., *Scientists Confront Creationism: Intelligent Design and Beyond* (New York: W.W. Norton, 2008). For discussions of the role of education in shaping us as persons, see Kwame Anthony Appiah, *The Ethics of Identity* (Princeton, NJ: Princeton University Press, 2007), especially ch. 5; and Martha Nussbaum, *Not for Profit: Why Democracy Needs the Humanities* (Princeton, NJ: Princeton University Press, 2010). Kent Greenwalt offers a clear survey of the legal history and a discussion of whether and how to include religion in classrooms in *Does God Belong in the Public Schools?* (Princeton, NJ: Princeton University Press, 2007).

References

American Association for the Advancement of Science. (2006, February 16). *Statement on the Teaching of Evolution.* Retrieved June 3, 2014, from http://archives.aaas.org/docs/resolutions.php?doc_id=443

Beckwith, F. J. (2006). It's the epistemology, stupid! Science, public schools, and what counts as knowledge. In W. A. Dembski, (Ed.), *Darwin's nemesis: Phillip Johnson and the intelligent design movement* (pp. 105–16). Downers Grove, IL: Inter-Varsity Press.

Behe, M. J. (1996). *Darwin's black box.* New York: Free Press.

Behe, M. J. (1997). The sterility of Darwinism. *The Boston Review, 22.* Retrieved June 3, 2014, from http://new.bostonreview.net/BR22.1/behe.html

Brighouse, H. (2005). *On education.* New York: Routledge.

Brighouse, H., Howe, K. R., & Haydon, G. (2010). *Educational equality.* New York: Continuum.

Callan, E. (2004). Citizenship and education. *Annual Review of Political Science, 7,* 71–90.

Catholic Church. (1997). *Catechism of the Catholic Church.* New York: Doubleday.

Costa, M. V. (2010). *Rawls, citizenship, and education.* New York: Routledge.

Curren, R. (2009). Education as a social right in a diverse society. *Journal of Philosophy of Education, 43,* 45–56.

Dembski, W. A. (2002). *Intelligent design: The bridge between science and theology.* Downers Grove, IL: Inter-Varsity Press.

Dworkin, R. (2006). Three questions for America. *New York Review of Books, 53.* Retrieved June 3, 2014, from www.nybooks.com/articles/archives/2006/sep/21/three-questions-for-america/

Forrest, B. (2011). The non-epistemology of intelligent design: its implications for public policy. *Synthese, 78*, 331–79.

Galston, W. A. (2002). *Liberal pluralism: The implications of value pluralism for political theory and practice*. Cambridge: Cambridge University Press.

Guidance on the place of creationism and intelligent design in science lessons. (n.d.). Retrieved June 4, 2014, from http://humanism.org.uk/wp-content/uploads/1sja-creationism-guidance-180907-final.pdf

Guttman, A. (1999). *Democratic education*. Princeton, NJ: Princeton University Press.

Hasker, W. (2009). Intelligent design. *Philosophy Compass, 4*, 586–97.

Hume, D. (1994). *Dialogue concerning natural religion*. J. C. Gaskin (Ed.). New York: Oxford University Press. (Original work published 1779)

Macedo, S. (2000). *Diversity and distrust: Civic education in a multicultural democracy*. Cambridge, MA: Harvard University Press.

Nagel, T. (2008). Public education and intelligent design. *Philosophy & Public Affairs, 26*, 187–205.

Nord, W. (1995). *Religion and American education: Rethinking a national dilemma*. Chapel Hill, NC: University of North Carolina Press.

Orr, H. A. (1997). Darwin v. intelligent design (again). *Boston Review, 22*. Retrieved June 4, 2014, from http://new.bostonreview.net/BR21.6/orr.html

Parliamentary Assembly of the Council of Europe. (2007). *Resolution 1580: The dangers of creationism in education*. Retrieved June 4, 2014, from www.assembly.coe.int/ASP/Doc/XrefViewPDF.asp?FileID=17592&Language=EN

Rawls, J. (1993). *Political liberalism*. New York: Columbia University Press.

Sloan-Lynch, J. (2010, Winter/Spring). Philosophers to the rescue? The failed attempt to defend the inclusion of intelligent design in public schools. *Philosophy & Public Policy Quarterly, 30*, 18–23.

Sober, E. (2007). Intelligent design theory and the supernatural: The "God or ET" reply. *Faith and Philosophy, 24*, 72–82.

7 Torture

For many reasons, human beings deliberately inflict extreme, debilitating, and often dehumanizing suffering on victims. They have done this as a form of punishment, to extract confessions, to terrorize a population, or to gather information. Writers sometimes describe these techniques as intending to "break" a victim. A person loses her commitment to key values as well as any sense of control over her life. She becomes a completely helpless victim.

Techniques of torture include methods that produce visible lasting physical damage. Victims might be put on a "rack," which stretches their bodies to the point of tearing tendons and ligaments, dislocating limbs, and sometimes tearing the limbs from the body altogether. People are sometimes mutilated: they may be branded, burned or crushed, in whole or in part. Parts of their bodies may be cut out or off. Dental drills may pierce their teeth without anesthesia. Other techniques produce no visible marks. Such techniques include administering electric shocks to sensitive body parts such as the genitalia. Victims might be deprived of the food or medicine that they need to survive. People might be waterboarded, which induces a paralyzing and panicked feeling of drowning. People might be raped, sometimes repeatedly. Other harsh treatments might involve sleep deprivation, sexual humiliation, lengthy exposure to loud noises or sensory deprivation, being forced to stand, sit, kneel, or crouch in uncomfortable positions, beatings, cuttings, piercings, shockings, and many other methods.

These techniques are not new. Historians have evidence that ancient civilizations practiced these techniques on their enemies. In the Middle Ages, European inquisitors developed torture into something of a scientific craft (Murphy, 2012). There were procedures for administering torture: physicians presided over the proceedings, clerks recorded the victim's cries and screams, and there were tactics for handling seemingly evasive victims. Some forms of torture have declined over the past few hundred years (especially punitive and confessional torture), but torture has hardly disappeared. The Nazis and Soviets continued the practices (Shalanov, 1994; Panné, Paczkowski, Bartosek, Margolin, Werth, & Courtois, 1999;

Spitz, 2005). The French are widely known to have tortured resistance fighters in Algeria in the 1950s (Aussaresses, 2004; Lazreg, 2007). Various Argentinian and Chilean governments used torture against political dissidents (Feitlowitz, 2011; O'Shaughnessy, 2000). The Israelis use many techniques often called torture (Public Committee against Torture in Israel, n.d.; Committee on the Rights of the Child, 2013). Recent history shows that the practice is not alien to Western democracies (Rejali, 2009). A nonpartisan group has concluded that "it is indisputable that the United States engaged in the practice of torture" after the September 11 attacks (Shane, 2013). Human Rights Watch and Amnesty International produce reports showing that technologies, training, tools, and methods continue to be developed.

What may have once seemed to be unspeakable barbarity has returned as a topic for serious scholarly and policy conversations. The discussions do not portray torture as a primitive fixture of a bygone era. Instead, we come face to face with the startling admission that torture is not an anachronism but a pervasive and contemporary practice that deserves current serious discussion.

Many writers now wonder whether an age of terrorism has changed the moral calculus. People ask whether torture can ever be justified and, in particular, what sort of *policy* regarding torture might be justified. Many writers recoil at such discussions; they think that to enter into such conversations is already to concede too much to proponents of torture. Henry Shue describes such worries as "a sort of Pandora's box objection": discussing torture at all threatens to make the unthinkable reasonable (Shue, 2004, p. 47). But as Shue correctly notes, the conversation is well underway. It is a topic worthy of study. If torture is indeed morally permissible, we should know that this is the case when considering policy options. And if it is not permissible, exploring the issues honestly may help relegate the practice to history.

The chapter begins with a brief discussion of the nature of torture. The chapter then considers some of the current policies on torture. Torture is forbidden, but there are important qualifications on what "torture" and "forbidden" mean. The chapter considers how recent writers have framed the torture debate and then argues that while particular acts of torture might seem justifiable in exceptional circumstances, it might be unwise to fashion policy based on appeals to such unusual cases. We must ask whether the promise of torture's success—even if never fulfilled—can count as a justification for a policy permitting torture.

Background

Many narratives of torture document how the procedures erode a victim's fundamental sense of self and the world. Where previously a person may have thought of herself as someone who is acting in the world according to her values and commitments, torture uses a victim's body or mind to induce a sense of helplessness and hopelessness that erodes all sense of self and commitment (Améry, 2009). Particularly in cases of interrogational and confessional torture, the goal is often to transform victims merely into a heap of needs that can only be satisfied by a complete surrender to the tormentor. Some victims think of it as a living death since the suffering annihilates whatever it is that makes one a person. "Torture is the worst thing we do to each other," Bob Brecher writes (Brecher, 2014, p. 268). Brecher expresses a compelling view that is common among many critics of torture—what we might call a sort of "torture exceptionalism"—which holds that if anything is absolutely forbidden in a world where freedom and the dignity of the individual are supreme values, torture is it.

This "torture exceptionalism" may motivate the absolute prohibitions on torture in various human rights documents. The UN Convention against Torture and Other Cruel, Inhuman or Degrading Treatment or Punishment defines torture as

> any act by which severe pain or suffering, whether physical or mental, is intentionally inflicted on a person for such purposes as obtaining from him or a third person information or a confession, punishing him for an act he or a third person has committed or is suspected of having committed, or intimidating or coercing him or a third person. ... It does not include pain or suffering arising only from, inherent in or incidental to lawful sanctions ...
>
> (United Nations, 1984)

Of note is how the UN Convention does not allow that any emergency could justify torture: "No exceptional circumstances whatsoever, whether a state of war or a threat of war, internal political instability or any other public emergency, may be invoked as a justification of torture" (United Nations, 1984). The Universal Declaration of Human Rights forbids the use of torture or any "cruel, inhuman, or degrading treatment or punishment" (Universal Declaration of Human Rights, 1948, article 5). Torture is forbidden by the laws of all Western democracies and many other countries. But many of the countries that forbid torture have been regularly accused of inflicting it. The recent disclosures of American conduct in Abu Ghraib and Guantanamo are but two examples. The United States is reported to have inflicted waterboarding, sexual humiliations, and beatings on Guantanamo detainees (Iacopino & Xenakis, 2011; Danner, 2004).

The key human rights documents that discuss torture often leave signatory states much discretion about what they may or may not do. In the case of the Convention against Torture, for instance, dozens of the signatory nations added qualifications or interpretations about their obligations (Allhoff, 2012, ch. 4). The task here is not to dwell on the details and logistics of various legal provisions at various levels of jurisdiction. A more fruitful focus is on whether there may be public policies that allow torture.

"Torture exceptionalism" strikes many critics as implausible. They argue that torture is sometimes, and maybe often, permissible and that a nation's policies and laws ought to acknowledge as much. They also maintain that torture "works," and in a conflict where the stakes are high enough, nations should not rule out a tool that can save thousands if not millions of people (Dershowitz, 2002; 2006).

What is torture?

Writers often linger on the boundaries of the notion of torture. This may matter because if policies forbid torture, people governed by the policies need to know what it is that they must not do. Many people will agree that torture is impermissible and should be forbidden by policy, but they may also think that some forms of harsh treatment are justified under certain circumstances. It is then important to figure out what, if anything, counts as permissible harsh treatment.

First, consider that many defensive or punitive uses of force are permissible. Some force seems justifiable in self-defense or to enforce the law. Someone being raped can fend off an attack with the use of lethal, disfiguring, ghastly force—even if such force is calculated to cause excruciating pain or permanent damage. Whether the victim can hunt down the attacker afterwards to inflict such pain is another matter. Any punishing activity seems to belong to the state.

Though people sometimes discuss horrific acts of brutality by one private citizen against another, it is the action or inaction of state agents where discussions of torture typically begin. The state, through its agents, often acts by force or the threat of it. Police officers may sometimes shoot escaping or threatening criminal suspects. Perhaps, though, they may never justifiably sodomize suspects with broomsticks (Fried, 1999). That might be a form of torture that no suspected criminal behavior can justify.

Human rights documents express the view that the prohibition on torture particularly applies to states. The UN Convention against Torture and Other Cruel, Inhuman or Degrading Treatment or Punishment, for instance, defines torture by focusing on acts inducing pain and suffering that are "inflicted by or at the instigation of or with the consent or acquiescence of a public official or other person acting in an official capacity" (United Nations, 1984). Focusing on states does not discount the moral significance of private acts by persons acting on their own. For the purposes of policy, however, we can consider what powers states may or may not have.

It seems the state may sometimes justifiably treat people in harsh ways. Police officers might reasonably make suspects *very uncomfortable* when interrogating them. This might encourage suspects to disclose important information. Inflicting some discomfort on a suspect seems justified provided it is proportionate to the value of the information she might have.

Where permissible harsh interrogation ends and torture begins is something that scholars and policymakers debate. Shining bright lights on suspects seated in uncomfortable chairs in uncomfortably warm rooms while yelling questions at them may strike many people as acceptable if doing so is necessary to extract information. Unnamed US intelligence officials claimed that interrogators may sometimes use "a little bit of smacky-face" with recalcitrant al-Qaeda suspects (Bravin & Fields, 2003). When and whether "smacky-face" becomes torture depends on how we specify what counts as torture. That there are challenging cases at the margins, however, need not undermine the fact that repeatedly delivering electric shocks to someone's genitals strikes most of us as torture.

It is difficult to find a precise boundary. It may vary depending upon the person or circumstance. Merely harsh treatment for one person may amount to torture for another. If harsh treatment is permissible but torture not (or less frequently so), then policy may need to specify a rubric for classifying treatments. Some definitions of torture focus on the intentions of the torturer (such as intending to "break" a victim's spirit). Others focus on the status of the victim (such as being defenseless or reduced to a feeling of helplessness). And still others consider the sort of force being used (such as by focusing on severity, duration, or the particular type of suffering inflicted).

Is there a way to set aside these terminological disputes? It seems there is. We can say generally that torture involves various deliberately intense coercive techniques (or threats of them) intended to punish, terrorize, extract information, and/or gratify a tormentor. For the purposes of analyzing how public policy might approach torture, we can work with certain uncontroversial examples and consider whether policies should ever permit them. We can then pass over some otherwise important disputes by asking a simple question: may public policies ever permit torture—however understood?

Whether torture "works" ... and how that figures in justification

If torture is justifiable, it had better "work." But we then need to be clear on what it takes for torture to be successful. It seems that whether or not torture is successful depends on what the torture is supposed to do. Consider then some of the various types of torture.

Sadistic torture aims to inflict suffering mainly for the pleasure of the tormentor. Such torture can take any form of deliberate cruelty that inflicts intense suffering on a victim. Such torture "works" if the victim suffers accordingly. Presumably such torture is forbidden at least as a form of assault.

Some critics, however, may quickly point to a vibrant BDSM culture (Bondage, Dominance, Sadism, and Masochism—though the letters sometimes stand for related ideas). Participants might engage in role play involving the infliction of suffering. They might say this is occasionally a form of torture (given the type of suffering), but that it ought to be permissible when parties freely consent (National Coalition on Sexual Freedom, 2013). There is a serious question about whether there can be such a thing as consensual torture and whether public policies should allow it. Some would appeal to a principle captured by the Latin phrase, *volenti non fit injuria*. This principle holds that where there is willing consent, there can be no wrong. Certainly, nonconsensual sadistic torture should be forbidden in public policy as a violation of rights and treated accordingly. Whether consensual torture should be forbidden depends first on whether the state is justified in keeping people from doing things state authorities regard as harmful, and second, and more specifically, whether BDSM activities are sufficiently harmful as to merit prohibition.

Sometimes the state does not allow consent to free parties to certain acts from punishment. Some examples include sales of banned substances and prostitution. Of course, we might argue that these sorts of acts ought to be legally permissible. Relatedly, the state might regard consent as beside the point for certain other acts, such as the taking of life. Perhaps then some forms of torture should be ruled out regardless of seeming consent? Minimally, we can imagine policies might reasonably presume sadistic torture is nonconsensual until shown otherwise. These policies might, for instance, permit or require police to intervene on discovering sadistic torture. This would protect potentially unwilling, vulnerable victims who are unable to express dissent freely from their treatment. For those other persons who seem to be eager and willing participants in BDSM activities, we might stipulate that it is torture but allow it as an important (though perverse) application of a commitment to personal freedom. Sometimes it may be best (and perhaps morally required) to give people the space to hurt themselves. The sort of sadistic torture that public policies rightly forbid are then those involving the unwilling participation of victims.

Punitive torture inflicts suffering as a form of punishment. The torture then works if the victim suffers in the way the tormentor wants. This is usually easy to determine. Witnesses need only look. (Abject suffering is typically hard to fake.)

Many people would find punitive torture impermissible as a violation of basic decency or perhaps of some fundamental rights that even the worst offenders never lose. Some writers, however, have argued that criminals may sometimes be justifiably tortured (Kershnar, 2002; 2012). Perhaps some criminals do not have rights against punitive torture, or perhaps policies may disregard such rights. A proper discussion of the merits of punitive torture policies would hang on the details of a theory of criminal justice and a theory of punishment, both of which are beyond the scope of this chapter. To explore the boundaries and possibilities of permissible torture policies, let us then stipulate that punitive torture works because it reliably does what some forms of justified punishment often do. They work because they make the victim suffer. Again, whether they are justified is something we postpone considering for a moment.

In cases of *terroristic torture*, tormentors hope to strike fear into victims and others so that they do what the tormentors want, such as surrendering their town without a fight. Torturers might brutalize prisoners unto death and leave their bodies for discovery by local communities. Or, captors might detain and torture prisoners and release them to instill fear in others. Torturers might also hope victims or observers stop obstructing tormentors or their allies through, say, dissident writings.

Whether terroristic torture works is a bit harder to determine since it depends on the actions of multiple parties, sometimes across much time, as well as on other contributing factors such as political will and social cohesion. Let us stipulate, however, that such torture works at least sometimes. Terroristic campaigns may be the decisive reason that people stop dissident activities. Terroristic torture might also be enough to get people to stop obstructing a drug trade. It may be enough to get people to surrender to the rule by some warlord. Let us also assume that terroristic torture is impermissible as a tool of tyrannies since they use it to achieve unjustified ends. Determining whether it is an acceptable tool of nations waging just wars, however, would require considering the rules of war. Some scholars describe many allied campaigns in World War II (such as Dresden and the two nuclear blasts) as cases of mass terroristic torture. Since such cases engage so many other issues that may confound a clear discussion of policies about terrorism, let us set them aside in order to examine cases where the stakes are much clearer.

In the case of *interrogational torture*, tormentors inflict suffering in order to extract information that may help avoid the suffering or deaths of innocent others. Does interrogational torture work? Scholars have long disagreed about this. Some argue that there is no reliable evidence that torture or the threat of it evinces anything but false confessions, lies, or information the victim simply thinks the interrogator wants to hear. Some writers warn that torture is at best a shortcut for more subtle and effective interrogation methods. Among the seminal sources for interrogation methods by US officials is a 1943 report by Marine Major Sherwood F. Moran, who describes at length the success he and his colleagues had when interrogating seemingly intractable Japanese prisoners. They succeeded not by torturing or threatening them, but by being very nice to them (Budiansky, 2005). He suggested that interrogators should make prisoners comfortable, befriend them, and cultivate mutual understandings and sympathy. Suspects have a story they want to tell. Set the stage right, and they will talk.

The problem is that some interrogators might not get what they need (or what they think they need) from some suspects through regular questioning. If the stakes get high enough, perhaps that is enough to license torture. Proponents point to cases where it seems to have worked. The French, for instance, uncovered valuable intelligence about the Algerian resistance using torture. The US government claims to have extracted valuable information from harsh interrogation of al-Qaeda suspects. In a noted 1995 case surrounding "Operation Bojinka," Philippine officials allegedly used harsh interrogation on one suspect to extract information that prevented a mass assault on multiple aircraft over the Pacific and an assassination attempt on the Pope (Brzezinski, 2001). Another case scholars frequently discuss concerns a 2002 case in Germany where Frankfurt police threatened and harshly interrogated a suspect to disclose the location of a boy, Jakob von Metzler, whom he had kidnapped. Hours of regular questioning produced nothing. Once police threatened the suspect with torture, he talked (Bernstein, 2003).

Let us suppose for argument's sake that these and other cases show that interrogational torture sometimes works. Scholars may dispute particular cases, but instead of bogging down in such details, let us consider granting the proponents of torture that it can produce real results that save lives. We must then ask two questions. Would success justify acts of torture? And would successful instances of torture justify a *public policy* permitting torture? The answers may very well differ.

Torture, ticking time bombs, and justification

Some authors treat torture as absolutely impermissible. They appeal to special rights that all persons enjoy, regardless of criminal status. International human rights documents specify unconditional rights against torture. These rights do not seem to fade when they clash with imagined greater social goods. As Robert Nozick writes, individual rights function as "side constraints": they set boundaries to the pursuit of some otherwise valuable goals (Nozick, 1974). Critics of torture might then insist that a suspect's right not to be tortured takes precedence over all other goals.

Many people will find this approach unpersuasive since it seems to suppose that rights are implausibly strong. In an oft-cited footnote (Nozick, 1974, p. 30), Robert Nozick wonders whether rights are absolute. Must rights prevail when threatened by what he calls "catastrophic moral horror"? Though many people will think that public policies should acknowledge the special—perhaps immense—significance of rights, they may deny that rights are always *infinitely stringent*. Your right to your property is not so strong as to forbid someone from using or taking it in certain emergencies. For instance, someone may have rights to her mountain cabin, but, following Joel Feinberg, her property rights are not necessarily so stringent as to deny that hikers might be justified in breaking in when innocently stranded by a sudden blizzard (Feinberg, 1978, p. 102)

Rights theory then need not rule out the possibility of permissible torture. Even if there is a right against torture, that right may be less weighty than the rights of others. It may then seem that the suffering or deaths of many (hundreds? thousands?) of innocent others is too high a price to pay to respect any supposed one individual's right against interrogational torture.

Much philosophical scholarship on torture revolves around elaborate hypothetical examples. We are to imagine interrogators considering whether to torture someone who has information that can prevent the deaths of many people. Often this suspect has planted a bomb somewhere. We are to imagine that there is no way to find or defuse the bomb without disclosures from the suspect. We are also to imagine that inter-rogators have tried standard techniques to get the suspect to talk with no success. Time is short. May they threaten or apply torture?

Many scholars question the structure or significance of these hypo-theticals. Henry Shue for instance, claims that these scenarios make several important but controversial assumptions, such as: interrogators know they have the right man, they know he has the knowledge they need, they know no other methods will be effective, and they know that the torture does not threaten to become inappropriately widespread (Shue, 2006, pp. 233, 235; Shue, 1978). Darius Rejali similarly argues that these sorts of implausible assumptions undermine attempts to justify torture in any circumstances (Rejali, 2009). Bob Brecher fervently argues that any such ticking time bomb example is uselessly abstract until given the flesh of more details. Once those are specified, the hypo-thetical shows, at best, that interrogational torture "*may be necessary*—that is all" (Brecher, 2007, p. 38). But, Brecher insists, this is never enough to justify torture.

Brecher and other critics may be right about many ticking time bomb cases. It is unclear how much to conclude from fanciful hypotheticals. We typically do not have the omniscience of the interrogators in contrived ticking time bomb cases. We do not know that we have the right suspect. We do not know that he has the knowledge we need. We do not know that torture will be effective. In the face of such uncertainty, it becomes difficult to justify something as serious as torture.

The problem with this reply is that it wrongly discounts particulars by appealing to correct generalizations. True: interrogators typically lack the knowledge they seem to need to justify interrogational torture. *But sometimes they have this knowledge.* It is not entirely fanciful to imagine, as in the German kidnapping case, that police interrogators know as well as anyone could be expected to know that they have the right man and that time is very short. Even in such cases we should add another stipulation, namely, that the interrogators are as good as they can be. If the interrogators are lazy, stupid, or inept, they may fail to get the information that better interrogators might extract without any harsh or torturous methods. Is the burden of justifying torture then inversely proportional to the talents of interrogators? This seems to pin not only suspects' fates—but also their *rights*—on the abilities of their interrogators. This is a conclusion that proponents of torture may have difficulty defending. Of course, they might bite the bullet and insist that the question is not about the suspect's rights but about what an interrogator is justified in doing.

Torture proponents might then admit that an interrogator's talents do affect justification for torture. Jack might justifiably believe someone under his control has ticking time bomb knowledge. Jack is an unskilled interrogator and has not persuaded the suspect to talk. Jack is, however, good with a baseball bat. On this view, Jack is then justified in threatening or actually beating the suspect if the stakes are high enough. On the other hand, there would not be similar justification in the same situation for Jill, a highly skilled interrogator who is equally good with a bat. In this way, justification for torture may vary depending upon the abilities of interrogators.

Consequentialism ... so, anything goes?

It may then seem that in rare but carefully specified cases, torture might be justifiable. Torture might be *very serious* and call for special justification, but, on this approach, if the stakes are sufficiently high, torture might be permissible. This sort of consequentialist reasoning leaves many writers uneasy. David Luban finds ticking time bomb arguments deeply problematic. Torture proponents use such arguments to challenge principled opposition to torture. But once someone concedes "that her moral principles can be breached, all that is left is haggling about the price" (Luban, 2009, p. 654). And, Luban adds, "Once you accept that only the numbers count, then anything, no matter how gruesome, becomes possible" (Luban, 2009, p. 656). Presumably, some things are off limits; otherwise, we lose a sense of what is valuable.

Critics of torture can then stipulate that sometimes, in very specific cases, torture might be justified. But they can deny that this should be reflected in the *policies* governing permissible conduct. What is justifiable in particular cases is not what matters. We have to consider what sort of institutions shall structure our lives. Are institutions that *ever* permit torture consistent with a fundamental understanding of how to structure our society? Are such institutions consistent with what we want and expect of our states?

Among the many moral considerations torture seems to challenge is the idea that human beings have a special sort of value, a *dignity*. What this notion means is much discussed among ethicists, but a common way of framing this idea is indebted to Immanuel Kant. He depicts persons as ends in themselves with a sort of incomparable and absolute worth (Kant, 1996; 2012). Recognizing this sort of worth might have us treating certain actions as *unthinkable*. It would seem unconscionable to treat persons merely as a means by tormenting them to extract information. Once we give up on a certain inviolability for persons—even for the most despicable persons—we have abandoned key values that make our self-understandings and our civilization possible. It is even worse to entrench this discounting of a person's worth in public *policy*. If anything, the proponent of "torture exceptionalism" might say, policy should be the expression of our most basic and nonnegotiable commitments.

Commenting on the Jakob von Metzler kidnapping case, German Interior Minister Otto Schily thinks that policies against torture must be unyielding: "If we begin to relativize the ban on torture … then we are putting ourselves back in the darkest Middle Ages and risk putting all of our values into question" (Bernstein, 2003). But does this mean that there can never be any justification for torture? Schily acknowledges that the police officer wanted to help an innocent child, which, he says, is "honorable" (Bernstein, 2003). The challenge to this sort of absolutist view, of course, is that torture is very thinkable. It might seem justified sometimes to torture or threaten torture.

Whether particular acts of torture are justified is one thing. That some such justification is sometimes available does not necessarily warrant establishing it with public *policies*. More is at stake than the fate of some innocent persons.

David Luban and Bob Brecher warn against establishing a policy to permit torture. Any such policy would need to set out guidelines for what to do, how to do it, when to do it, and who may do it. Torture does not simply happen. Someone needs to know what to do. There needs to be a "torture culture" in order to train interrogators, study techniques, and teach them to students. Luban warns against normalizing torture; it would undermine our sense of the fundamental inviolability of human beings. It would turn us back to a barbaric past in which human dignity was not a serious part of the moral calculus.

A further worry is that licensing torture invites escalation. Alan Dershowitz, a proponent of legalized torture through judge-granted "torture warrants," acknowledges the loss of moral currency were the United States or other Western democracies to permit torture. It becomes difficult to persuade other less free nations to curtail their torturous practices (Dershowitz, 2002, p. 145). But Dershowitz thinks we can avoid sliding down pernicious slippery slopes by appealing to "a principled break" (Dershowitz, 2002, p. 147): with sufficiently clear but demanding criteria, we can stop state officials from too easily resorting to torture on fishing expeditions for potentially useful knowledge.

The problem with Dershowitz's "principled break" is that it is not self-interpreting. As the *Economist* wrote in a 2003 editorial, "[t]o legalise is to encourage" (Is torture ever justified? 2003). Any policy permitting torture will apply to fallible people acting in conditions of uncertainty. These are persons who will decide whether to administer torture, and these are people working in organizations susceptible to bureaucratic pathologies and who, as fallible agents, are vulnerable to rent-seeking, turf-protecting, career-advancing, self-justifying, cognitively biased behaviors that social scientists routinely document. When the stakes are high enough, these fallible persons may needlessly or unjustifiably give in to the worst sides of their characters.

This sort of argument worries about unleashing the powers of the state. States do many things, but they typically claim a monopoly on the use of coercion in a particular territory. If they are even sometimes permitted to perform torture, the critic may worry, then we would have no principled basis for insisting on the inviolability of certain constraints.

But consider a reply to this worry: appeals to the imprecision of policies and the fallibility of state actors may threaten to prove too much by undermining the state's claim to do *anything*. After all, even though policies are sometimes ambiguous and people make mistakes, to many people it seems state officials can be justified in teaching math to schoolchildren, regulating the content of pharmaceuticals, garnisheeing the wages of deadbeat dads for child support, or doing any of the many other things that legitimate states do, including shooting fleeing criminal suspects. Perhaps states can be justified in doing such things because they do not threaten our fundamental ways of living our lives and structuring our relationships. But this is what normalizing the practice of torture may do. So, an appeal to the fallibility of state actors and imprecision of policy might derail attempts to justify torture while preserving the state's powers to do many other ordinary things.

David Luban cautions about a torture culture. He warns of a fundamental normative shift in how people conceive the sorts of reasons available to them and the people who govern them. If policies were to permit torture in extreme circumstances, the torturers who administer it would be doing something important in the service of justice. The torturers would become *heroes* (Luban, 2009, p. 654). This would change how people think of what a state may do to people in its jurisdiction.

Torture critics worry about how institutionalizing certain acts can invite a reorienting of fundamental moral outlooks. This reorientation shifts the structure of practical reasoning. It alters the terms by which we justify what we can do to one another. Isaiah Berlin discusses the bargains we make in seeking some perfect justice:

> To make mankind just and happy and creative and harmonious forever—what could be too high a price to pay for that? To make such an omelette, there is surely no limit to the number of eggs that should be broken—that was the faith of Lenin, of Trotsky, of Mao, for all I know, of Pol Pot ... You declare that a given policy will make you happier, or freer, or give you room to breathe; but I know that you are mistaken, I know what you need, what all men need; and if there is resistance based on ignorance or malevolence, then it must be broken and hundreds of thousands may have to perish to make millions happy for all time.
>
> (Berlin, 1988)

Proponents of torture would discount these worries as overblown. They do not see a single act of torture—or even *policies* permitting occasional torture—as portending doom. They seem to discount the challenges of interpreting policies that touch on fundamental features of our moral outlook. But torture as a *policy* raises precisely these concerns about the boundaries of what state institutions may claim *legitimately* to do. Surely, there are some limits, but it is unclear how to describe and uphold them with any policy permitting torture.

Many critics warn about certain forms of consequentialist reasoning that emphasize *maximizing* certain values in a political morality. These critics suggest that, sometimes, value maximization is not the way to go. A proper concern with promoting human life must rule out public policies that license some state actions that come at the expense of human life. Doctors, for instance, are not free to kill their patients to harvest their organs to redistribute to needy others—this despite the many lives that might otherwise be saved. Presumably, such organ harvests are out of the question—even if, hypothetically, we can suppose doctors could "get away with it." Now, to be sure, a consequentialist might insist that longer term views justify forbidding such a practice. This is how keeping certain possibilities beyond the pale may help everyone overall. This can provide a consequentialist argument against *policies* permitting torture—ever—even if one act might seem to promote the greatest good.

People leery of this pattern of moral reasoning may prefer instead appeals to the dignity and value of human beings. Proper public policy would respect such moral values and so rule out permitting torture—ever. Policies that cut against this inviolability may undermine our sense of what counts most of all. In our fanciful philosophical moments we might think that some particular act of torture might do well to promote dignity overall, but dignity may seem to rule out any torture for anyone—no matter how depraved.

Final reflections about torture policies

It might be true that specific acts of torture can save lives. It might, however, be better not to acknowledge that in policy. Refusing to craft policies that ever permit torture may capture the special value of human beings.

Of course, it is one thing to forbid torture. Policies must still specify in what torture consists and how, when, and whether merely harsh treatment is permissible. This might be no small task, but allowing uncomfortable interrogations does not seem to threaten a fundamental moral reorientation (some may say, *disorientation*) that comes from licensing torture. Being able to fashion policies with such criteria need not cut against a commitment to the fundamental value of human beings. In the end, torture might be exceptional. It might threaten to undermine a central commitment of the liberal view that individual human beings are inviolable.

Critics of torture exceptionalism may insist that refusal to permit any torture is a naïve form of absolutism. But it need not be naïve. It can be tied to the conclusions of social science about the effectiveness of torture and the limits of imperfect persons acting in institutions empowered to wield lethal force. It can also be tied to a view that leaving some things beyond the pale helps us all in the long run to be better off.

Further reading/screening

Michel Foucault's *Discipline and Punish* (New York: Vintage, 1995) offers an account of how contemporary prisons arose partly in response to the political costs and public misgivings about punitive torture. For a seminal discussion of the rules of war and responses to terrorism, see Michael Walzer, *Just and Unjust Wars*, 4th ed. (New York: Basic Books, 2006). The 1971 Clint Eastwood film *Dirty Harry* features a villain responsible for brutally assaulting and burying a girl alive. Eastwood plays the police officer who uses some harsh methods to get the suspect to disclose the girl's whereabouts. The film tests the boundaries of our commitment to rules governing police investigations and the use of force. Judith Jarvis Thompson considers the strength and boundaries of rights in many of the essays in her *Rights, Restitution, & Risk* (Cambridge, MA: Harvard University Press, 1986). Mark Bowden describes a case where US interrogators gained valuable information after extensive questioning—without torture—of al-Qaeda suspects in "The Ploy," *Atlantic Magazine*, May 2007. John Harris offers a compelling challenge to the limits of consequentialist reasoning in his "Survival Lottery," *Philosophy*, 50 (1975), pp. 81–7. David Schmidtz considers the limits and demands of consequentialist reasoning in "Islands in a Sea of Obligation: Limits of the Duty to Rescue," *Law and Philosophy* 19 (2000), pp. 683–705.

References

Allhoff, F. (2012). *Terrorism, ticking time-bombs, and torture: A philosophical analysis.* Chicago: University of Chicago Press.

Améry, J. (2009). *At the mind's limit.* Bloomington, IN: Indiana University Press.

Aussaresses, P. (2004). *The battle of the Casbah: Terrorism and counterterrorism in Algeria 1955–1957.* New York: Enigma Books.

Berlin, I. (1988, March 17). On the pursuit of the ideal. *The New York Review of Books, 35*(4).

Bernstein, R. (2003, April 10). Kidnapping has Germans debating police torture. *The New York Times*, p. A3.

Bravin, J., & Fields, G. (2003, March 4). How do US interrogators make a captured terrorist talk? *Wall Street Journal*, p. B1.

Brecher, B. (2007). *Torture and the ticking time bomb.* Malden, MA: Blackwell.

Brecher, B. (2014). Torture and its apologists. In A. I. Cohen, & C. H. Wellman (Eds.), *Contemporary debates in applied ethics* (2nd ed., pp. 260–71). Malden, MA: Wiley-Blackwell.

Brzezinski, M. (2001, December 30). Bust and boom. *Washington Post*, p. W09.

Budiansky, S. (2005, June). Truth extraction. *Atlantic Magazine*, pp. 32–5.

Committee on the Rights of the Child. (2013). *Concluding observations on the second to fourth periodic reports of Israel, adopted by the Committee at its sixty-third session (27 May–14 June 2013).* New York: United Nations Convention on the Rights of the Child.

Danner, M. (2004). *Torture and truth: America, Abu Ghraib, and the War on Terrror.* New York: New York Review Books.

Dershowitz, A. (2002). *Why terrorism works.* New Haven, CT: Yale University Press.

Dershowitz, A. (2006). Tortured reasoning. In S. Levinson, (Ed.), *Torture: A collection* (pp. 257–80). New York: Oxford University Press.

Feinberg, J. (1978). Voluntary euthanasia and the inalienable right to life. *Philosophy & Public Affairs, 7*(2), 93–123.

Feitlowitz, M. (2011). *A lexicon of terror: Argentina and the legacies of torture, revised and updated with a new epilogue.* New York: Oxford University Press.

Fried, J. P. (1999, December 14). Volpe sentenced to a 30-year term in Louima torture. *The New York Times.* Retrieved June 4, 2014, from www.nytimes.com/ 1999/12/14/nyregion/volpe-sentenced-to-a-30-year-term-in-louima-torture.html

Iacopino, V., & Xenakis, S. (2011). Neglect of medical evidence of torture in Guantánamo Bay: A case series. *Public Library of Science Medine, 8*(4).

Is torture ever justified? (2003, January 9). *The Economist*, p. 11.

Kant, I. (1996). *Kant: The metaphysics of morals.* (M. J. Gregor, Ed.). Cambridge: Cambridge University Press.

Kant, I. (2012). *Groundwork of the metaphysics of morals.* (M. Gregor & J. Timmerman, Trans. and Ed.). Cambridge: Cambridge University Press.

Kershnar, S. (2002). *Desert, retribution, and torture.* Lanham, MD: University Press of America.

Kershnar, S. (2012). *For torture.* New York: Lexington Books.

Lazreg, M. (2007). *Torture and the twilight of empire: From Algiers to Baghdad.* Princeton, NJ: Princeton University Press.

Luban, D. (2009). Liberalism, torture and the ticking bomb. In M. Zwolinkski (Ed.), *Arguing about political philosophy* (pp. 647–63). New York: Routledge.

Murphy, C. (2012, Jan/Feb). The torturer's apprentice. *Atlantic Magazine.*

National Coalition on Sexual Freedom. (2013, February 15). *Statement on consent.* Retrieved November 11, 2013, from https://ncsfreedom.org/images/stories/ pdfs/Consent%20Counts/CC_Docs_New_011513/ConsentStatement.pdf

Nozick, R. (1974). *Anarchy, state and utopia.* New York: Basic Books.

O'Shaughnessy, H. (2000). *Pinochet: The politics of torture.* New York: New York University Press.

Panné, J.-L., Paczkowski, A., Bartosek, K., Margolin, J.-L., Werth, N., & Courtois, S. (1999). In M. Kramer, (Ed.), *The black book of communism.* (J. Murphy, Trans.) Cambridge, MA: Harvard University Press.

Public Committee against Torture in Israel. (n.d.). *1999 to the present.* Retrieved November 11, 2013, from stoptorture.org.il: www.stoptorture.org.il/en/ skira1999-present

Rejali, D. (2009). *Torture and democracy.* Princeton, NJ: Princeton University Press.

Shalanov, V. (1994). *Kolyma tales.* New York: Penguin.

Shane, S. (2013, April 16). U.S. practiced torture after 9/11, nonpartisan review concludes. *The New York Times*. Retrieved June 4, 2014, from www. nytimes.com/2013/04/16/world/us-practiced-torture-after-9-11-nonpartisan-review-concludes.html

Shue, H. (1978). Torture. *Philosophy & Public Affairs, 7*(2), 124–43.

Shue, H. (2004). Torture. In S. Levinson (Ed.), *Torture*. Oxford University Press.

Shue, H. (2006, March). Torture in dreamland: Disposing of the ticking bomb. *Case Western Reserve Journal of International Law, 37*, 231–9.

Spitz, V. (2005). *Doctors from Hell: The horrific account of Nazi experiments on humans*. Boulder, CO: Sentient Publications.

United Nations. (1984). *United Nations Covention against Torture* and Other Cruel, Inhuman or Degrading Treatment or Punishment. Retrieved June 6, 2014, from http://www.ohchr.org/EN/ProfessionalInterest/Pages/CAT.aspx

Universal Declaration of Human Rights. (1948). Retrieved June 4, 2014 from www.un.org/en/documents/udhr/

8 Reparations and restorative justice

The pages of the book of human history are marked by plenty of blood and suffering. Human beings have shown stunning cruelty and oppression. Unfortunately, the sufferings from injustice are not merely bygones of a sad past.

For hundreds of years, millions of Africans were kidnapped from their homelands, torn from their families, and shipped to the Americas to serve as slaves. But slavery is not ancient history. The effects of such subjugation endure among the slaves' descendants today in countless ways. Among other populations, there is also significant evidence that forced labor continues today with child labor, sex trafficking, and debt bondage.

For thousands of years, Jews have contended with tyrants and intolerance all over the globe. In Europe in the mid twentieth century, millions succumbed to Hitler's sacrificial furnaces. Their fortunes were stolen, their communities destroyed, and their lives incinerated.

Indigenous populations in the Americas, Australia, New Zealand, and elsewhere were decimated by the European influx. Natives lost their land, their communities, and their culture. They often lost their lives.

Other examples of massive human rights violations include wholesale killing of early-twentieth-century Armenians in Ottoman Turkey, the deaths of the Ukrainian "kulaks" of the 1930s, the 1970s victims of Cambodia's killing fields, the victims of South Africa's twentieth-century apartheid policies, and those who perished in China's mid-twentieth-century campaigns such as the Great Leap Forward. And there are plenty of other examples, omitted here for reasons of space but not insignificant. More sharply, genocide is not distant history. We need only look to Rwanda, East Timor, North Korea, the former Yugoslavia, or many other recent sites for the wholesale destruction of groups.

People are increasingly coming to terms with such histories. The victims and their descendants often demand that their voices be heard, that their losses be acknowledged, and that some material steps be taken to compensate them for harms done. In some cases, nation states with violent histories have officially embraced such tasks. These movements are often immensely controversial. They make people confront the legacies of state injustice and their complicity in oppression. They invite people to come to terms with their victimization. They often involve restitution, compensation, or both. These challenges may partly explain the many cases where there has been little if any acknowledgement or reconciliation for wholesale injustice.

These new calls to reckon with the past do not simply dwell on state injustices. They also increasingly focus on individual criminal offenders. In addition to and sometimes instead of traditional criminal punishment, many jurisdictions experiment with ways of promoting reconciliation and repair among harmed persons, their communities, and offenders. These various approaches often aim to heal victims and (re)establish appropriate relationships. The United States, Rwanda, South Africa, Ireland, New Zealand, and many other countries have had some success with such programs. But they are sometimes in tension with the demands of criminal justice and the interests of third parties.

This chapter focuses on some of the challenges facing various contemporary reparative justice policies. Such policies provide rules and guidelines for reckoning with and repairing past injustice. The programs and policies face numerous difficulties yet offer intriguing opportunities for moral progress. Sometimes it is difficult to isolate harms, assign responsibility, or identify victims. Some measures of reparation threaten undue harm to communities or innocent third parties. On the other hand, such policies may promote greater respect for human dignity, better opportunities for victims to get on with their lives, and help to prevent future atrocities.

We should note what this chapter will not do. It will not offer anything near an inventory of the various approaches to reparations and restorative justice. It will only glimpse some examples as springboards for reflection. Further, though businesses are increasingly coming to terms with their own tainted histories, the chapter will not consider the many opportunities for policy reform among corporations and nonstate actors who were complicit in injustice. Instead, the chapter discusses how ethics identifies and frames some of the difficulties for *states* in overseeing a reckoning with the past. States administer criminal justice systems. And states are often guilty of creating or abetting the worst atrocities in human history. We can then consider the difficulties for states in fashioning some policies that might reduce controversy while satisfying widely shared moral concerns for repair and reconciliation. The first section outlines some of the key concepts at work in discussions of moral repair and policies for reparation. The second section discusses some of the central difficulties confronting any efforts at moral repair for historic injustice. The third section briefly sketches aspects of the developing movement for "restorative justice" and how it offers an alternative or supplement to traditional criminal justice. The fourth section highlights some of the difficulties in emphasizing *material* compensation for historic injustice. The fifth section offers some closing thoughts about the potential for policy to promote some moral repair.

Some of the terms of discussion

Ideal vs. nonideal theory

In Chapter 3, we cast distributive justice as the subject of a group of theories that offer various justifications for what individuals must do and what they may claim from others. We noted that distributive justice was not the only moral dimension relevant to assigning responsibilities and benefits to residents of a political community. Others included charity, criminal justice, and restorative justice. This chapter focuses on aspects of the latter consideration. It is not charity when victims of injustice receive some measure of repair. And criminal justice is often not enough or inapplicable for some oppressive pasts, as we shall see shortly.

Discussions of just relationships, including those about just allocations of goods and positions of power, often imagine that persons in a society interact in a peaceful and respectful fashion. But as we know, these relations sometimes break down. Sometimes they never fully existed, if even at all. Many theories of justice will bracket these possibilities. Theorists sometimes begin with a form of "ideal theory" that identifies what should guide the understandings and institutions of justice. They might then pass over the messy and bloody specifics that come up in discussions of violent actual histories.

There are many different approaches to ideal theorizing about justice (Schmidtz, 2011; Valentini, 2012). Among them is, first, treating theory as a simplifying device that avoids dwelling on what John Rawls calls "distracting details" (Rawls, 1993, p. 12). As David Schmidtz notes, theorizing in this sense abstracts from particulars and focuses on the essentials that matter to us (Schmidtz, 2011). A second way to understand theorizing as an ideal is to imagine that everyone behaves justly and so the main theoretical task is only to specify what justice is so that people may comply. A third view of ideal theorizing revolves around objects of aspiration, as when a theory defends appropriate distributions of wealth or opportunities to own or access vital goods. On this understanding, a theory of justice indicates the ideal; figuring out how to realize it is another matter. Sometimes those "feasibility" considerations have little or no bearing on a theory of justice.

Any reckoning with oppressive pasts starts with a clear departure from an ideal: people have behaved horribly to one another. What to do about this may be omitted from a theory of justice altogether. Or it might enter in a secondary way as part of a theory of criminal justice, which discusses how a group of people may establish institutions to correct past wrongs. But criminal justice is often not enough when facing the past for two reasons. First, fallible persons inhabit institutions of criminal justice. They sometimes make mistakes. The institutions sometimes leave some wrongs uncorrected or punish the innocent. Second, when confronting violent pasts, we are often considering people and institutions that over a long time systemically ignored or deprived others of basic human rights. Sometimes, criminal justice systems were defective, corrupt, or tools of a pernicious regime. Third, criminal justice typically stresses punishment, not restoring *victims* and their relationships with others. Theorizing about past injustices thus typically involves or requires departures from ideals in many of the senses of ideal theorizing.

If a theory of justice is silent about what to do when coming to terms with wholesale slaughter, it may strike people as irrelevant. Injustice is the history many of us face, either as victims, bystanders, perpetrators, or simply as individuals enmeshed in complex relationships with persons who were parties to injustice in some way. When reflecting about such histories, we are thus engaging in what writers often call *nonideal theorizing*: we are figuring out what to do given a very particular troubled past. This involves addressing people who were unjust, allowing victims to recover, and considering how to move forward in some way that represents a moral improvement. But we can still draw on the more "ideal" theories to specify where we should be going and to constrain how we get there.

Compensation, restitution, reparations, punishment

Several related processes and ideas are linked to moral repair. Here we distinguish among them. This helps us to set the terms for discussion.

Compensation

Compensation is something of value that a person receives to make up for some setback. Any persons can provide compensation to someone who suffered a loss if they are able. If a family suffers a loss from a devastating fire, they can be compensated by their government, by an insurance company, by neighbors, or by the person(s) who somehow caused the fire.

Restitution

Restitution is the process of returning what has been wrongly taken from a victim. Suppose Western museums are in possession of antiquities that were inappropriately removed from Egypt, Greece, or elsewhere. (To be clear, establishing this is deeply controversial.) Restitution may involve returning the antiquities.

Reparations

Reparations are the steps or measures taken to undo the effects of some wrong. Reparations may include compensation, restitution, or additional measures to repair moral relations among wrongdoers, victims, and communities. Reparations address someone as a victim of wrongdoing and not merely as someone who has suffered harm. Thus, reparations call for acknowledging the harm as a wrong. They then often require apologies by the wrongdoer to the victim. They may also involve some symbolic elements such as memorialization or commemoration.

Reparations typically have one of two possible goals. They can attempt to put a victim into the position she would have occupied had the wrong not occurred. Alternatively, they can attempt to put the victim back into the situation she was in prior to the wrongdoing.

One essential feature to reparations is that they must be provided by the wrongdoers to their victims. If Jill steals Jack's bicycle, it is not reparations if sympathetic neighbors buy Jack a new bicycle. That would be compensation. It is also not reparations if all that the police do is find Jill and put her in jail. Jack would then still be without his bicycle. In this sense there can be no vicarious reparations. Except as an expression of sympathy, bystanders cannot apologize for injustice nor provide reparations to victims of injustice. Reparations for historic injustice thus do not cross generations. After his death, Jack's descendants might receive his stolen bicycle to compensate for the previous wrong, but this would not be reparations directly to Jack. (Nothing can be done directly to someone who is dead.) If, however, there can be rights of or duties to the dead, then returning the bicycle to Jack's descendants might very well be a form of reparations to Jack.

Punishment

Punishment is the process whereby a person(s) with authority imposes measures intended to make someone suffer for having violated some rules. Though there are many theories of punishment, reparation is not punishment. Whereas reparation targets the victim and is intended to make her whole, punishment targets a wrongdoer and attempts to correct him in some way. As John Locke once wrote, the right of reparation uniquely belongs to the victim. Rights of punishment, however, may be claimed by duly appointed authorities or, absent those, anyone who wishes to uphold people's rights (Locke, 1988, chap. 2).

Inheritance vs. reparations

When we speak of historic injustice, we often have in mind one of two possibilities. First, we might target a long-standing unredressed wrong visited on deceased members of distant generations. Second, we might be thinking of a continuing injustice that can be causally traced to something that started many generations ago. Often, cases of reparation involve both concerns.

African slavery, for instance, inflicted horrific wrongs on the slaves. But the slaves are dead. Those slaves, however, were entitled to reparations and compensation for the wrongs they suffered. On many common understandings of inheritance, their descendants would be entitled to the value of those unsatisfied claims. Of course, determining what those claims included would be no easy matter. The value may increase over time if the damages from the original loss are compounded. In any case, a descendant who merely claims the value of her ancestors' unsatisfied claims might then merely be calling for what she is due as her inheritance.

Reparations, however, are what a victim is owed to make her whole. The descendant of a victim of injustice may only claim *reparations* for the wrongs she has personally suffered. Those wrongs may be causally linked to something her ancestors suffered. Descendants of African slaves, for instance, might claim reparations for pernicious inequalities and discrimination that have their roots in African slavery. But they cannot claim reparations for slavery. They might claim the value of unsatisfied reparations claims that their ancestors were owed, but those would be their inheritance, not reparations for slavery.

Calls for moral repair often involve some or all of compensation, restitution, or punishment. They variably invoke appeals to inheritance or reparation. Here we pass over discussions of punishment and focus on various features of the other processes. We will consider some recent challenges for policies regarding moral repair.

Some challenges facing calls for moral repair

Supersession

The historic injustices that come up in discussions of reparations are not just great wrongs but long-standing unredressed wrongs. Time sometimes heals wounds. People move on. Time also sometimes makes moot some wounds. All the victims or all the perpetrators may have died or forgotten earlier wrongs. But time sometimes leaves wrongs untouched or even deepens them. The victims might continue to suffer and their setbacks might adversely impact others such as their children and communities. It may then seem that they should be able to claim some recognition of their wrongful deprivations. They may even be due some form of restitution, compensation, or both.

We commonly hold that victims should receive some repair for unjustly inflicted misfortune. We take it that justice should protect them from such setbacks and that when people suffer them, justice typically demands that the effects of such wrongdoing be undone—preferably by the wrongdoer. Of course, the remedies for such setbacks may vary, but the point is that misfortune is a moral problem because we commonly think that it is a matter of justice that people should be able to plan and live their own lives (Boxill, 2014). As John Rawls puts it, people have a fundamental interest in being able to have, plan, and revise their own "conception of what is of value in human life" (Rawls, 2001, p. 19). Misfortunes undermine their opportunities to fulfill this interest. Injustice compounds misfortune as it typically involves an additional strike against one's dignity by devaluing one's moral, social, or political standing.

A concern with victims' misfortunes is but one aspect of addressing long-standing injustice. Time changes things. It does not change the significance of individuals' interests in leading their own lives. But time does complicate assessments of the weight and content of various interests. As time goes on, it may become difficult if not impossible to identify wrongdoers, victims, or what has been lost. Consequently it may become impossible to figure out what if anything is needed to make victims whole. This is a special challenge for historic injustice.

Perhaps descendants of victims of historic injustice are due some compensation. In the case of African slavery, the European takeover of indigenous lands, and the destruction of native cultures, the amounts might be staggering. They might seem to require a fundamental reorganization of civilizations. Of course, difficulty is itself no argument against moral repair. If Jill stole Jack's bicycle and hid it in a location that is very difficult to get to, that is not an argument that Jill need not return the bicycle to Jack.

Of course, stolen bicycles do not compare to the wholesale violations involved in generations of slavery or colonialism. It may then be difficult to figure out how to fix things or even whether one should try. Some people point to passage of time and say that it is now *impossible* to disentangle who did what to whom. There is an "epistemological fog" that blocks us from figuring out how to make victims whole (Loury, 2007, p. 102). In the case of indigenous populations, for instance, we simply cannot put victims into the position they occupied before the unjust violations. Most of those victims are dead. In the case of chattel slavery, the challenges are equally daunting. Attempting to make victims whole is deeply problematic. As Glenn C. Loury notes for the case of the United States,

> How would one even begin to demonstrate in quantitative terms the nature and extent of injury? Given the wide economic disparities to be observed among white Americans of various ethnic groups, who can know how blacks would have fared but for the wrongs of the past? Who can say what the out-of-wedlock birth rate for blacks would be, absent chattel slavery? How does one calculate the cost of inner-city ghettos, of poor education, of the stigma of perceived racial inferiority? The damage done by slavery and its aftermath is at once too subtle and too profound to be evaluated in monetary terms.
>
> (Loury, 2007, p. 88)

Though Loury and others argue for material measures intended to address the situation of contemporary persons of color in light of the troubled history, others argue that dwelling on the past serves no purpose. We should let bygones be bygones. It is too hard to sort out who did what to whom and so we should move on.

Others make a stronger moral claim. They argue that people can sometimes acquire legitimate title over time in a way that rivals claims to compensation or restitution. Individuals sometimes build their lives around improvements to things that can be causally linked to an injustice. This is especially true of land or the inherited wealth that might be traced to the depredations of slavery or violence against indigenous peoples. It is impossible to separate out what part of the land and what part of contemporary holdings can be traced to earlier injustices.

So much has happened in the generations since earlier injustice that claims to compensation or restitution might then be "superseded" with time (Waldron, 1992). Determining who owes what to whom is further complicated by intermarriage and blurring of group boundaries. The wrong might then fade in some way. Furthermore, correcting some wrongs might involve undue burdens on the perpetrator. How or whether the wrongs fade is something that calls for considerable discussion, especially in light of fraught power dynamics. After all, victims and their descendants rarely invoke supersession. They might be in an environment where the wrong is hardly historic. It might be rehearsed at family meals and gatherings. That history might now be part of their culture.

"Nonidentity" problems

To claim reparations, one must be a victim of some injustice. Many critics of reparations warn that contemporary descendants of victims of injustice are thus ineligible for reparations. They were not victims of the original injustice.

Consider the pernicious violations of African chattel slavery. Descendants of the slaves cannot claim reparations for slavery. Those reparations were owed to the slaves, but all the slaves are dead. Moreover, contemporary descendants of those slaves cannot claim to have been harmed by slavery since in many cases they owe their existence to slavery.

One of the typical ways of understanding harm involves some "counterfactual" reasoning. We think of a person's current opportunities and welfare and compare them to what that person would have had but for the harm. Compensating the person for the harm attempts to make up for that difference. In the case of some historic wrongs, however, this type of calculation might be conceptually impossible.

Successful reparations either restore a victim to her condition before a wrong or put her into the situation she would have been in had the wrong not occurred. Consider Sam, the child of two former slaves. Sam cannot complain about slavery if he was never enslaved. (No doubt, in our world Sam can complain about many other things traceable to slavery.) If Sam's parents die without receiving reparations for slavery, Sam might be entitled to some compensation for his parents' unsatisfied reparations claims. But Sam, as a child of former slaves, might not be entitled to reparations for slavery.

Suppose Sam's parents were shipped to the Americas from different parts of Africa and would not have met had there been no African slave trade. Sam would then not have been conceived had there been no slavery. There is no world we can imagine in which Sam exists had the injustice of slavery never taken place. It is then meaningless to attempt to restore Sam to the condition he was in before slavery or the condition he would have been in had there been no slavery. At best we can imagine two alternatives had there been no slavery: (1) Sam was never conceived, or (2) another person was conceived, somehow instead of Sam, and that person's existence does not depend on the historic wrong. (That person would not be identical to Sam, and this is partly why philosophers call the relevant challenge the "nonidentity problem.") But in either case, Sam cannot claim compensation for a wrong that seems to have been a condition of his existence. Existence can rarely if ever be a harm in itself. (But see Benatar, 2006 for the view that coming into existence is always a great harm.)

This sort of problem does not derail all claims regarding historic injustices. Inheritance claims might still persist. Furthermore, contemporary descendants of victims of past injustice might have independent claims to redress for wrongs they (and not their ancestors) suffered. These sorts of violations need not founder on "nonidentity" problems. Indeed, often the violations their ancestors suffered were not one-off events. They typically persisted long after the original injustice and were compounded with additional injustices on subsequent generations. The key is that those subsequent injustices can be traced to earlier ones. Establishing causal linkages in such cases is no easy matter. However, there may still be excellent grounds for some form of moral (perhaps material) repair for living generations.

Theorists have offered other responses to nonidentity problems. (See Roberts, 2013, sec. 3 for a careful overview.) Among them is to construct a notion of a wrong that does not presuppose some comparative notion of harm. The wrong might instead involve the expression of some vice or involve treating someone with disrespect. In such cases, there may be room for reparations claims. Another is to hold people to account for wrongly setting back overall well-being.

Another way to address nonidentity challenges is to acknowledge history: typically the harms involved in persistent injustices were inflicted on people because of group membership. We might then treat the harm as something that was done *to the group*. Sometimes that harm might not be easily understood in terms of the sum of harms done to individuals. This might be clearest in cases of indigenous populations such as those of the Americas, Australia, and New Zealand. In each case, the histories involved not just murder and depredations on individuals but harms to the groups to which the victims belonged. Children were taken from their families and forced to assimilate to the ways of dominant white peoples. They were forbidden to speak their families' languages, dress in their traditional clothing, or know the ways of their culture. Their native cultures and languages suffered as a result. We might then say that those *groups* are now due moral repair. Members of each group might then claim the repair on the group's behalf.

This is only a sketch of a deeply controversial issue in social theory. Some thinkers find this approach quite promising (Tan, 2007; Thompson, 2002). It avoids some of the problems in establishing causal chains and identifying appropriate specific claimants. But there are important challenges to this approach that we may need to overcome if we wish to pursue moral repair as part of a policy of *reparations*.

First, any appeal to group rights of repair must be mindful of the danger that *individuals* would wield such rights. In some cases, the most salient individuals are those in positions of power or authority. But allowing them to claim such rights and distribute the proceeds may risk entrenching current pernicious power dynamics within the group (Kukathas, 2007, chap. 6). This is not an argument against a group-rights-based approach to moral repair so much as it is a cautionary note in establishing policies that take the group as the locus of repair.

A further problem is that appeals to groups do not overcome all non-identity worries. Indeed, they create new ones. Consider the Māori people of New Zealand. The group's identity has changed considerably because of contact with Europeans. To say that the *group* has been harmed as a result of such a history requires understanding how the group can have interests independently of its members. More troublesome, speaking of group harm might be deeply problematic because the harm often changes what the group is. The contemporary Māori are causally linked to the Māori prior to European contact, but they might be importantly different groups. If their cultural identity has changed crucially from European contact, it might be difficult to understand how the current group has been harmed as a result of that contact. There might be no meaningful way to compare the current group's identity and status to some such identity or status of a pre-injustice group (Perez, 2014, pp. 206–10).

Suppose such nonidentity worries do not rule out moral repair for various historic injustices. There are still important questions involving what form if any moral repair might take, who should receive it, and who should provide it. We turn to a sketch of some such challenges.

Determinacy problems, limitations on compensation, and alternate forms of repair

Independently of any philosophical challenges to validating reparation claims, there are daunting problems in specifying the proper form and extent of such claims. It might be impossible to indicate any formula for resolving these problems in advance. Resolving the challenges in any satisfactory way for purposes of policy will surely require careful and patient discussion.

In cases of identifiable theft, it is usually reasonably easy to figure out how to take important and perhaps sufficient steps toward repair. Suppose Jill steals Jack's bicycle, which had been the basis of Jack's business. Jack has reparation claims against Jill to recover the bicycle as restitution and claims to additional compensation for the losses associated with not having had the opportunity to earn a living. Jill also owes Jack an apology of some sort for disrespectful treatment.

Obviously, this simple one-on-one case passes over the complications of massive rights violations that persist over time. In such cases, there are increasing chances that people would have made choices to upset the status quo prior to the injustice. This may impact our sense of what they are due as compensation. Indeed, victims, had they not been victimized, might have gone on to squander their wealth or opportunities. But we typically discount such possibilities and suppose for the purposes of calculating compensation that history would not have seen drastic changes. Even with this simplifying assumption, it can be extremely difficult to calculate the appropriate compensation for historic wrongs. Slaves, for instance, did not merely lose the wages they should have been given for their labor. They lost their freedom, their communities, and often their lives. It seems difficult to put a price on those losses. Indeed, attempting to do so may seem to cheapen the meaning and value of what was lost. For related reasons, some Jews resisted initially taking reparations from Germany for the Holocaust (Colonomos & Armstrong, 2007).

Emphasizing material compensation for historic wrongs comes up against additional challenges. Over the generations, there has been some intermarriage. It is then sometimes difficult to separate out victims, perpetrators, and bystanders. Indeed, some might argue that few if any of us have clean hands. The land we occupy may have a tainted history. The products we use and consume may depend importantly on exploitation or subjugation of impoverished persons in the developing world. Our ancestors might have suffered, but they also might have been complicit in grievous rights violations. And so on. This might be the start of an argument not to dwell too much on the past. After all, few people have a grievance with the Norman invasion of England in 1066. On the other hand, there are plenty of historic injustices whose persistence has current victims today calling out for repair. Those would seem to be good candidates for attention (Spinner-Halev, 2012). This is not to discount the injustice of various historic events for which people do not demand repair. It is to say that those events are not clear candidates for policy attention.

Even if we can identify some criteria for persons to be candidates for receiving compensation for historic wrongs, critics may warn against pursuing this enterprise in some cases. It might involve creating or entrenching worrisome group identities instead of encouraging persons to think of themselves as equal members of a single cooperative political community. More worrisome is the danger that creating policies for compensation for historic wrongs might distort behavior. Such policies threaten to create incentives for people to shift their energies away from independently productive activities that might create new wealth and instead toward fabricating or exaggerating a group identity for themselves mainly for the purposes of qualifying for the compensation. Of course, this might simply be an argument against poorly designed compensation policies.

Policies to compensate people for historic wrongs might also sweep too many persons into the group of the supposedly culpable. One common complaint against black reparations in the United States, for instance, is by persons who argue that neither they nor their ancestors owned slaves. Perhaps their ancestors "got off the boat" from the old country in the early twentieth century and so, they argue, they cannot be held accountable for the evils of slavery.

Among the responses to such criticisms is an appeal to "unjust enrichment": whites in the United States enjoy the benefits of various forms of illegitimate "white privilege." In this way they might be complicit in and have benefitted from the ill-gotten gains against which the slaves and their descendants have claims. Another reply is to speak of the political community as a forum for achieving mutually justifiable goals within shared institutions. When a portion of that political community has suffered in straitened conditions for generations in a way that can be traced to a historic wrong the political community made possible, everyone may have an important reason to support measures intended to remedy the legacy of those injustices. This appeals not so much to unjust enrichment but to the benefits and burdens of membership in political society. Of course, neither of these approaches tells us how much and in what form compensation should be provided.

Whatever the remedies for the historic injustice, they likely come up against important limits. John Locke describes how victims of injustice have a right of reparation against wrongdoers. Their right is constrained by the legitimate interests of third parties. As Locke writes when speaking of a just war, the victors may claim what is necessary for reparation, but limited by "the right of the innocent wife and children" (Locke, 1988, sec. 182). The limiting right here is not to everything innocent persons might be holding. After all, they cannot claim a right to stolen goods. But it would seem that satisfying reparation may not deny innocent third parties their opportunities to satisfy basic needs. If, for instance, reparation for some injustice would leave others to starve, then it would seem reparation claims may not be (fully) satisfied. This sort of limitation might be especially relevant when considering how (much) to compensate descendants of African chattel slavery and European colonization.

Locke's idea about the limits of reparation suggests a few general restrictions on redress. Repair must not impose undue moral costs. The repair must not impose excess costs on offenders. It must be proportionate to the original offense. The repair must also not impose undue serious disadvantages on third parties. If Lee wrongly punches Sam in the nose, Lee needs, among other things, to undo the damages to Sam. This may mean, for instance, that Lee must pay to fix Sam's broken nose and provide lost wages. If Lee had hoped instead to use those resources to purchase a vacation in some tropical paradise, this is hardly an undue burden on Lee. The fulfillment of Sam's right of reparation might, however, take second place were Lee to need to use those resources to provide life-saving emergency care for his or her child. That does not mean Sam's rights of repair disappear but that their fulfillment may be delayed or limited in some way. A policy specifying how and when rights of reparation may be suspended, delayed, or cancelled would then need to avoid excess costs on others. In lieu of exhaustively specifying relative moral and political weights, the policy might only attend to basic rights to clear moral minimums.

Many of the challenges that come up with moral repair turn on who shall *pay* and how much. One way of avoiding some of these problems and taking some concrete steps toward moral progress is to consider other forms of repair. Much of what is damaged with injustice is any appropriate moral relationship; victims are devalued and denied their equal moral and civil status. Among the ways of repairing such relationships are truth-telling, memorializations, and commemorations. These processes can help to (re)establish the proper place of victims of injustice. There are plenty of examples of each of these, including South Africa's transition from apartheid toward greater freedom and political inclusiveness. The Truth and Reconciliation Commission's work there helped document history. But the promise they offered of amnesty for truth was deeply controversial, leaving some victims feeling as if their sufferings were discounted.

These commissions are illustrations of various programs for testimony and community-based restorative justice. The programs do not always work well in some or many respects. Some communities are not stable enough to permit such testimony. Sometimes the programs arbitrarily exclude certain offenders from their jurisdiction (Human Rights Watch, 2011). Some communities simply do not want to air the past. Some victims believe that airing the truth only revictimizes them. Others believe that justice requires not the truth but the application of sanctions on their offenders. Many complain that truth without compensation is empty. Honest investigation and publicity, however, have often gone far toward validating the suffering of victims. These programs have provided a forum for victims to confront their offenders and for there to be some measure of reconciliation.

Investigating and speaking the truth is hardly the only alternative or supplement to material compensation. Other options have included public apologies, the creation of museums or national holidays, establishing days of remembrance, or additions or changes to school curricula. Australia, for instance, has recently confronted its deeply troubled history with the Stolen Generations ("Bringing them Home Report," 1997). There is now a series of regular events to remember how Australia forcibly removed indigenous children from their communities. The investigations, testimony, discussions, and apologies have helped shift the national conversation about history and about how to address the legacies of previous injustice. This is but one example of the various ways political communities can grapple with history.

When considering past injustices by states, these options each call for particular state acts and policies. Executing them with any measure of success often requires negotiations with victims. Success here means providing some measure of moral repair. When the victims are still alive, their say is crucial in determining what can count as repair and what would be an empty gesture or worse.

Restorative justice

Restorative justice is a recent movement that explores substitutes or supplements for traditional criminal justice. It takes many forms. It typically includes extensive victim and community involvement in determining how to repair an injustice. There have been sentencing conferences, facilitated mediation, community oversight, and other measures intended to promote repair and reconciliation between offenders and those whose lives they have altered. Various forms of restorative justice have had some success in the United States, Ireland, the UK, Australia, and elsewhere. The movement represents a partial shift away from the notion that the state is the main complainant for injustice. There are victims who have suffered. Incarceration may do little if anything to restore them. Restorative justice then presents important opportunities for moral progress but presents some challenges. However, since it is typically a response to criminal activity, it requires state policy.

In many cases of restorative justice, there are institutions that stakeholders hope will achieve both some consensus about how to repair damaged relationships and a measure of reconciliation. Attendant discussions give victims a special role in identifying their loss and determining how to repair it. In some cases, there are conferences that substitute for typical criminal penalties. Often they have served in an especially compelling advisory capacity (Van Ness & Strong, 2010; Zehr, 1990).

These conferences allow for offenders to learn about the impact of their injustices. They can allow victims to have their suffering validated. They can also help communities to figure out how to reintegrate offenders in a way that promotes healing and reduces recidivism. They can also fruitfully depict responses to injustice not as a one-off event but as a process that calls for continuing commitment to acknowledge the past while moving forward.

Among the challenges for such processes are the potential coercion involved for both offenders and victims to participate, the distortive classification of "community" in determining who may have stakes in determining acceptable restorative outcomes, the potential creation or entrenchment of pernicious power hierarchies within communities, the worry that the processes discount the significance of crime, and the general misgiving that they do not provide adequate if any punishment. There are also some concerns about whether the processes provide appropriate healing for victims or actually reduce recidivism over standard criminal retribution (Levin, 2005; Morris, 2002; Strickland, 2004). Some of these concerns hang on the findings of empirical social science, whose conclusions emerge with unfolding social scientific investigations.

There are public policy opportunities given the early signs of success in some cases. States can permit experimentation with such measures, which might foster further study about what seems to promote healing and what problems to avoid. Here too we are likely to find that no one policy will suit all cases. Healing is a particularized phenomenon; what sorts of things work in various communities will surely vary depending upon local norms and distinct histories. Public policies can promote some moral progress and reconciliation partly by acknowledging that criminal reprisals are not the only (or perhaps even the best) way to achieve widely shared goals.

Material reparations for the legacies of historic injustice

The United States apologized for WWII-era Japanese internment camps. Ireland continues to confront the many decades of forced labor and incarceration of women in Magdalene asylums. Germany has provided reparations for Nazi atrocities. These are some of the many examples of nation states coming to terms with mass injustices. There are continued calls for some official honest discussion and repair regarding the legacies of many other injustices.

There has been no official apology by the United States government for its role in the African slave trade. Various government officials have expressed remorse, and particular states and corporations have acknowledged their role in fostering the injustice. Some writers and lawmakers have continued to call for some form of black reparations, either involving an apology or some material redress (Brooks, 1999; Coates, 2014). No doubt, apologies do not undo the damage, but, as many would argue, they can begin to validate the historical record and initiate a conversation about how to achieve some repair. Many people have misgivings about such political apologies. They might misrepresent the views of many citizens or perpetuate pernicious hierarchies that helped make the original injustices possible. These are cautions against insensitive moral repair, not reasons not to pursue it at all.

Several Caribbean nations have recently called for reparations from several European countries for the history of colonialism (Blake, 2014; Gibb, 2014). Spokespersons for the Caribbean consortium called Caricom demand compensation for centuries of depredations and for the modern legacies of colonialism, including lasting public health problems and adverse impacts on economic and cultural development. Some critics worry that Caricom represents little more than a cash grab, but their efforts might be the start of honest reflection about the enduring impact of historic injustice. What comes out of it might depend on difficult conversations about how to respond to history while allowing all parties to move on with their lives.

The Caricom demands and calls for black reparations illustrate that reckoning with injustice is complex and painful. Inheritors of privilege understandably resist confronting a past that may challenge their status and the wealth they hold. This is why calls for moral repair often meet with great resistance. Victims worry about commodifying their losses; offenders and their descendants worry about losing what they believe should be theirs. Now, on the one hand, it is not an objection to moral repair that one may lose access to some of one's current holdings. After all, stolen goods belong to the people from whom they were taken. But, on the other hand, beginning calls for moral repair with demands for material compensation might block progress toward reconciliation. Documentation, testimony, and symbolic measures might be helpful first steps toward the healing that many parties crave. Public policies can promote this progress not by foisting a single solution on a political community but by allowing for dialogue. And in any case, given how bloody history is and the many opportunities for moral progress, policy might focus first on those inequities that have their roots in enduring historic injustice (Spinner-Halev, 2012).

Conclusion

History is rife with injustice. There are plentiful narratives of subjugation, servitude, and wholesale slaughter. It can overwhelm the most well-meaning student of history. But the darkness of much of the past is not a reason to turn away. The injustices live on in the memories of victims and their descendants. They often shape the identities of persons and communities. They are often key factors responsible for persistent and morally suspect inequalities. Such injustices might make salient which harms deserve policy priority for remedies. Indeed, framing harms as a product of injustice might give added significance to certain remedies. How Western nations might address climate change, for instance, continues to be deeply controversial. But if climate change can be understood as a product of some historic injustice, it may become a platform for concrete remedies for those peoples who are threatened with serious harms (Harris, 2014).

We often cannot make whole what has been demolished. Moral repair faces daunting challenges, whether the offender is a person, a corporation, or a state. But public policies can permit and perhaps encourage experimentation with different forms of reparation. Some of these might succeed at reducing the incidence and costs of law enforcement, as well as promoting healing and reconciliation among offenders, victims, and communities.

Many discussions of reparation and restorative justice confirm that moral repair is not a one-off event. It is typically a *process*. As Michael DeGagné notes, we can move from a time where injustices simmer without validation to a time where people face the history and legacies of injustice. It is never easy: "This is how we move forward—this messy, awful business of making things better one day, one person, one community at a time" (DeGagné, 2012). When policymakers are open to such possibilities, they can promote the reconciliation that people can find mutually justifiable.

Further reading

Investigations of modern-day servitude are available in many spots, including Kevin Bales and Ron Soodalter, *The Slave Next Door: Human Trafficking and Slavery in America Today* (Berkeley and Los Angeles: University of California Press, 2010) and Siddharth Kara, *Sex Trafficking: Inside the Business of Modern Slavery* (New York: Columbia University Press, 2010). For context about vexing reparations, consider any documentation of communism, Nazism, slavery, or colonialism. Stéphane Courtois edited an acclaimed but controversial book, *The Black Book of Communism* (Cambridge, MA: Harvard University Press, 1999), which documents the body count of communism in the twentieth century. Among the seminal pieces on the devastation and legacies of colonialism is Frantz Fanon's *The Wretched of the Earth*, originally published in 1961 and now in reprint, which offers a Marxist analysis of liberation struggles in the developing world. Howard Zehr's book, *Changing Lenses: A New Focus for Crime and Justice* (Scottdale, PA: Herald Press, 1990), is widely credited as a major resource for the growing restorative justice movement. He urges people to rethink traditional paradigms of retributive punishment. The power and pitfalls of truth and reconciliation commissions are documented in extensive literatures, including, for instance, Priscilla Hayner, *Unspeakable Truths: Facing the Challenges of Truth Commissions*, 2nd ed. (New York and Abingdon: Routledge, 2010), which documents the work and impacts of dozens of truth commissions and how the investigations and testimonies are sometimes in tension with justice. A similar earlier book offers an excellent collection of scholarly commentaries in Robert I. Rotberg and Dennis Thompson (eds.), *Truth v. Justice: The Morality of Truth Commissions* (Princeton, NJ: Princeton University Press, 2002). Paul Tullis documents the gripping case of a victim–offender conference where a murderer met his victim's parents (Tullis, 2013), which had an impact on sentencing.

References

Benatar, D. (2006). *Better never to have been: The harm of coming into existence.* Oxford; New York: Clarendon Press; Oxford University Press.

Blake, M. (2014, March 10). Caribbean leaders are to sue Britain for its part in the slave trade. *Mail Online.* Retrieved March 30, 2014, from www.dailymail.co. uk/news/article-2577312/Caribbean-leaders-sue-Britain-slave-trade-150-years-abolished.html

Boxill, B. (2014). Compensation and past injustice. In A. I. Cohen & C. H. Wellman (Eds.), *Contemporary Debates in Applied Ethics* (2nd ed., pp. 191–202). Malden, MA: Wiley-Blackwell.

Bringing them home report. (1997). Text. Retrieved March 30, 2014, from www.humanrights.gov.au/publications/bringing-them-home-report-1997

Brooks, R. L. (1999). *When sorry isn't enough: The controversy over apologies and reparations for human injustice.* New York: New York University Press.

Coates, T.-N. (2014, May 21). The case for reparations. *The Atlantic.* Retrieved June 4, 2014, from www.theatlantic.com/features/archive/2014/05/the-case-for-reparations/361631/

Colonomos, A., & Armstrong, A. (2007). German reparations to the Jews after World War II: A turning point in the history of reparations. In J. Miller & R. Kumar (Eds.), *Reparations: Interdisciplinary inquiries* (pp. 390–419). New York: Oxford University Press.

DeGagné, M. (2012, December 14). Implementing reparations: International perspectives. Retrieved March 30, 2014, from www.humanrights.gov.au/ implementing-reparations-international-perspectives

Gibb, F. (2014, March 10). Two centuries on, Caribbean leaders prepare to sue Britain over slave trade. *The Times* (London). Retrieved July 6, 2014, from www.thetimes.co.uk/tto/law/article4028282.ece

Harris, G. (2014, March 28). Facing rising seas, Bangladesh confronts the consequences of climate change. *The New York Times.* Retrieved July 6, 2014, from www.nytimes.com/2014/03/29/world/asia/facing-rising-seas-bangladesh-confronts-the-consequences-of-climate-change.html

Human Rights Watch. (2011, May). Justice compromised: The legacy of Rwanda's community-based Gacaca courts. Retrieved March 30, 2014, from www.hrw.org/node/99189

Kukathas, C. (2007). *The liberal archipelago: A theory of diversity and freedom.* Oxford: Oxford University Press.

Levin, M. (2005). Restorative justice in Texas. Texas Public Policy Foundation. Retrieved March 30, 2014, from www.texaspolicy.com/center/effective-justice/ reports/restorative-justice-texas

Locke, J. (1988). *Locke: Two Treatises of Government.* (P. Laslett, Ed.) (3rd ed.). New York: Cambridge University Press.

Loury, G. C. (2007). Transgenerational justice. In J. Miller & R. Kumar (Eds.), *Reparations: Interdisciplinary inquiries* (pp. 87–113). New York: Oxford University Press.

Morris, A. (2002). Critiquing the critics: A brief response to critics of restorative justice. *British Journal of Criminology*, *42*(3), 596–615. doi:10.1093/bjc/42.3.596

Perez, N. (2014). Must we provide material redress for past wrongs? In A. I. Cohen & C. H. Wellman (Eds.), *Contemporary debates in applied ethics* (2nd ed., pp. 203–15). Malden, MA: Wiley-Blackwell.

Rawls, J. (1993). *Political liberalism.* New York: Columbia University Press.

Rawls, J. (2001). *Justice as fairness: A restatement.* E. Kelly (Ed.). Cambridge, MA: Harvard University Press.

Roberts, M. A. (2013). The nonidentity problem. In E. N. Zalta (Ed.), *The Stanford encyclopedia of philosophy* (Fall 2013). Retrieved June 4, 2014, from http://plato.stanford.edu/archives/fall2013/entries/nonidentity-problem/

Schmidtz, D. (2011). Nonideal theory: What it is and what it needs to be. *Ethics*, *121*(4), 772–96.

Spinner-Halev, J. (2012). *Enduring injustice.* Cambridge; New York: Cambridge University Press.

Strickland, R. A. (2004). *Restorative justice.* New York: Peter Lang.

Tan, K.-C. (2007). Colonialism, reparations, and global justice. In J. Miller & R. Kumar (Eds.), *Reparations: Interdisciplinary inquiries* (pp. 280–306). New York: Oxford University Press.

Thompson, J. (2002). *Taking responsibility for the past: Reparation and historical injustices.* Cambridge: Polity.

Tullis, P. (2013, January 4). Can forgiveness play a role in criminal justice? *The New York Times.* Retrieved from www.nytimes.com/2013/01/06/magazine/can-forgiveness-play-a-role-in-criminal-justice.html

Valentini, L. (2012). Ideal vs. non-ideal theory: A conceptual map. *Philosophy Compass*, *7*(9), 654–64. doi:10.1111/j.1747–9991.2012.00500.x

Van Ness, D. W., & Strong, K. H. (2010). *Restoring justice: An introduction to restorative justice.* New Providence, NJ: LexisNexis: Anderson Pub.

Waldron, J. (1992). Superseding historic injustice. *Ethics*, *103*(1), 4–28.

Zehr, H. (1990). *Changing lenses: A new focus for crime and justice.* Scottdale, PA: Herald Press.

9 Markets in human body parts and tissues

In November of 2013 in the United States, nearly 77,000 persons were "active waiting list candidates" for crucial human organs such as a heart, kidney, lung, or intestine (Organ Procurement and Transplantation Network, n.d.). In the UK, the number exceeded 10,000 persons (See e.g. "Transplants Save Lives," 2013). Each year, however, thousands of people die while waiting for such organs.

The laws in most countries forbid treating human body parts as commodities for sale. That is the key feature of policies about human body parts. Some critics argue that such policies are responsible for the needless deaths of thousands of human beings each year. Every day, vast numbers of potentially useful human organs or tissues worldwide are buried or burned with the dead bodies that contain them. Additional healthy organs and other human tissues (such as blood, bone marrow, and kidneys) from the living could be available were it legal to buy and sell them. This chapter considers some of the many ways such markets might be structured and what if anything some vital ethical considerations might suggest about the merits of such markets.

There are multiple important dimensions to the possibility of selling human body parts and tissues. There are concerns about whether such markets are feasible and how the markets would affect the availability and safety of human tissues. There are additional vital moral concerns, which hinge on the appropriateness of turning body parts into commodities, the transfer of resources from poor to rich, and whether certain persons can freely consent to participate in such exchanges. There are more basic disputes about how public policy should account for distributive justice in regulating healthcare resources.

This chapter offers an overview of some such policies and moral concerns. It considers the potential benefits of markets for body parts and tissues and how to begin to grapple with some ethical worries. It explores whether some such markets can be justified. There may be many sets of institutions to satisfy the needs and concerns of potential participants in markets as well as third-party bystanders. Whether any such institutions are appropriate hangs on crucial disputes about what we owe to and may claim from each other.

Background

Transplants and physiological challenges

Human organs or tissues fail because of disease, injury, birth defect, or abuse. Some failures have less of an impact on life expectancy than others. The loss of corneas or limbs to accident or disease can certainly have a tremendous impact on quality of life. But restriction or loss of function in organs such as the liver, intestines, kidneys, or heart is often thoroughly incapacitating and life-threatening. In order to survive, a human being needs to absorb nutrients from food, process and store energy, pump and cleanse blood, take in oxygen, and so forth. Given current technology, when vital organs fail, they must be replaced through transplant.

Organ transplants have recently become increasingly successful. Patients now routinely receive single or multiple organ transplants with impressive long-term success. Indeed, recently, physicians have also been successful in transplanting joints, limbs, and faces.

The first successful transplants date to the early twentieth century and involved tissues such as the cornea. Later attempts at whole organ transplants often failed because of rejection, in which a host body takes steps to destroy unfamiliar tissue. Scientists have since developed immunosuppressant drugs that curtail or prevent the rejection response. Recipients of donor organs must take these drugs for the rest of their lives. While these drugs leave patients vulnerable to other infections, a life with a new heart and immunosuppressants is usually better than the alternative, which is quick decline until death.

One way of avoiding the immune response is to use perfectly compatible tissues such as from an identical twin. Transplants between identical twins present little if any risk of rejection. (The first successful kidney transplant was between identical twins.) Another way to reduce post-operative complications is to use the patient's own cells. A patient can use her own tissues with grafts of skin, bone, or blood vessels. More commonly patients might "bank" their tissues in advance of surgery. This is a common procedure with blood. Doctors may also relocate or temporarily remove body parts to preserve function during treatment for cancers. For instance, doctors have moved ovaries or ovarian tissue to a patient's arm while she was treated for cervical cancer. More commonly, doctors have removed a patient's bone marrow during treatments for some forms of leukemia and returned it to the patient later.

Another way of avoiding the immune response is to construct a new organ or part using a patient's own cells. Recent exciting developments in medicine involve bioengineering replacement parts (such as the bladder, ear, nose, or trachea). (See e.g. Naik, 2013; Fountain, 2012). Scientists use a patient's stem cells to grow a new organ on a "scaffold" harvested from a cadaver that has been cleansed of its own cells. Scientists are hopeful that such procedures will become possible with dense tissue organs such as kidneys or hearts, but for now the only replacement for a kidney or a heart is another person's kidney or heart.

Transplants and economic challenges

Economists tell us that shortages of any good arise when demand exceeds available supply. Sometimes shortages arise because of distribution problems. This is common after natural disasters when victims cannot receive the food or medical care they might want. Sometimes it is temporarily difficult or impossible to move the goods to the people who want them. At other times, the supply can be moved, but governments enact policies that make it difficult for people to get the things they want or need.

As an example of how public policies can restrict the availability of needed goods, consider how states sometimes impose price ceilings. Price ceilings are maximum legal prices on goods or services. Price ceilings might make little difference in a market. If, for instance, a state were to announce that from now on, no apple may sell for more than $500,000 (roughly €390,000 or £328,000), this would not have much if any impact on the apple market. It might affect apples that are collectors' items, but not ordinary apples. If, however, a state were to enforce a price cap of .01 (in dollars, pounds, or Euros), the number of apples available for purchase would decline. Growers would not bother to grow apples and bring them to market. It would not pay. Many apples would simply rot on the ground after falling from their trees; growers would not tend to them.

As economists note, when a price ceiling is set below what some sellers believe their good is worth, they will not sell the good. They will hold on to it, use it themselves, or let it spoil. Price ceilings then can restrict the supply brought to market and so keep willing buyers and sellers from connecting (see e.g. Gwartney, Stroup, Sobel, & Macpherson, 2012).

Here is why this matters for markets in human organs: with few exceptions, the market price someone may receive for her organs or tissues is zero. That is because most jurisdictions forbid their sale. Most of the time, organs or tissues may only be acquired through donation.

Organs or tissues can be harvested from cadavers. But the main problem with cadaver organs/tissues is that they are rarely as good as those from living donors. Still, they can sometimes be very valuable to recipients. An organ from a dead person is often much better than no organ at all.

Residents in nearly all jurisdictions have the option of becoming a donor upon death. Sometimes this option is mandatory; in other words, sometimes anyone who wants a driver's license must choose whether or not to be an organ donor. In other jurisdictions with "presumed consent" public policies, physicians may harvest a resident's organs when they become available upon death—unless that resident had previously taken some steps to "opt-out." If she had done nothing, her parts become eligible for transfer to needful others upon her death.

Nearly all countries rely on donation for human organs. They have detailed policies regarding the allocation of any organs once they are available. The UK and the United States, for instance, have panels of experts determining priorities for distributing organs. Children typically go to the front of the line. Geographical proximity often matters; the longer an organ must travel to its recipient, the more it is likely to degrade. The Human Tissue Act of the UK and the National Organ Transplant Act in the US detail such policies. Unfortunately, areas that rely exclusively on donation still suffer a chronic and growing shortage of organs and tissues. This is true even for countries (such as many in Europe) that have "presumed consent" laws regarding tissues and organs from the dead. But the laws forbid sales of organs. Consequently, the scarcity persists.

One recent attempt to overcome scarcity has come through "linked" donations. Suppose Mary needs a kidney, but no one in her willing family is a match. Suppose hundreds of miles away, the same is true for Jack. But imagine Jack's father is a perfect match for Mary, and Mary's sister is a great match for Jack. They can arrange linked donations. This sort of swapping can work quite well; networks have emerged to serve as clearinghouses for tissue matching. Somewhat similar to linked donations are chain donations, which begin when the unreciprocated kindness of one donor initiates a lengthy chain of linked donations. *The New York Times* recently reported on a series of linked transplants that involved 60 persons (Sack, 2012).

The problem is that these measures are not enough. Even with chain transplants, linked transplants, presumed cadaveric donor consent, and exhorting living people to make donations now, there is still a desperate shortage of organs. People are dying, and there are organs available that they might receive.

But consider how in ordinary circumstances, there is no scarcity of apples. True, some apples cost more than others, and some locations (such as those near apple-growing areas) enjoy lower costs for apples. But it is extremely rare for a willing and able buyer of an apple not to find a willing seller. That is significantly because there is no price ceiling on apples. Some theorists have thus suggested amending policies to lift the price ceiling on human tissues and organs.

The obvious challenge, of course, is that kidneys and hearts are importantly unlike apples.

Quality worries and the possibility of profits for markets in human organs and tissues

There are two models for what markets in human tissues might look like. One is legal, and the other is illegal. While illuminating in many respects, even together these are incomplete indicators of what the markets might become. Advocates often claim that we do not know what these markets would look like because public policies forbid people from fully exploring what might work.

The illegal trade in human organs gives mixed indications of the merits and drawbacks about markets in organs. This "black market" has poor persons in developing nations selling their organs, often to wealthy foreigners. There are cases of "transplant tourism," where a recipient visits a seller's country for a transplant. Relatedly, a seller might visit a recipient's country for a paid transplant under the pretense of donation.

This illegal trade does not always work out well. Some studies of sellers from India show impaired postoperative health and feelings of regret. Often the proceeds from the sales are used to pay down debt. But sometimes health complications after the surgery keep sellers from staying reliably employed, and so the payout yields little net gain (See e.g. Goyal, Mehta, Schneiderman, & Sehgal, 2002; Kumar, 1994). A further concern is that such illegal markets may trade in organs from sellers whose participation is sometimes questionably voluntary (Goodwin, 2006). There are plenty of allegations of unfulfilled promises of payment and harvest from prisoners of conscience (See e.g. the controversial book by Matas & Kilgour, 2009).

Appeals to various black market norms are poor indicators of what a legalized market might look like and how sellers might be treated. Black markets by their very nature are illegal and so offer sellers little recourse when someone reneges on an agreement to pay them a fee or provide postoperative care. The black market is also underdeveloped because successful transplants require access to substantial medical resources and expertise. It is difficult to perform a back-alley liver transplant. What is revealing, though, is the immense demand and potential resources buyers bring to any market for such organs. When their lives or those of their loved ones are at stake, vast sums of money are available. These could potentially be used to help needy sellers. But as we will see later, we might worry that this model of allocating goods is entirely misguided.

Beyond black markets, we should consider legal markets where people can buy and sell human tissues. There are versions of such markets. One context for such legal markets involves middlemen and healthcare providers. They profit from trading in human organs. Vendors sell human tissues and organs they have acquired from donation, and those vendors are compensated for their efforts. Physicians are paid for their services and time. Pharmaceutical companies, device manufacturers, nurses, and a whole host of intermediaries and healthcare providers receive compensation for their work with human tissues and organs. Often, though, the person who is the source of the tissues or organs does not get much if any compensation. Another context for legal markets allows sellers to be compensated for their tissues or organs. Proponents of markets in body parts even argue that profit incentives can help improve provision and delivery of needed goods. To see how profit might help provision of needed human tissues, consider some examples.

Selling blood?

The Red Cross and Red Crescent are networks of not-for-profit organizations dedicated to providing humanitarian assistance to the needy. They also support healthcare projects throughout the world. They perform outstanding services, but perhaps they have room for improvement.

Among the many valuable projects of the American Red Cross are their blood services, which gather and distribute a considerable portion of the blood products available in the United States. They sell blood. They sell it to hospitals and other medical facilities in order to recoup their costs (Engber, 2006). But, since such organizations are often dominant providers in the market, hospitals sometimes face shortages for important surgeries. Sometimes the Red Cross is the sole provider but does not furnish the number of expected units.

Shortages are one side of a blood market with insufficient profit motives. On the other side are wasteful surpluses. This was an unfortunate consequence of blood drives in the US after the 9/11 attacks. Many people donated blood but the networks did not efficiently allocate the supply, so more blood than usual was discarded from spoilage (Young, 2002).

Some entrepreneurs have introduced for-profit blood services to compete with the distribution networks of the Red Cross and community blood banks (Carlyle, 2012; Rebeck, 2012). They hope to avoid problems in distribution. They also have an immensely powerful incentive to provide quality products on time and where needed. Their reputation is everything. Their incentives toward efficient delivery can also help reduce waste and healthcare costs ("Expediting the blood flow," 2012). Profit drives these and other companies efficiently to provide needed products.

This is one model for compensating people for providing needed human tissues. But the compensation here only goes to intermediaries. Might donors also be compensated for their blood? There are legal models that can serve as examples. In the United States, a significant portion of the blood supply once came from paid donors until studies began to show that their blood was more likely to carry transmissible disease (van der Poel, Seifried, & Schaasberg, 2002). Nowadays, all whole blood in the US comes from donations.

People may nevertheless legally sell blood plasma. They undergo a process where the plasma is extracted from their blood, and the remaining blood products are returned to their bloodstream. The reimbursements vary, but sellers might make as much as $30 per visit, up to twice per week. This market operates efficiently and produces quality products. Blood plasma donors are subjected to rigorous health screenings. They are connected to databases to prevent more frequent donations that might jeopardize their own health.

There is rarely a shortage of quality blood plasma in the US. Indeed, the United States is a major source of blood plasma for the world (Farrugia, Penrod, & Bult, 2010, p. 205). Now, part of the reason quality is not threatened in a source-compensated plasma market is that blood plasma is not a good vector for disease. Whole blood, however, is, and so too are human organs. This turns us toward frequently cited concerns about the quality of the fully commoditized tissues and organs.

Paid donors and inferior products?

Critics sometimes worry that introducing monetary incentives will threaten the quality of human tissues by encouraging subpar donors into the market. This sort of worry dates back at least to Richard Titmuss. His still-frequently cited book from the early 1970s, *The Gift Relationship*, argued that altruistic (i.e., uncompensated) donation was more likely to produce healthy tissues and organs for use than by paying people.

Intuitively, Titmuss's argument seems compelling. We want healthy organs and tissues available for needy others. But introducing compensation might encourage persons with questionable health histories to offer products for sale. Systems that rely exclusively on altruistic donation, it may seem, would more likely produce healthy organs since healthy donors would primarily be the ones who would go to the trouble of contributing. Presumably, someone with a transmissible disease would not bother to donate.

There are many empirical claims here. And they turn out to be misguided if not mistaken. Recent studies make several points against the Titmuss sort of view.

First, there is *some* compensation for donors of all sorts. Even whole blood donors get snacks, modest public recognition, occasional door prizes, chances in raffle drawings, and, in the case of some European countries, paid time off. Of course, these may seem different than paying someone €5000 for a kidney, but the point is that blood donors are not completely denied compensation. If we worry that any compensation invites marginal donors into the mix, we need to acknowledge that most current systems include some compensation for blood donations.

Most public policies have a narrow notion of compensation, but it seems that compensation is not simply a monetary payout. When your loved one gets a kidney from your linked donation to a stranger, that might count as a form of compensation. We might also count the benefit of having loved ones around longer as a form of compensation.

A second strike against the Titmuss sort of view draws on recent studies challenging the idea that financial compensation threatens the quality of tissues and blood products (Farrugia, Penrod, & Bult, 2010; Tabarrok, 2004; Becker & Elias, 2007). Current technologies allow for rigorous tests of human tissues or organs for contamination. This sort of technology is used to test reproductive cells whose donors have been compensated (sometimes handsomely). Sperm donors are not paid much, but ova donors are, given the difficulties in harvesting the cells. (For narratives, see Cohen, 2002; Howley, 2006). There is some controversy about whether such compensation is appropriate, and, indeed, some countries ban the practice. But the point is that markets have, with reasonable assurances of safety and effectiveness, connected eager buyers with willing sellers.

Of course, many people will think there is greater moral urgency in safely providing vital organs than reproductive cells. But note that in any market where providers are compensated for their tissues or organs, tests for safety will never be perfect. Some diseases may pass unnoticed. Some people might die when receiving contaminated organs. (For instance, current tests for HIV cannot detect a very recent infection.) But this problem confronts current systems that forbid payment to donors. The data seem to challenge the easy assumption that payment jeopardizes quality. If compensating donors does not threaten quality, and if such compensation might increase supply, there might be a moral reason to consider it. Meanwhile, entrepreneurs might devise institutions and tests that could further increase supply without jeopardizing quality. As advocates of these market measures might note, however: We do not know. People have not been allowed to try.

Markets and consumer needs

Good evidence for the promise of markets in human organs comes with other markets. Consider food. Multiple providers in many markets are able to satisfy diverse tastes at various price points. For the most part, people in most countries do not suffer from want of food. No doubt, some have limited opportunities to enjoy champagne and caviar, but in most countries unmarked by war, it is rare to see mass numbers of people suffering on the brink of starvation. They are able to grow their own food or buy and trade with others to get what they want.

We must admit that some persons deliberately or by accident sell contaminated food. We must also admit that many people cannot get everything they want, or even enough to satisfy basic caloric needs. But most of humanity (and, fortunately, an increasing share) has access to a minimum amount they need to survive. This is not the case for persons on queues for human organs. They often die waiting.

In the developed world, hundreds of thousands of persons undergo repeated and time-consuming dialysis to make up for poorly functioning kidneys. The numbers are expected to rise with the increasing incidence of diabetes and the development of better dialysis. All this costs a lot of money. It costs the patients money, and so too their insurance companies and government-paid healthcare services. Transplants (even with expensive immunosuppressant drugs) for many of these patients would be less expensive. But in the current system where the compensation cap to donors is zero, there are not enough kidneys to go around.

One perhaps surprising example of how markets in human organs might function comes with Iran (Hippen, 2008). Since the late 1980s, Iran has allowed modest compensation for persons willing to offer a kidney. It is a heavily regulated market that is only open to Iranians. If a living donor is unavailable, and if a deceased donor kidney is still unavailable after a six-month wait, vendors are identified after a rigorous screening process. The Iranian system has a nonprofit intermediary who connects prospective vendors with recipients and transplant professionals. This helps minimize any conflict of interest. Vendors are eligible for compensation that ranges from somewhere between the equivalent of US\$2,000 and US\$6,000. Part of this fee is paid by the Iranian government. The other part is provided by recipients, but if they lack sufficient funds, various charities provide the funds. Vendors receive some free state-sponsored medical care after the surgery for up to one year. Of special note: there is no longer any waiting list in Iran for kidneys.

The example from Iran invites consideration for some such system elsewhere in the developed world. Policymakers need not necessarily legislate all details of an infrastructure; they might allow stakeholders to explore which alternatives might work. Even within a jurisdiction, there need not be a single institution for gathering and distributing organs.

The markets may take many forms and feature varying institutions to cater to different needs. A *cadaveric* market might yield more organs were families given financial incentives to allow their recently deceased loved ones' tissues to be used. In a *current* market, payment can be made to persons now for use of their organs/tissues now. (Such is the case for kidneys in Iran or plasma in the United States.) In a *futures* market, payments are tendered to persons now who then grant an agency rights to the use of their organs upon death. The specific forms those markets might take would vary, as surely as the specific agreements parties would make. Australia is now experimenting with limited payment to current donors. The payment is not for their organs but their time. They are given the equivalent of minimum wage compensation for the recuperation period. And they must first have a job (Yosufzai, 2013).

In case direct payments strike parties as unseemly, there are noncash forms of compensation that might be provided (Buyx, 2009). Such compensations are available now to whole blood donors in many developed countries. Organ donors also now sometimes receive rebates on driver's license fees (as in parts of the United States for consent to cadaveric donation). Consider other forms of compensation that might increase availability of organs now. There can be public calls for donors (who need not be called "sellers"). The donors might also benefit from reputation boosts through favorable publicity. This is a common tactic with blood drives, which offer self-congratulatory stickers as door prizes. Rewards with more tangible financial value might come through tokens, gifts, or vouchers for other items of value (such as concert tickets, rebates for big-ticket purchases, and so forth). Unlike cookies and t-shirts for blood drives, the compensating items might be especially valuable for donors of organs. They might be given the promise of payment for future funeral expenses, vouchers to send their children to school, a paid vacation, or other items of value. We do not know what sorts of valuable items might change hands, but as the economists tell us, people respond to incentives. If we had the right incentives, we could eliminate the queues for human organs.

The National Organ Transplant Act in the United States forbids payment to donors of human organs and bone marrow. When the act was first passed in the 1980s, bone marrow required an invasive procedure involving needles penetrating bone. Today bone marrow can be extracted in a fashion that is quite similar to regular blood donations. Many people await marrow donations even though plenty of people seem to be willing donors on lists. But often these recipients die when perfect matches back out at the last moment. Some activists had pushed to allow for limited compensation. Indeed, a recent 9th Circuit Court decision ruled that the act does not prohibit compensating donors who provide marrow with the new technique (Schmitz & Naggiar, 2013; Rowes, 2012).

The head of the National Marrow Donor Program in the US opposes paid compensation. He believes that allowing compensation would deny American patients access to millions of prospective donors worldwide because of current international norms that forbid compensation. He also warns that compensating people will provide the wrong incentives. Meanwhile, however, insufficient donors are available and people some-times die as a result. Whether a paid system would provide more donors is very much an empirical question.

A mother pursued policy change on behalf of her daughters, all of whom needed transplants. As her attorney argued, "Bone marrow is just like anything else in the world ... it's valuable. And if you compensate people for it, you're going to get more of it, it's just that simple" (Schmitz & Naggiar, 2013). One possibility is to explore alternative or deferred compensation, such as donating to a charity on a donor's behalf or contributing to a scholarship fund. We do not know what will work because these alternatives have not been fully explored. Perhaps policies can permit the space to find out.

Even if paid compensation might work for marrow, people may draw the line at organs. After all, marrow replaces itself. Kidneys do not. And many critics object to the idea of turning human body parts into com-modities. Even if we could somehow overcome quality worries (and some critics say that we cannot), there are important and specifically ethical challenges. Human organs are not apples. Treating them both as commod-ities that belong to the same sphere may be deeply problematic because of concerns about justice, fears of coercion, and the value of humanity. It is to such worries that we now turn.

Moral concerns about markets in human body parts

The discussion so far has outlined some features of the shortage in human body parts. It has speculated about what shapes such markets might take. In many respects, we can only imagine various markets where people are able to buy the parts or tissues they need from sellers. Indeed, as propo-nents of such markets might argue, our imaginations have not been unleashed because many such markets are against the law. Abandoning prohibitions on sales in human tissues and organs might reduce shortages and give the needy access to important resources.

Many critics find the prospect of any organ markets pernicious. They typically raise several sorts of worries. Among their concerns are: (a) any market in human tissues or parts would unfairly privilege the rich over the poor and deepen the desperate situation of the chronically poor; (b) any market where human organs can be sold would in and of itself involve coercion or increase the threat of coercive pressures on the poor; and (c) any market that treated human body parts or tissues as commodities would cheapen humanity and pollute all caring relationships with the totalizing and contaminating logic of the marketplace.

Each of these is a proper concern for public policy because each touches on important features of the social and political landscape. Public policies can shape such landscapes or set boundaries to what shapes they might take. Right now, the policies forbidding sales in human organs shape the landscape by setting roadblocks no one may pass. Eliminating those obstacles, however, might save lives. The remaining parts of this section consider these worries and some challenges to them.

Objections appealing to justice

Justice is that body of norms that considers, among other things, what people owe to one another and what they may claim from one another. Justice is at least, in part, a feature of appropriately structured relationships among human beings. Surely we owe a measure of decency and respect to one another, and it would seem justice forbids us from creating, profiting from, or deepening exploitative relationships. We do not need a full theory of justice to consider whether policies that might allow organ sales are committed to licensing oppression and exploitation.

This sort of concern about markets can take many specific shapes. Critics may fear, for instance, that organ markets will disadvantage the poor by introducing financial incentives for them to take steps to make harmful choices. This is especially worrisome for the desperately poor. Critics might then appeal to studies showing many organ donors in the developing world come to regret their decision and find themselves financially worse after the surgery because of declining health from poor postoperative care or because the funds they acquire only perpetuate a cycle of indebtedness. Offering them money as a path out of abject poverty may strike some people as a sort of unconscionable offer, something a bit like offering rescue to a drowning person on condition that she submit to sexual slavery. They may then argue that organ markets should be banned to prevent these morally worrisome consequences.

This is only a sketch of a more detailed worry about organ markets. But it is not necessarily the start of an argument against organ markets. It might be the start of an argument against markets with inadequate protections from exploitation. Legal markets might require a minimum commitment of providing (or paying for) some amount of postoperative and follow-up care. Public policies might set price floors for kidneys, sensitive to local conditions. They include age restrictions. They might foster national or international institutions that prevent exploitative intermediaries from creating or profiting from oppressive relationships. It is unclear what precise form these markets might take because public policies currently forbid exploration of the options.

Critics may still worry that offering money to the desperately poor amounts to unjust exploitation. Whether this is an objection to organ markets hangs partly on *why* they are desperately poor. If the buyer has induced or is complicit in the abject poverty that makes someone more inclined to sell his/her organs, then there is reason to worry that organ markets may perpetuate oppressive relationships. But this is not an argument against organ markets. It is an argument, first, against allowing people to deprive others of the opportunity to live a decent life and, second, against allowing people to profit from having previously deprived others of the opportunity to live a decent life. Organ markets may offer the poor important opportunities by giving them access to resources they might not otherwise have. To object that they should not make a choice to give up parts of their bodies for money is a different sort of objection, which comes up in a moment.

Another sort of justice-based worry about organ markets hangs on distributive justice concerns. Were organ markets opened up, the argument may begin, organs would be very expensive and so mainly available to the rich. Indeed, organ markets may strike some observers as an unwholesome transfer of body parts from the poor to the rich.

This also is only a sketch of a more developed argument about the appropriate amount of access the poor may have to healthcare resources. But even when fully developed, it would not necessarily be an argument against organ markets. It could be an argument against leaving the poor without access to much needed organs in an organ market. We can easily imagine publicly funded institutions that make such organs available to the poor. Some such institutions are already in place in Iran. And in the United States, the UK, and other developed nations, where the state is often a major purchaser or provider of healthcare services, organ transplants often turn out to be much less expensive in the long run than continued palliative care. This is especially true for patients with diseased kidneys. A market could help reduce healthcare costs overall and extend the lives of or provide needed resources for willing participants in market transactions.

Coercion

Coercion is deeply problematic as it embodies an unjust use of power. There are considerable debates about what coercion means. Many leading accounts understand coercion as involving certain offers. The person making the offer wrongly compels a choice between two or more unpalatable alternatives. (Specific theories of coercion would give different accounts of the various terms in that broad statement.) Paradigmatic cases of coercion involve "your money or your life" scenarios at the point of a gun. But other cases might not be so obvious. Would organ markets involve coercion?

We can set aside apocryphal tales of tourists waking up in tubs of ice after their kidneys had been stolen. These have never been verified, and obviously, they would be grievous violations. They are also currently forbidden by the laws of any country. The more frequently cited concern about coercion is that sellers would be forced to make a desperate choice because of their economic circumstances. Critics concerned with the poor may propose forbidding organ markets to prevent unfair desperate choices. They might draw on an idea that inequality itself presents coercive circumstances; it makes the disadvantaged contemplate and pursue choices that they would not have otherwise made. Call this the *coercive inequality* view. It holds that inequality as such, not simply persons making offers, can count as coercive.

The *coercive inequality* view is a crucial challenge to any market in human body parts. Indeed, it represents a challenge to many (perhaps nearly all) other markets, such as that for healthcare, education, and labor. If being in an unequal position represents a sort of coercion, then the choices one makes in such circumstances would lack the moral force we typically ascribe to those by mature adults who voluntarily agree to arrangements with others. Public policies may then need to address this moral imbalance, either by remedying the inequality in the first place or by somehow compensating for the unequal bargaining positions, perhaps with careful oversight and/or subsidies or prohibitions of some sort that equalize the positions of parties to any agreement. However it would proceed, the view would need a hearing in any fuller account of exploitation and coercion.

Some thinkers might challenge the coercive inequality view. They may wonder how circumstances can coerce. They may hold a view that *only other persons can coerce.* On this view, coercion seems to be something only *persons* inflict on one another. (Taylor, 2005, provides a helpful discussion of whether poverty creates coercive exchanges.) True, people colloquially use the idea of circumstances "forcing" a choice, such as in describing how "she had no choice but to slam on the brakes to avoid the collision" or "her cancer forced her to undergo chemotherapy." But, according to this view, these do not seem to be cases of coercion. They are unfortunate situations. Misfortune need not necessarily entail injustice.

In the *only other persons can coerce* view, people may be more open to risks because of their judgment about their circumstances. That people take risks others would not contemplate is not itself a sign of such coercion. Activities with similar risks of injury or death (such as high-risk construction jobs, hang gliding, and skydiving) are legal (Taylor, 2005: Ch. 6).

Proponents of the *coercive inequality* view likely will not find these sorts of responses compelling. They and advocates of other accounts of coercion critical of the possibility of markets in human body parts might return to worries about perpetuating oppressive relationships. Consider a circumstance of chronic poverty where organ markets become widespread. In such an environment, it may be more difficult to refuse participation in kidney markets when, for instance, moneylenders demand one's kidney as collateral (Cohen, 2003). This can be especially problematic in cases where women are in subordinate social, political, and economic circumstances. Their husbands or fathers may unduly pressure them to offer their kidneys as collateral or for sale. Organ markets might then perpetuate the cycle of poverty and subjugation that defines many women's lives in poor countries.

This is an important worry about how to structure organ markets. Whether it amounts to a decisive objection to expanded markets in human body parts is unclear. It might, for instance, be an objection to oppressive gender relations. That some persons might misuse market opportunities is not necessarily a reason to deny everyone the chance to enjoy such opportunities. It is an invitation for constructing institutions that help to curtail such oppressive circumstances. Perhaps, as in the Iranian case, disinterested intermediaries might interview prospective donors alone and solicit informed consent. What would work would depend heavily on local norms and the willingness of participating parties. But notice again that closing off organ markets for fear of misuse threatens to deny people important resources. The capital that a family might realize from collateralizing a kidney might help a girl to get an education, escape the cycle of poverty, and avoid a life of prostitution.

This brief discussion hardly settles the matter of in what coercion consists, nor does it pretend to offer an exhaustive characterization of various accounts of coercion. But critics might still worry that people should not be faced with choices such as those that might be available with markets for body parts to get the resources they need. They might argue that distributive justice requires rethinking what sorts of opportunities the poor should have to access key goods (especially for healthcare and education). This may require a fundamental reevaluation of the institutions and norms by which we structure our society.

Worries about commodification

Many concerns about organ markets turn on worries about wrongly treating body parts as commodities. A commodity is something that has a market value and can be bought, sold, and traded. Apples are commodities. They have a price. Typical trade in apples neither demeans participants nor degrades the apples or trees on which they grow. But body parts might be different. Allowing them to be bought and sold may disrespect human beings.

Worries about commodification might root many people's repugnance at the thought of organ markets. Some things are unfit for sale. Treating them as commodities misunderstands particular values. As Elizabeth Anderson notes (1993), there are many "spheres" of value. The market is one such sphere. But it need not be all encompassing. Problems emerge when we wrongly treat certain objects or experiences as having a market value. We then distort the value of those things and undermine our ability to live well and form healthy and enriching relationships shaped by the appropriate values.

Imagine, for instance, a long-term intimate relationship where one partner paid the other for sex. This may seem to distort the special value of sexual intimacy; perhaps it should instead be spontaneous, mutual, and freely given. Someone who thought sex can or should be bought and sold in marriages, for instance, may seem to have fallen short of understanding the value of marital unions.

This may be the start of argument against allowing the sale of sex. While it may seem that such voluntary transactions among consenting adults harm no one, critics worry that even in ideal circumstances, markets where sex is a commodity may seem to dehumanize participants, objectify women, and degrade everyone's humanity. But note that even if this argument succeeds, it would not show that public policy should forbid the sale of human body parts. Consider first the sale of sex. That some *other* people buy and sell sex does not necessarily cheapen the intimacy two partners experience when they freely (and for free!) have sexual relations. The same may be true of body parts. If selling body parts is degrading, it need not contaminate everyone.

Critics will warn that this is mistaken. Norms shift when attitudes do. When it is commonplace to buy and sell body parts, people will be less likely to think of their bodies as special. Public policy, the argument may run, should foster appropriate attitudes to our bodies as bound up with our essential humanity—a value that should resist commodification. As one set of critics warn:

> To sell the body is to sell what the body does for us and its significance for us. This sale of significance, in turn, degrades the level of respect merited to the human body and takes away the true importance of the body to the human being. If our bodies are able to be monetized, it seems that anything has the ability to be allocated a monetary value, destroying a sense

of human respect and significance that can only come from outside the market place.

(Campbell, Tan, & Boujaoude, 2012, p. 172)

This captures much of the worry about commodifying bodies while also showing the important ambiguities of such a view. It is unclear why selling a body part is degrading. To degrade is to bring something down in value. In the case of human bodies, what is unclear is what value the body supposedly has that must resist commodification. Now, some persons might think the body is somehow sacred. (Consider, relatedly, how many persons would never consider selling themselves for sex.) But the problem is that others might not think that way. To forbid those others from taking steps to do what they believe will improve their condition is then to impose one set of values on them. This can deny people their autonomy—which partly involves the chance to live their lives as they see fit. But in the case of forbidding the sale of human body parts, the cost might be measurable in dead bodies. We need only consider the thousands of people who die each year waiting for organs. We must ask whether one particular conception of the value of the human body is so important as to dominate public policy at the expense of the lives of disagreeing others. The challenge is then to show how reasonable people cannot object to policies that forbid them or others from the opportunities to receive resources from exchanging parts of their bodies.

Critics may need to show that expanding markets in body parts will undermine other spheres of value. This speaks to the supposed phenomenon of "crowd out." Social scientists can measure it. We need to assess the evidence that expanding the market suffocates other spheres of value. The assessment is partly empirical and importantly evaluative. Proponents of expanded markets will argue that people can still act on those other spheres. Patients might still await donor organs; donors might refuse to take payment for their services; physicians might only work with donor organs. For-profit markets might exist alongside other forms of procurement and distribution. Indeed, economics suggests this is exactly what can and will happen (Taylor, 2005, chap. 8).

That you can buy a nice meal does not undermine the special value you might realize by preparing and sharing a home-cooked meal with loved ones. That an out-of-town friend might stay in a hotel when she visits does not undermine the hospitality you might show her by inviting her to stay in your home. In fact, the ready availability of these options might *deepen* your opportunity to realize non-market values.

Many critics, however, will continue to defend public policies that forbid organ sales. They might argue that organ markets degrade human beings. If that is the justification for the prohibition, it needs to overcome a challenge that prohibitions seem wrongly to use public policy as a vehicle for imposing values on others who reasonably disagree.

Proponents will urge us to imagine that expanded markets need not degrade everyone or anyone. We might not know what shape such markets will take, but there is a strong chance they might save thousands of lives and give others a better shot at a better life. What might work and be acceptable is still unclear.

Conclusion

Current public policies throughout the developed world forbid the sale of most human body parts and tissues. Arguments for such policies appeal to quality of the product, the seeming injustice of exploiting desperately poor persons, the fear of creating or deepening oppressive relations, and the thought that bodies should not be treated as commodities. There are important reasons to resist these sorts of concerns. Ethical principles of freedom, self-improvement, and care for the poor might favor reconsidering the prohibition. The prohibition might be responsible for the deaths of thousands of people each year.

Many worries about organ markets might be worries about something else (such as coercion or oppression). Some objections to organ markets are objections to poorly structured or ineptly regulated markets. Market institutions might emerge to supply unmet demand and satisfy multiple ethical concerns. We do not know exactly what such markets will look like, though we do have some indication by looking at other medical markets and at the vibrant diversity of markets for other goods. We do not know because public policies forbid people from exploring and experimenting. Meanwhile, people are often dying while prohibitions on organ markets remain in place.

Any policy in this area would, however, need to proceed cautiously, especially in light of critics' concerns with the potential coercive features of inequality as such. These critics challenge us to consider what we can and should provide to each other and what public policy might do in fostering distributive justice. These critics might agree that it is a shame that people die waiting for organs. They may argue, however, that the solution is not to expand markets in a way that might create or deepen worrisome oppressive relationships.

Much of this dispute hangs on empirical details about what works. But there are more fundamental ethical questions at stake regarding the proper reach of public policy and what if anything should constrain the function of markets. Bringing such ethical considerations into the foreground can help us to understand more of what is at stake and what frames continuing disputes about how to satisfy crucial human aspirations and needs.

Further reading

Debra Satz offers an engaging discussion of problems with market norms in *Why Some Things Should Not Be for Sale* (Oxford: Oxford University Press, 2010). Arguments on related themes are in Michael J. Sandel, *What Money Can't Buy: The Moral Limits of Markets* (New York: Farrar, Straus and Giroux, 2012). A glance at some of the sociology and law surrounding human organs and the impact on persons of color can be found in Michelle Goodwin, *Black Markets: The Supply and Demand of Body Parts* (Cambridge: Cambridge University Press, 2006) and Ronald Munson, *Raising the Dead: Organ Transplants, Ethics, and Society* (Oxford: Oxford University Press, 2012). Among arguments favoring markets in human tissues and organs, Mark Cherry offers a helpful historical overview and canvasses many of the arguments on the issues in *Kidney for Sale by Owner: Human Organs, Transplantation, and the Market* (Washington, D.C.: Georgetown University Press, 2005). For a discussion of ethical arguments against such markets, see for instance, T. L. Zutlevics, "Markets and the Needy: Organ Sales or Aid?" *Journal of Applied Philosophy*, 39 (2001), 461–71. Janet Radcliffe-Richards discusses many of the leading arguments against markets in human body parts but finds many of them hanging on questionable emotional responses in "Nepharious Goings On: Kidney Sales and Moral Arguments," *Journal of Medicine and Philosophy*, 21(4) (1996), 375–416.

References

Anderson, E. (1993). *Value in ethics and economics*. Cambridge, MA: Harvard University Press.

Becker, G. S., & Elias, J. J. (2007). Introducing incentives in the market for live and cadaveric organ donations. *Journal of Economic Perspectives, 21*(3), 3–24.

Buyx, A. (2009). Blood donation, payment and non-cash incentives: Classical questions drawing renewed interest. *Transfusion, Medicine and Hemotherapy, 36*, 329–39.

Campbell, A. V., Tan, C., & Boujaoude, F. E. (2012). The ethics of blood donation: Does altruism suffice? *Biologicals, 40*, 170–72.

Carlyle, E. (2012, July 12). The guys who trade your blood for profit. *Forbes*.

Cohen, J. (2002, December). Grade A: The market for a Yale woman's eggs. *The Atlantic*.

Cohen, L. (2003, September). Where it hurts: Indian material for an ethics of organ transplantation. *Zygon, 38*(3), 663–88.

Engber, D. (2006, September 11). *The business of blood*. Retrieved November 11, 2013, from Slate.com: www.slate.com/articles/news_and_politics/explainer/2006/09/the_business_of_blood.html

"Expediting the blood flow." (2012, July 24). *Carlson {University of Minnesota} School News.*

Farrugia, A., Penrod, J., & Bult, J. (2010). Payment, compensation and replacement—the ethics and motivation of blood and plasma donations. *Vox Sanguinis, 99,* 202–11.

Fountain, H. (2012, September 16). A first: Organs tailor-made with body's own cells. *The New York Times,* p. A1.

Goodwin, M. (2006). *Black markets: The supply and demand of body parts.* Cambridge: Cambridge University Press.

Goyal, M., Mehta, R. L., Schneiderman, L. J., & Sehgal, A. R. (2002). Economic and health consequences of selling a kidney in India. *Journal of the American Medical Association, 288*(13), 1589–93.

Gwartney, J. D., Stroup, R. L., Sobel, R. S., & Macpherson, D. A. (2012). *Economics: Private and public choice.* Mason, OH: Cengage/South-Western Publishing.

Hippen, B. E. (2008, March 20). Organ sales and moral travails: Lessons from the living kidney vendor program in Iran. *Cato Policy Analysis* (164).

Howley, K. (2006, October). Ova for sale. *Reason.*

Kumar, S. (1994). Curbing trade in human organs in India. *The Lancet, 344*(8914), 48–9.

Matas, D., & Kilgour, D. (2009). *Blood harvest: Organ harvesting of Falun Gong practicioners in China.* Woodstock, Ontario: Seraphim Editions.

Naik, G. (2013, March 22). Science fiction comes alive as researchers grow organs in lab. *Wall Street Journal.*

Organ Procurement and Transplantation Network. (n.d.). Retrieved September 23, 2013, from http://optn.transplant.hrsa.gov/

Rebeck, G. (2012, September). Five minutes with David Mitchell. *Delta Sky Magazine,* 28.

Rowes, J. (2012, August). *IJ wins a life-saving victory for cancer patients and their families.* Retrieved November 11, 2013, from Institute for Justice: www.ij. org/l-l-8-12-ij-wins-a-life-saving-victory

Sack, K. (2012, February 19). 60 lives, 30 kidneys, all linked. *The New York Times,* p. A1.

Schmitz, A., & Naggiar, S. (2013, March 15). *Mom of girls in need of transplants wins fight to compensate bone marrow donors.* Retrieved November 11, 2013, from Rock Center with Brian Williams: http://rockcenter.nbcnews.com/_news/2013/03/15/17315965-mom-of-girls-in-need-of-transplants-wins-fight-to-compensate-bone-marrow-donors

Tabarrok, A. (2004, April). How to get real about organs. *Econ Journal Watch, 1*(1), 11–18.

Taylor, J. S. (2005). *Stakes and kidneys.* Burlington, VT: Ashgate.

"Transplants Save Lives." (n.d.). Retrieved September 23, 2013, from NHS Blood and Transplant: www.organdonation.nhs.uk/newsroom/fact_sheets/transplants_save_lives.asp

van der Poel, C., Seifried, E., & Schaasberg, W. (2002). Paying for blood donations: Still a risk? *Vox Sanguinis, 83*(4), 285–93.

Yosufzai, R. (2013, April 7). *Live donors to get financial support.* Retrieved November 11, 2013, from *The Australian*: www.theaustralian.com.au/news/breaking-news/living-donors-to-receive-financial-support/story-fn3dxiwe-1226614172117

Young, E. (2002, February 21). September 11 blood donations "wasted". *New Scientist.*

10 Factory farming of animals

Each year, Confined Animal Feeding Operations (CAFOs) raise and slaughter billions of land animals and fish. These industrial farms efficiently provide animal products at low prices to consumers worldwide whose demand for meat increases each year. However, there are important costs to these CAFOs, some of which are not fully visible to the public. Among other concerns, industry critics cite environmental degradation, foodborne illness, and decreased effectiveness of pharmaceuticals. There are also important concerns about the welfare of the animals, whose conditions in CAFOs are frequently documented in horrifying videos and disturbing news reports.

Various public policies enable the spread and consolidation of such industries. These policies touch on environmental impacts, pharmaceutical use, and various subsidies. Independently of any concerns about the merits of alternative diets, and the moral status of animals, there are possibilities to adjust some public policies so that CAFOs bear more of the costs they impose. This might take some small first steps toward reducing some of the industry's most worrisome impacts.

This chapter begins by offering some background about the industrial production of animal products. The chapter will consider only a few aspects of the complex industry to highlight some of the many dimensions of the controversies surrounding CAFOs. It will suggest that there are opportunities for some moral and policy progress, at least through changing institutions that foster practices people widely view as deeply problematic. In some cases, however, additional policies may be needed to reduce the extent to which people risk uncompensated harms to others. The aim of this chapter is modest: It proposes neither the eradication of an industry nor the redirection of global diets. Instead, it explores some of the challenges for regulating CAFOs and considers whether developed societies can do more about the impact of CAFOs through public policies that encourage people and industries to bear the costs their actions impose on others.

Some background

This section surveys a bit of the history of ideas about the moral status of nonhuman animals. With broad strokes, it focuses on intellectual traditions that warrant giving nonhuman animals a second-class moral status. It only gestures to some of the many potentially worrisome impacts of CAFOs on our environment.

Children's storybooks sometimes romanticize the tasks of animal husbandry. However, making animal products available for human consumption is often a dirty business. It involves dealing with living creatures. Just as any other living creatures, the animals we eat suffer pain, contract disease, and produce waste. In today's common CAFO facilities, there is plenty of each. Of course, handlers must also slaughter the animals. This involves processes of varying effectiveness and impacts on welfare.

CAFOs may have brought greater industrial efficiency to some of these challenges. The industry produces animal products with efficiencies unparalleled in history. CAFOs feed billions of people and bring them historically inexpensive sources of animal protein. But, the impacts on the environment are substantial, and the tolls on human and nonhuman animal welfare are worrisome. The industry produces vast quantities of untreated toxic waste. It generates many foodborne illnesses. It devastates water supplies and watersheds. It produces massive amounts of airborne pollutants. We must also not forget the animals the industry so efficiently produces. Billions of these animals suffer in dark polluted conditions with open sores, broken bones, chronic diseases, and frustration of their natural impulses. These animals wallow in their own filth as they mature for slaughter. Their slaughter is sometimes slow, and sometimes they live through much of the process.

Why do people allow this? We typically do not need animal products to survive. CAFOs have become so successful because most human beings enjoy the taste of meat and other nonhuman animal products. But taste is only one part of the story. Eating certain foods in a certain way is bound up with our ideas of who we are and what our lives mean. Enjoying foods together is often an important part of family life and cultural tradition.

What are some of the cultural trends that inspired and justified the industrial production of animals? Some writers point to a family of views common among many cultures. In this group of views are varieties of anthropocentric accounts of the proper relationship of human to nonhuman animals. The nonhuman animals are of secondary, if any, moral concern. Often they exist to satisfy human ends.

The creation narrative in the Judeo-Christian tradition is one example. In the Bible, God creates beasts, cattle, and all manner of "creeping thing" before creating human beings, whom He then tells to "Be fruitful, and multiply, and replenish the earth, and subdue it: and have dominion over the fish of the sea, and over the fowl of the air, and over every living thing that moveth upon the earth." God further tells people that they may consume the flesh of "every moving thing" (Genesis 1:24–8, Standard King James Bible).

The Christian theologian Thomas Aquinas echoed this view by arguing that the beasts are subordinate to and properly the slaves of beings with superior (more intellectual) natures. There is no sin, he said, in killing the "dumb animals"; they exist for human consumption. But Aquinas did not think humans may be cruel to nonhuman animals. This is not because humans owe to such animals any special moral regard. The prohibition on cruelty is because of a concern with how humans ought to treat each other. Cruelty to the dumb animals brings about cruelty to human beings (Aquinas, 1993).

Immanuel Kant had a similar idea about how we should treat other animals. Nonhuman animals "are not self-conscious and are there merely as a means to an end. That end is man" (Kant, 1963). Just as Aquinas, Kant held that people ought to be kind to animals because it promotes morally appropriate behavior to other human beings. As Kant notes, "he who is cruel to animals becomes hard also in his dealings with men" (Kant, 1963). On this account, any duties we have regarding animals are not owed *to them*. Kindness to animals is required because it cultivates dispositions to behave in the right way to other human beings. Nonhuman animals are merely the beneficiaries of the fulfillment of duties that humans owe to one another.

Other thinkers from the Western world have discounted the moral status of animals. A notorious example of this view is that of René Descartes, who likened nonhuman animals to machines. They are only sophisticated "automata" devoid of soul or intellect. Each is like an elaborate clock whose inner mechanisms resemble complex pulleys, springs, and levers. The internal structures of these machines help to explain why nonhuman animals seem to respond *as if* they were experiencing pain. Lacking minds and souls, however, they are incapable of genuine experience. Consequently, there is no moral problem with eating animals (Descartes, 1998).

Commonly cited accounts of our relationship to nonhuman animals have evolved since such early modern writers. Even by the nineteenth century, thinkers such as Jeremy Bentham shifted away from considering whether moral status depends on having a soul or on the capacity to reason. Instead, Bentham simply rooted moral reasons to treat any creature well in its capacity to suffer. He likened evolving attitudes toward all animals with the then-developing views against racism. Just as the color of one's skin should have no impact on the treatment a human being receives, so too might a creature's species membership be morally irrelevant (Bentham, n.d.). Bentham's view finds an echo in the notable contemporary ethicist Peter Singer, whose many works on animal liberation emphasize the moral disvalue of suffering—no matter who experiences it (Singer, 2009). Parallel to such trends in moral theorizing is an evolving science of animal biology and cognition, much of which shows that animals are far more sophisticated than we had suspected. (See e.g. Boehm, 2011; de Waal, 2009; Morell, 2013.)

There is plenty of other ethical theorizing about the moral status of nonhuman animals. The many robust scholarly conversations track how nowadays, people—especially in wealthier countries—seem increasingly receptive to the ideas that we ought to treat other animals with certain care and that our failure to do so *wrongs the animals*. Despite these trends, it is still hardly outlandish to hold that the suffering of other animals is ultimately less morally significant than that of human beings. This notion may partly underwrite (critics may say, rationalize) some of the inattention to the conditions of factory-farmed animals.

Some trends in factory farming of meat and animal products

More animal products are more widely available to human beings now than at any time in history. This is the product of a historic achievement of industrialization. But there are numerous critics who flag the costs of such practices for human beings, the environment, and nonhuman animals. This section highlights only a few of these complexities as a prelude to considering some of the many tradeoffs involved in producing, feeding, slaughtering, and delivering tens of billions of land animals for human consumption each year. To be sure, we approach this from the standpoint of lay observers to get a sense of what marks the controversies about CAFOs.

According to many sources, human population from the mid twentieth century to the early twenty-first century has more than doubled, rising from around 3 billion in 1961 to nearly 7 billion in 2009 ("Trends–United Nations Population Division," n.d.). Though there are important variations by country (such as from the devastating toll of war and HIV/AIDS), human life expectancy has overall increased in the past 50 years, linked to global gains in wealth, reductions in poverty and hunger, and better access to healthcare. Of note, though, is that the global population has only approximately doubled, but its consumption of animal products has grown significantly faster.

Increasing numbers of people are eating increasing quantities of meat and other animal products. The Food and Agriculture Organization of the

UN tracks rates of consumption for different meats, fishes, and animal products, across nearly 200 countries and over the past 50+ years. In nearly every country, people are getting more animal protein and more calories by consuming more meat and animal products. These upward trends are especially pronounced among newly developed countries.

For all measured nations, the food supply quantity of bovine meat produced per year rose from 28.4 million tonnes in 1961 to 63.8 million tonnes in 2009. There are now more eggs produced, rising from 13.8 million tonnes in 1961 to over 4 times the amount at 59.3 million tons in 2009. There are striking increases in quantities of pig meat produced annually, which rose from 24.4 million tonnes worldwide in 1961 to 105.5 million tonnes in 2009. Most stunning are the gains in poultry, which started at 8.8 million tonnes supplied worldwide in 1961 and increased more than 10 times that by 2009, to 90.7 million tonnes (FAOSTAT Emissions Agriculture database, n.d.).

Though there has been population growth and increasing quantities of animal products for developed countries, much of the growth in production comes with developing nations, especially from nations such as India and China. Their rising wealth and increasing populations brought substantial increases in the production and consumption of animal products. While the population of China rose from around 600 million in the 1960s to around 1.3 billion in 2009, growth in the supply of animal products typically far exceeded the growth in population. For instance, the annual supply of pig meat in China rose from 1.6 million tonnes overall to 17.2 million tonnes. The annual cow-meat supply started at 84,000 tonnes in 1961 and grew over 77 times to 6.5 million tonnes in 2009 (FAOSTAT Emissions Agriculture database, n.d.).

A good bit of what has made all of these changes possible is the celebrated but sometimes controversial "green revolution" in agriculture, which produced massive increases in agricultural yields in the twentieth century. With increased and more efficient production of grains such as wheat and (especially) corn, farmers have been better able to provide food for people and for the increasing numbers of animals whose products they consume. Without such improvements, many experts concur there would have been greater incidence of hunger and malnutrition over the past 50 years (Ridley, 2011, pp. 121–56; Vietmeyer, 2011). There is continued discussion about the mixed blessings of the green revolution (Shiva, 2000; Smil, 2001). Commentators note with concern the increasing use of synthetic pesticides and fertilizers, greater focus on "monoculture" farming (which is more vulnerable to outbreaks of disease), and a global shift in diets to higher fat foods. Critics wonder whether such trends are sustainable.

While there are many reasons for some worry, we should first consider whether these trends might signify substantial improvements in human welfare. People are living longer and have access to more protein (or, at least, more animal protein). That the production of animal products has outpaced population growth suggests that providers have done well at satisfying changing human preferences for more food, and it suggests that more people have the means to satisfy desires for items that were previously out of their reach. This development is *prima facie* a good thing, though if our desires are systematically misguided, it might signify a problem.

The green revolution is part of the increasing intensification of agri-culture. More yields are coming from smaller inputs. This helps to cope with vastly increasing demand for food products. Among the benefits of such intensification is that farmers can get more from less and thus have less incentive to convert land untouched by humans into farmland for crops or pasture for animals.

CAFOs are an increasing source of our animal products, and the size of such CAFOs continues to grow. In many locations, typical farms raise over 10,000 pigs or over 200,000 chickens. In the United States, the number of animal farms shows striking industry consolidation. In the early 1960s, for instance, there were about 1 million hog farms; 4 decades later, there are a tenth as many (Foer, 2010, p. 162). These trends are not confined to the United States and other developed countries; increased factory farming of animal products is a global phenomenon (Food & Water Watch, 2010; Nierenberg, 2003; Steinfeld *et al.*, 2006).

Throughout the world, confinement, changes in feed, and selective breeding have allowed farmers to produce more meat less expensively. The time it takes for animals to mature has decreased and so have their feeding needs. This is clearest in poultry production, especially for chickens. From 1935 until the end of the twentieth century, weight of "broilers" (chickens raised for consumption) increased by 65 percent, but the time to market went down by 60 percent. By manipulating lighting conditions, farmers can substantially increase egg output in turkeys and chickens to twice or thrice what it would be in the wild (Foer, 2010).

These and other trends toward greater production of animal products at lower costs stem from the increasing efficiency and concentration of animal operations. People can grow heavier animals faster and at lower costs. Keeping these improvements in mind, let us now consider some of the costs of such operations.

Some of the tradeoffs of agricultural intensification: pollution

The farming of animals is very much an industry, and as with any industry there are some tradeoffs. Among the costs of increased and more efficient production are waste, pollution, and other threats to human health from the incidence or susceptibility to disease. Intensification allows for an overall increase in these problems, even if it controls their extent by improving on earlier techniques of farm management. For instance, according to John Robbins, cattle raised in CAFOs take just a few months to get to market weight, but on the open range they would require several years. Raising beef cattle on the open range would have called for more land on which they would range, which would threaten current undeveloped forests. And, anytime cattle graze, they threaten to degrade the land (McWilliams, 2010, chap. 4).

The increasing production of grain for human and animal consumption is possible significantly because of the increasing use of synthetic pesticides and fertilizers. This requires considerable extraction and processing of fossil fuels, which involve well-documented impacts on the environment. The use of such chemicals sometimes threatens water supplies and watersheds. Some people point to such costs as regrettable necessities given human population growth.

Perhaps because of these and other impacts, some critics defend allowing more animals to roam on pastures, eat grasses, and so enjoy a more organic upbringing. But Norman Borlaug, father of the green revolution, warns that organic fertilizers alone could never sustain food production for a population like what we have today, and certainly could not support a population that is forecasted to reach over 9 billion within this century (Bailey, 2000).

Of special note for CAFOs is the production of waste. All animals produce waste of some sort, and factory farms produce *massive* quantities of it. CAFOs in the United States, for instance, produce more waste than all human residents of the country (Sayre, 2009). Many industrial hog facilities produce more waste than that of large cities (Foer, 2010). Unlike human sewage, which must be extensively treated before being discharged into the environment, animal waste is minimally treated, if at all. Producers typically store the waste in open-air pits and disperse them on nearby fields as fertilizer. Critics often complain that the fields to which such waste is applied get more than they can handle. These setups often contribute to dangerous buildups of toxins in the soil and threats to the environment from spills, leaks, and runoff (Gurian-Sherman, 2008).

This animal waste is a source of numerous airborne pollutants, many of which scientists claim are potent greenhouse gases. Cows and sheep are notorious producers of methane, which is a byproduct of their digestion. Estimates of worldwide production of methane from ruminant digestion are in the range of 86 million tonnes/year. While hardly the source of the majority of methane emissions worldwide, ruminant burps and flatulence increase as we raise more animals for meat. Of note, though, is that agricultural intensification has reduced the extent to which such emissions might otherwise be a problem. Because of faster maturation rates and industrial feed, there is less methane and other emissions from burps, flatulence, and waste than there might otherwise be (McWilliams, 2010, chap. 4; Steinfeld *et al.*, 2006, pp. 96–7). Put simply and crudely, when farmers raise faster growing cows, there are fewer burbs and farts to make a steak.

Industrial handling of animal waste is also a notorious source of airborne ammonia, which besides stinking up the landscape for neighbors is, many scientists say, a powerful greenhouse gas. Moreover, working the land to grow the grain to feed the animals for human consumption is itself an important source of nitrous oxide (Steinfeld *et al.*, 2006, pp. 103–5). But again, improved agricultural intensification keeps down the emissions of these and other pollutants over what they might have been from cattle raised on open pasture. With CAFOs, cattle grow faster and so require less land (and fewer resources such as water and fertilizer) to grow the grain to fatten them up.

Producing animal flesh for human consumption is still expensive in several ways. Besides costing resources such as water, energy, and time, it requires a lot of grain to produce animals fit for food. The amount of grain needed to produce meat varies. In CAFOS, it takes just under 2 kilograms of grain to produce a kilogram of fish, around 2 kilograms of grain for a kilogram of poultry, and about 7 kilograms of grain for a kilogram of cattle (Brown, 2009, chap. 9). Some critics point to such statistics to argue that forsaking animal flesh is a key way to reduce the environmental impact of one's food sources (Singer, 2009). But, again, the environmental burden of producing animal protein decreases as technology improves.

The polluting effects of CAFOs are well documented. Pollution, noxious stinks, and damage to natural resources such as water are what economists call *externalities*. People who might not have agreed to suffer the costs have to bear them anyway. There are various tools available to control such externalities, such as special taxes, permits, fees, or a system of property rights over a resource. Common law also includes provisions for allowing people to recover when others have imposed costs on them without their consent. Stench (and the subsequent decline in property value) is one such cost. So are the contaminating effects of spills and leaks from animal waste lagoons. Among the mechanisms available to minimize the impact of such industries are applications of liability norms. For instance, when producers are liable to lawsuits for losses they impose on others, they take steps to minimize those costs. If the activities of producers impact a resource to which others have some rights (such as to a watershed or to air free of stench and volatilized ammonia), they would need to pay for the right to impose such costs. The shapes that such liability norms and property rights take might vary from one jurisdiction to another, but the key is to get producers to internalize the costs of their activities.

This is but a glimpse of a very complex topic in environmental policy, but CAFOs need not be treated any differently than any other polluting industries. When polluters pay for the privilege to pollute, they will take steps to control their pollution. And when they still impose losses on others, they can be held accountable (see Schmidtz, 1994; 2000).

Some of the tradeoffs of agricultural intensification: antibiotics

Other notable impacts of industrialized animal production come with the increased use of antibiotics. In 2011 in the United States, for instance, manufacturers sold 7.7 million pounds of various antibiotics to treat human illness. However, they sold 29.9 million pounds for meat and poultry production. There might be more annual antibiotic use per unit of human weight than there is per unit nonhuman animal weight. Still, people worry about the considerable amount devoted to animal production. Some of the medications treat animal illness, but the vast majority is for nontherapeutic uses. Adding antibiotics to feed increases an animal's weight gain rate (Foer, 2010; Philpott, 2013). Unfortunately, the manure from animals in CAFOs contains resistant pathogens, which can be passed on to humans in the water supply or when used as fertilizer for growing crops.

Regardless of who gets the drugs, the risk from increased use of antibiotics is creating a population of bacteria that can resist their effects. This is no small problem. In the United States, for instance, antibiotic resistant strains cause a significant number of the 2 million or so annual cases of infections originating in hospitals. About 99,000 people die each year from such infections (Gurian-Sherman, 2008; Harris, 2012).

Scientists have, at best, an incomplete understanding of the exact relationship of antibiotic use in food animals to the impacts on human beings (Anderson, 2013; Animal Health Institute, n.d.). There is some linkage between the use of some antibiotics in animals and the emergence of resistant strains and outbreaks (de Waal & Grooters, 2013; Vieira et al., 2011). Because of such worries, antimicrobials are increasingly restricted. Some European countries forbid nontherapeutic use of the drugs. Some people suggest a complete ban of antibiotic use in livestock and poultry, but this may be premature. Outright bans of certain classes of antibiotics may backfire with decreased health of herds or flocks. This might have been the case with some localized bans in Europe. Some industry groups point to scholarly literature that suggests some bans are ineffective or worse. (See, for instance, some of the references at www.ahi.org). Meanwhile, in the United States and other developed countries, scientists and regulators already monitor the prevalence of resistant strains of bacteria.

Antibiotic resistance is part of a collective action problem where what seems to be individually rational is collectively suboptimal. Widespread use of antibiotics contributes to resistant strains through basic evolutionary pressures. The organisms antibiotics do not kill will tend to multiply. Now, the private use of antibiotics produces private gains by curing disease. There are also gains for second parties when users get better: those second parties are less likely to be exposed to the user's disease. However, the costs of antibiotic use are distributed to many others now living and yet to be born. Even responsible antibiotic use increases the chances that others will be exposed to resistant strains. Critics ultimately worry that the current widespread use of antibiotics is unsustainable (Anomaly, 2009; Philpott, 2013; "Resistance to Antibiotics," 2011).

Unfortunately, there are fewer new antibiotics in development now than in the twentieth century. Part of the explanation for this comes from the economics of pharmaceutical patenting, which may be open to revision. (See Chapter 2 in this book, "Pharmaceuticals and the developing world.") Meanwhile, the science on antibiotic use is still developing. Greater study of the impact of European bans is needed. But it seems clear that microbial resistance is on the rise.

As the science unfolds, one possible tactic is to exhort people to be more diligent in using antibiotics. But exhortation is rarely as effective as users bearing the costs of their behavior up front. Some scholars propose a tax on antibiotics. This could be a sort of user fee whose rates would be calculated to encourage users to minimize the behavior that imposes costs on others (Anomaly, 2009; Rudholm, 2002). The precise structure of those fees might vary depending upon the type of antibiotic. Perhaps, for instance, first-line medicines might be taxed at a lower rate than the medicines of last resort. The fees for such medicines might then fund prizes for the creation of new antimicrobial medications. To be truly effective, though, such a system may need to be internationalized (Anomaly, 2010).

Industrial agriculture commentators may warn that increasing the cost of antibiotics will increase the cost of meat. Perhaps this is as it should be, since omnivores are imposing indirect costs on others through their meat consumption. But when the costs of antibiotics rise, producers will consider alternatives that reduce or remove the need for antibiotics. This might require changing the foods animals eat or the conditions in which they live. With increased prices, people would direct resources to the most highly valued uses. This might help to allow everyone to enjoy the benefits of antibiotics without imposing undue costs on others. And when people do use antibiotics or rely on processes that might do the same, they would pay for the privilege of doing so.

Another alternative in addition to or instead of a tax is more modest. Public policy might restrict or forbid the nontherapeutic use of antibiotics. In late 2013 for instance, the United States took small steps in that direction by phasing in a ban on the use of the drugs merely to make food animals bigger. Veterinarians will be required to prescribe antibiotics, but only for specific conditions. Critics warn the ban is ultimately meaningless since the regulations permit use of the drugs to keep animals from getting sick. Reports are that similar such bans in Europe had little impact on overall antibiotic use (Tavernise, 2013). Further study and experimentation about the impacts of various policies (including stronger nontherapeutic bans) might be warranted.

Animal welfare

The discussion so far has focused mainly on the impact CAFOs have on humans, but we must not forget the living creatures the industry produces and prepares for human consumption. Few people nowadays have a "Cartesian" view of nonhuman animals. Most of us acknowledge that all the land animals we eat are capable of feeling pain. Many of us would also have to admit that our food animals are capable of what we regard as fairly sophisticated forms of experience and interaction, including understanding social hierarchies, building and establishing trusting relationships, caring for and about one's young, planning for the future, and communicating meaningfully with others (Grandin & Johnson, 2006). The evidence about animal cognition forces us to realize that food providers routinely slaughter on our behalf billions of creatures who can and very often do feel pain. This matters to us since we believe that pain is bad—and that it is not just bad for ourselves.

Reports of animal welfare on factory farms are riddled with stories of pain (Eisnitz, 2007; Foer, 2010; Singer, 2009). The pain comes from, among other things, crowded living conditions, features (or the barrenness) of their environment, disease, and the conditions of slaughter. In many cases, the pain seems avoidable. (See many of the reports by Temple Grandin available at www.grandin.com.) Industry critics can point to plenty of gruesome and disturbing videos depicting ghastly animal suffering.

Chickens are raised in massive sheds where they are crowded into spaces that provide little opportunity for them to perform many of the behaviors critics take as appropriate to chickens, including wing stretching, scratching the ground, or preening. Some chickens live in large crowded areas where they often wallow in their own waste. The concentrated environment and accumulation of waste generates a buildup of toxic amounts of airborne ammonia, which gives the chickens respiratory problems. Other chickens are raised in battery cages by themselves or in small groups, often allowing each chicken less space than the size of a standard sheet of paper. The amount of space chickens receive varies from one country to another. Some countries have banned battery cages and created regulations requiring greater space per chicken and more stimulating fixtures in their environment.

Stories of the conditions hens experience in confined environments inspire much sympathy in readers and viewers. Hens frequently suffer skeletal abnormalities or broken bones. The techniques to inspire more egg-laying include starvation diets and tinkering with light cycles. Nearly all egg-laying birds that survive culling after hatching (the male birds are destroyed) are debeaked to prevent them from harmfully pecking one another in confinement. Debeaking typically involves using a heated blade to remove the tips of their beaks without anesthetic. Later the birds are mechanically slaughtered after being hung upside down and placed in isolation cones, but sometimes the machines are ineffective and human workers must catch the misses. Even then, however, the workers might miss surviving birds, so some hens are alive as they go through the slaughter process that includes scalding, feather removal, and dismemberment.

Cows are raised in confined conditions as well. Some, such as veal cows, are often raised in pens so small they cannot turn around. Some cows do graze on pastures, but most mature cows live on feedlots where they spend most of their time in crowded conditions and routinely walk in plenty of waste. Without anesthesia, the cows' horns are removed (again, to prevent harmful behaviors in confinement). The cows are tagged or branded.

Cows' diets in CAFOs feature high quantities of corn and other grains. Cows are grass eaters; feeding them grain often produces various digestive maladies featuring buildup of painful quantities of gas and ulcers. For slaughter, cows are transported long distances without food or water. The cows are typically incapacitated using electrical shocks to the head or various types of bolt pistols applied to the forehead—some of which penetrate the head to destroy parts of the brain. In the best conditions, these procedures render the animal immediately unconscious. They are then hung up by their legs and prepared for slaughter. Their bodies are drained of blood and their skins are removed. Even the respected animal scientist Temple Grandin confirms reports that a substantial number of cattle survive initial efforts to kill them and so experience their own slaughter (Eisnitz, 2007; Foer, 2010, p. 229ff; Vogel & Grandin, 2008).

The conditions of industrial pigs do not inspire much admiration from lay observers either. Some jurisdictions allow pigs to be confined to crates that are so small they cannot turn around. Producers sometimes confine pigs when they are farrowing to keep them from crushing their young to death. In some cases, continuous contact with the sides of the crates causes ghastly open sores. When pigs are to live in group pens, their tails are sometimes removed and teeth clipped (usually without anesthesia) to prevent the cannibalistic behaviors common in close confinement. The consensus among animal scientists is that pigs are highly intelligent creatures, but the sparse and crowded conditions of confinement prevent pigs from pursuing their usual behaviors of digging, wallowing, nesting, and exploring. Some critics complain that such confinement conditions leave pigs bored and frustrated.

Such conditions strike many of us as deeply troubling. As if standard animal husbandry were not sufficiently disturbing, reports of gratuitous cruelty make the news. Videos featuring abuses circulate around the internet. People can find videos of slaughterhouses featuring poultry workers drop-kicking birds and cattle handlers using electric prods or forklifts to goad sick cows. There are secretly made videos showing chickens treading upon the partially decomposed carcasses of birds in poultry sheds, diseased cattle sitting in their own waste, and pig workers "thumping" piglets by bashing their heads against the floor to cull the sick or slower growing animals. New videos might be increasingly difficult to find (and so make independent oversight challenging), as many jurisdictions are passing laws to forbid the photographing or video recording of conditions inside industrial animal facilities (Oppel, Jr., 2013; The Humane Society of the United States, n.d.).

When cruel behaviors come to light, slaughterhouses face recall and immense public backlash. Industry critics say this should be no surprise since involvement in butchery often deadens a person to others' pain. Immanuel Kant reports that butchers were not allowed on juries in his day. Perhaps this was because people worried that butchers were inured to the suffering of others. Moreover, as Jonathan Safran Foer notes, historically, the task of ritual slaughter was rotated so that no one person had to suffer the common debilitating effects of being the agent of death (Foer, 2010).

To be sure, it is not standard practice for workers to torture the animals they process. But the standard practices still bother many people. Perhaps, as some critics suggest, modern consumers are detached from the process of manufacturing animal products. We are accustomed to the products showing up in nice pieces in clean packaging. We do not much like the idea that a living creature had to be slaughtered and dismembered to come to us. Some writers suggest that we might reacquaint ourselves with animal husbandry and slaughter and so better appreciate the attendant tasks and important responsibilities (Hanel, 2013; Pollan, 2006).

Of course, the modern economy is structured to cater to consumer preferences, and people typically dislike blood and whimpering creatures. Moreover, we often are "detached" from many things which, closer up, are disturbing, disgusting, or horrific, such as sewage disposal, garbage collection, crime-scene cleanup, mortuary science, or legislative negotiations. It might be an achievement of our specialized global economy that most of us do not have to pay much attention to such things. We pay someone to do our dirty work.

Apologists for CAFOs might add that many of the animals we eat would not exist but for human manipulation. This is not simply a matter of humans inseminating animals to get them pregnant. It is a matter of creating breeds whose products are better adapted to efficient production and human consumption. The common broiler chicken, for instance, is a cross of some breeds in order to produce quickly lots of breast meat. The industrial pig is another human creation, but, like many other industrial-raised animals, has many features that make it unsuited for life outdoors. The common broiler chickens' skeletons are incapable of supporting the animal much beyond adolescence. The common turkey is also bred for growth and efficient production of meat, but it is such an oddity that it is physiologically incapable of breeding on its own (Foer, 2010; Grandin & Johnson, 2006). So, advocating that animals have more access to the outdoors may offer little if any improvement for such unnatural creatures (McWilliams, 2010).

That these animals depend on human beings does not excuse maltreatment, the apologist might admit, any more than it would be permissible for human parents to torture their children. But, the apologist might say, standard conditions in confined animal facilities, while hardly luxurious, are in some respects better than the more "natural" alternatives. As Mark Sagoff writes, "Mother Nature is so cruel to her children she makes Frank Perdue look like a saint" (Sagoff, 1984, p. 303). Nature's typical rule for animals is predation and suffering.

Appeals to the harshness of nature may seem a bit too fast. Perhaps we must also pay people to do our dirty work, but maybe there are some policy remedies available to reduce how dirty it is. Let us suppose that factory farms typically lower the quantity and intensity of a chicken's pain over its life as compared to life in the wild. (This is a claim industry critics would vigorously dispute.) Perhaps adjusting confinement conditions, slaughterhouse practices, or oversight regimes can offer some improvements. Of course, industry advocates ask us to consider questions of cost. But many critics warn that welfare concerns should not take second place to cost (Sagoff, 1981). Perhaps some government regulations can provide some welfare improvements.

There is already a variety of public policies in place. States control the process of animal husbandry and slaughter to protect human and animal welfare. Some regulations govern living space and living conditions. Many industry observers agree that confinement saves money but involves significant tradeoffs for animal and human welfare. There are disputes about the cost savings of certain regulations. For instance, some commentators argue that requiring greater space for animals will increase costs, but others argue that reduced skeletal and other injuries would reduce loss from sick or injured animals.

In her many works for lay and scholarly audiences, Temple Grandin documents how efficient animal husbandry requires diligent care and attention to the animals' needs. Keeping livestock calm, respecting their natural dispositions, and building facilities to minimize stress will keep costs down and improve animal welfare. But it still may seem that, even when well-managed, there is a reason to minimize the extent to which human beings permit the slaughter of living creatures simply to gratify what is ultimately merely a dispensable taste. After all, as numerous nutritionists have shown, people can acquire all the nutrients they need from a vegetarian diet. Why not then take policy steps to encourage it?

Perhaps developing trends would help us avoid such a stark reorientation in diet. Scientists are making impressive strides in developing synthetic meat, sometimes called "shmeat." Scientists have harvested cells from living creatures and put them in environments to replicate. They are still experimenting with texture and taste, and the current price is a bit high at about £200,000/burger (Ghosh, 2012). But the environmental and welfare impacts of mass "shmeat" production would be only a fraction of those involved in CAFO-produced animal products (Tuomisto & Teixeira de Mattos, 2011). As of 2014 the venture capitalist firm Modern Meadow is exploring how to monetize bioengineered food. Were they and others like them to succeed, CAFOs could become a thing of the past.

In the meantime, it is interesting that big players in the industry have already initiated changes in response to consumer pressure. Animal welfare becomes a selling point. Major restaurant chains such as Burger King have insisted on improvements in the conditions in which the animals they purchase are raised and slaughtered. Major meat-product producers such as Smithfield have committed to improvements in their facilities as well (Cone, 2012). In supermarkets, consumers can already search out organic meat and antibiotic-free animal products. Though initially a boutique phenomenon, organic and antibiotic-free meat might be priced quite competitively with products from animals reared under standard (and more worrisome) conditions (Chapman, 2012; "Majority of Americans want meat without antibiotics," 2012).

But still: we have billions of animals raised, confined, and slaughtered on farms. Should policies curtail the consumption of the products of such facilities? Because reasonable people disagree about the moral weight of animals' interests in not living in captivity, or in not being slaughtered for human consumption, any such policy proposal would be fraught. Many people would object to policies that increase the cost of their dietary choices when others use the political process to impose their conflicting values about food animals. The single parent struggling to raise children might reasonably object to measures that make it more difficult to provide low-cost protein to the family. Of course, this is disputable. Meantime, there is one step that policymakers can take to curtail the adverse impacts of CAFOs. It involves not new policies but *undoing* policies that encourage CAFOs.

Agricultural subsidies

Throughout the world, governments subsidize agriculture. They do this indirectly, by imposing tariffs on products from other nations. They also do this directly by giving farmers cash payments or by subsidizing the purchase of crop insurance. Some advocates justify these policies as devices to protect domestic agriculture. But the policies have profound impacts on the marketplace and artificially reduce the cost of producing meat.

The United States, for instance, subsidizes a variety of crops with direct payments, crop insurance subsidies, disaster subsidies, and other payouts. The subsidies help producers of livestock (totaling $4.1 billion from 1995–2012). But there are also subsidies for the producers of the grains that livestock eat. This keeps feed costs artificially low. From 1995 to 2012, various US Department of Agriculture programs paid out over $27.8 billion for soybean subsidies and, most notably, $84.4 billion for corn—a major ingredient in poultry and cattle feed. Other subsidies come from the continuing Environmental Quality Incentives Program, which subsidizes CAFOs' costs in controlling and disposing of the vast quantities of manure their operations generate. Of special note: the bulk of American subsidies go to a handful of large industrial farms, leaving smaller operations at a competitive disadvantage. Moreover, federal funds subsidize the transport of waste from areas where there is too much to areas that might otherwise use it (EWG Farm Subsidy Database, n.d.; Imhoff, 2010). There are further subsidies for irrigation and surplus crops, each of which encourages production beyond what the marketplace would have otherwise inspired. The glut of cheap grain holds prices lower than they would otherwise be. Even those producers that feed animals outside have sometimes benefitted from federal subsidies; ranchers have been allowed to graze cattle at below-market costs to access rangeland (Myers & Kent, 2000, pp. 49–50). This makes meat cheaper to produce and so less expensive at the market. All this encourages further consumption of meat as well as further breeding, captivity, and slaughter of food animals.

These subsidies are hardly unique to the United States. Many countries have similar such programs in place, often defended with appeals to domestic food security. Brazil, for instance, subsidizes agriculture with low-cost loans, production subsidies, price floors, and substantial import tariffs. China waives transportation taxes, port fees, and value added taxes for some agricultural products. Japan subsidizes soybeans so that revenue always meets costs of production. Mexico supports corn up to a certain production level for any producer. And so on (EWG Farm Subsidy Database, n.d.). In each of these cases, government policies encourage the production of more commodity grains and agricultural products than there might otherwise have been.

Economists have no problem explaining the origin and persistence of such programs: the benefits are concentrated and the costs dispersed. Those who stand to gain from the programs lobby politicians; those who stand to lose do not spend the time to oppose policies whose impact on them is nominal. But people respond to incentives, and the upshot is that these policies artificially inflate the supply of agricultural goods. In the case of CAFOs, the result in many cases is that the cost of production is lower than what it would have been without the supporting public policies.

When we subsidize the production of a good, we will typically get more of it. This seems to be happening for meat and animal products. Meat is so cheap because it is cheap to grow animals, cheap to store and clean up their excrement, and cheap to water the crops that grow the cheap feed that nourishes them. Consumers respond to price signals, too. They buy meat, and as any economist will point out, consumers will buy more meat when the price comes down. But, with prices kept so artificially low, there are more animals on CAFOs.

By ending all of the subsidies, and thereby making producers and consumers bear more of the costs of manufacturing animal products, we can begin to curtail the scope and impact of CAFOs. This would likely raise the price of meat and reshape the industry. But it need not be economically devastating. In the 1980s, New Zealand eliminated nearly all agricultural subsidies. And while there was some adjustment, the agricultural sector of New Zealand is thriving today (Sayre, n.d.).

Removing subsidies would have a beneficial side effect: it would allow agricultural production to take place where it is most efficient. In some cases, farmers in the developing world may then have better opportunities to sell their products at competitive prices. This would help poorer persons to earn a livelihood. Ultimately, though, removing the subsidies might very well allow animal products to be priced in a way that reflects more of their costs of production. This might reduce demand for such products, thus decreasing the number of animals raised in CAFOs. Given the moral and environmental costs of the industry, perhaps this would be a good thing.

Closing thoughts

Industrial agriculture is complex and engages many sectors of the economy. This chapter has not discussed several dimensions of related fields, including aquaculture, biodiversity, soil degradation, use of pesticides, genetically modified organisms, and the impact of the growth of CAFOs on global diets. This chapter has also not discussed the complexities of competing regulatory regimes. (But see, for instance, Chapter 2 in this book, "Pharmaceuticals and the developing world.") The discussion selectively highlighted some leading controversies surrounding the industrial production of meat and animal products. Ultimately, there are substantial tradeoffs in raising large quantities of animals for human consumption.

The industrialization of animal production has made low-cost meat widely available. But the industry generates important and worrisome environmental impacts and health tradeoffs. When institutional norms encourage producers and consumers to internalize the costs of their choices, there will be fewer unwilling bystanders.

The science on antibiotic resistance is unsettled, but there are some good reasons to consider policies targeting reduced use of drugs among all animals. Removing subsidies would allow people to choose their food with clearer price signals and a better sense of the costs of production. Such changes may help people take responsibility for their choices. The changes may encourage improvements in food animal welfare as well.

Further reading

The literature on this industry is vast. Anyone wishing further grounding in the moral issues might start with writings about the moral status of animals. Tom Regan, for instance, has several compelling works on the topic, such as his *Empty Cages* (Lanham, MD: Rowman and Littlefield, 2005), which offers a detailed defense and discussion of animal rights. Animal scientist Temple Grandin has several works on the inner lives of animals and how to treat food animals. Her book with Mark Deesing, *Humane Livestock Handling* (North Adams, MA: Storey Publishing, 2008), gives discussion and diagrams of how to manage food animals in industrial facilities. David Kirby's *Animal Factory* (New York: St. Martin's Press, 2011) documents the impacts of CAFOs in communities throughout the United States with the eye of a journalist. Eric Schlosser's *Food Inc.* documentary gives a gripping and deeply disturbing look at industrial animal operations. Readers hoping for some uplifting news, even about agriculture, might check Charles Kenny's *Getting Better: Why Global Development Is Succeeding—And How We Can Improve the World Even More* (New York: Basic Books, 2012). Alex Renton's 2013 Kindle book, *Planet Carnivore: Why Cheap Meat Costs the Earth (and How to Pay the Bill)* considers some recent trends and suggests possible improvements. Christopher Leonard documents the worrisome impacts of the US meat industry's business model in his 2014 book, *The Meat Racket: The Secret Takeover of America's Food Business* (New York: Simon & Schuster). Finally (though hardly all that there is on this subject), people eager for technical economic and epidemiological discussions of antibiotic resistance might look at the essays in Ramanan Laxminarayan's edited collection *Battling Resistance to Antibiotics and Pesticides: An Economic Approach* (Washington, D.C.: Resources for the Future, 2003).

References

Anderson, K. (2013, May 9). Opinions on antibiotics vary widely. *Brownfield*. Retrieved November 4, 2013, from http://brownfieldagnews.com/2013/05/09/opinions-on-antibiotics-vary-widely/

Animal Health Institute. (n.d.). Animal antibiotics. Retrieved November 4, 2013, from www.ahi.org/issues-advocacy/animal-antibiotics/

Anomaly, J. (2009). Harm to others: The social cost of antibiotics in agriculture. *Journal of Agricultural and Environmental Ethics, 22*(5), 423–35.

Anomaly, J. (2010). Combating resistance: The case for a global antibiotics treaty. *Public Health Ethics, 3*(1), 13–22.

Aquinas, T. (1993). Differences between rational and other creatures. In R. Botzler (Ed.), *Environmental ethics: Divergence and convergence* (pp. 278–80). Boston: McGraw Hill.

Bailey, R. (2000, April). Billions served: Norman Borlaug interviewed by Ronald Bailey. *Reason*. Retrieved June 4, 2014, from http://reason.com/archives/2000/04/01/billions-served-norman-borlaug

Bentham, J. (n.d.). Principles of morals and legislation. Retrieved November 3, 2013, from www.constitution.org/jb/pml_17.htm

Boehm, C. (2011). *Moral origins: Social selection and the evolution of virtue and shame.* New York: Perseus Books Group.

Brown, L. R. (2009). *Plan B 4.0: Mobilizing to save civilization.* New York: W. W. Norton.

Chapman, S. (2012, February 16). Food and conscience. *Reason*. Retrieved November 7, 2013, from http://reason.com/archives/2012/02/16/food-and-conscience

Cone, T. (2012). Burger King to eliminate gestation crates, chicken cages by 2017. *Huffington Post*. Retrieved June 4, 2014, from www.huffingtonpost.com/2012/04/25/burger-king-gestation-crates_n_1451703.html

de Waal, C. S., & Grooters, S. V. (2013). *Antibiotic resistance in foodborne pathogens*. Center for Science in the Public Interest. Retrieved from http://cspinet.org/new/pdf/outbreaks_antibiotic_resistance_in_foodborne_pathogens_2013.pdf

de Waal, F. B. M. (2009). *The age of empathy: Nature's lessons for a kinder society*. New York: Three Rivers Press.

Descartes, R. (1998). Discourse on method. In *Discourse on method and meditations on first philosophy*. (D. A. Cress, Trans.) Indianapolis, IN: Hackett.

Eisnitz, G. A. (2007). *Slaughterhouse: The shocking story of greed, neglect, and inhumane treatment inside the U.S. meat industry*. Amherst, NY: Prometheus Books.

EWG Foreign Subsidies Database. (n.d.). Retrieved November 7, 2013, from www.depts.ttu.edu/ceri/index.aspx

FAOSTAT Emissions Agriculture database. (n.d.). Retrieved October 21, 2013, from http://faostat3.fao.org/faostat-gateway/go/to/download/Q/QA/E

Foer, J. S. (2010). *Eating animals*. New York: Back Bay Books/Little, Brown and Co.

Food & Water Watch. (2010). Factory farm nation: How America turned its livestock farms into factories. Retrieved from http://documents.foodandwaterwatch.org/doc/FactoryFarmNation-web.pdf

Ghosh, P. (2012, February 19). Synthetic meat grown in Dutch lab. Retrieved July 6, 2014, from www.bbc.co.uk/news/science-environment-16972761

Grandin, T., & Johnson, C. (2006). *Animals in translation: Using the mysteries of autism to decode animal behavior*. Orlando, FL: Harcourt.

Grandin, T., & Johnson, C. (2010). *Animals make us human: Creating the best life for animals*. Boston: Mariner Books.

Gurian-Sherman, D. (2008). CAFOs uncovered: The untold costs of confined animal feeding operations. Cambridge, MA: Union of Concerned Scientists Publications. Retrieved November 4, 2013, from www.ucsusa.org/assets/documents/food_and_agriculture/cafos-uncovered.pdf

Hanel, M. (2013, April 4). The proper way to eat a pig. *The New York Times*. Retrieved June 4, 2014, from www.nytimes.com/2013/04/07/magazine/the-proper-way-to-eat-a-pig.html

Harris, G. (2012, April 11). Antibiotics for livestock will require prescription, F.D.A. says. *The New York Times*. Retrieved from www.nytimes.com/2012/04/12/us/antibiotics-for-livestock-will-require-prescription-fda-says.html

The Humane Society of the United States. (n.d.). Anti-whistleblower bills hide factory-farming abuses from the public. Retrieved November 6, 2013, from www.humanesociety.org/issues/campaigns/factory_farming/fact-sheets/ag_gag.html#id=album-185&num=content-3312

Imhoff, D. (Ed.). (2010). *The CAFO reader: The tragedy of industrial animal factories*. Berkeley, CA: Watershed Media.

Kant, I. (1963). Duties to animals and spirits. In *Lectures on ethics*. (L. Infield, Trans.) (pp. 239–41). New York: Harper & Row.

"Majority of Americans want meat without antibiotics." (2012, June 20). *Consumers Union*. Retrieved November 7, 2013, from http://consumersunion.org/news/majority-of-americans-want-meat-without-antibiotics/

McWilliams, J. E. (2010). *Just food: Where locavores get it wrong and how we can truly eat responsibly*. New York: Back Bay.

Morell, V. (2013). *Animal wise: The thoughts and emotions of our fellow creatures*. New York: Crown.

Myers, N., & Kent, J. (2000). *Perverse subsidies: How tax dollars can undercut the environment and the economy*. Washington, D.C.: Island Press.

Nierenberg, D. (2003, June). Factory farming in the developing world, *World Watch, 16*, 10–19.

Oppel, Jr., R. A. (2013, April 6). Taping of farm cruelty is becoming the crime. *The New York Times*. Retrieved from www.nytimes.com/2013/04/07/us/taping-of-farm-cruelty-is-becoming-the-crime.html

Philpott, T. (2013, February 8). The meat industry now consumes four-fifths of all antibiotics. *Mother Jones*. Retrieved November 4, 2013, from www.motherjones.com/tom-philpott/2013/02/meat-industry-still-gorging-antibiotics

Pollan, M. (2006). *The omnivore's dilemma: A natural history of four meals*. New York: Penguin Press.

"Resistance to antibiotics: The spread of superbugs." (2011, March 31). *The Economist*. Retrieved June 4, 2014, from www.economist.com/node/18483671

Ridley, M. (2011). *The rational optimist: How prosperity evolves*. New York: Harper Perennial.

Rudholm, N. (2002). Economic implications of antibiotic resistance in a global economy. *Journal of Health Economics, 21*(6), 1071–83. doi:10.1016/S0167-6296(02)00053-X

Sagoff, M. (1981). At the shrine of Our Lady Fatima, or why political questions are not all economic. *Arizona Law Review, 23*, 1283–98.

Sagoff, M. (1984). Animal liberation and environmental ethics: Bad marriage, quick divorce. *Osgood Hall Law Journal, 22*, 297–307.

Sayre, L. (2009). The hidden link between factory farms and human illness. *Mother Earth News*, (232), 76–83.

Sayre, L. (n.d.). Farming without subsidies in New Zealand. Retrieved November 7, 2013, from www.newfarm.org/features/0303/newzealand_subsidies.shtml

Schmidtz, D. (1994). The institution of property. *Social Philosophy and Policy, 11*(2), 42–62.

Schmidtz, D. (2000). Natural enemies: An anatomy of environmental conflict. *Environmental Ethics: An Interdisciplinary Journal Dedicated to the Philosophical Aspects of Environmental Problems, 22*(4), 397–408.

Shiva, V. (2000). *Stolen harvest: The hijacking of the global food supply*. Cambridge, MA: South End Press.

Singer, P. (2009). *Animal liberation: The definitive classic of the animal movement*. New York: Harper Perennial.

Smil, V. (2001). *Feeding the world: A challenge for the twenty-first century.* Cambridge, MA: MIT Press.

Steinfeld, H., Gerber, P., Wasenaar, T., Castel, V., Rosales, M., & de Haan, C. (2006). *Livestock's long shadow: Environmental issues and options.* Rome: Food and Agriculture Organization of the United Nations.

Tavernise, S. (2013, December 11). F.D.A. restricts antibiotics use for livestock. *The New York Times.* Retrieved from www.nytimes.com/2013/12/12/health/fda-to-phase-out-use-of-some-antibiotics-in-animals-raised-for-meat.html

"Trends – United Nations Population Division." (n.d.). Retrieved November 4, 2013, from www.un.org/en/development/desa/population/theme/trends/index.shtml

Tuomisto, H. L., & Teixeira de Mattos, M. J. (2011). Environmental impacts of cultured meat production. *Environmental Science & Technology, 45*(14), 6117–6123. doi:10.1021/es200130u

Vieira, A. R., Collignon, P., Aarestrup, F. M., McEwen, S. A., Hendriksen, R. S., Hald, T., & Wegener, H. C. (2011). Association between antimicrobial resistance in *Escherichia coli* isolates from food animals and blood stream isolates from humans in Europe: An ecological study. *Foodborne Pathogens and Disease, 8*(12), 1295–1301. doi:10.1089/fpd.2011.0950

Vietmeyer, N. (2011). *Our daily bread: The essential Norman Borlaug.* Lorton, VA: Bracing Books.

Vogel, K., & Grandin, T. (2008). 2008 restaurant animal welfare and humane slaughter audits in federally inspected beef and pork slaughter plants in the U.S. and Canada. Retrieved November 6, 2013, from www.grandin.com/survey/2008.restaurant.audits.html

11 Conclusion

Making public policy is inherently controversial. The outputs include rules, norms, and institutions that govern people's behavior, often by restricting their choices. People do not simply disagree about means. Even the experts disagree about the impacts of alternative public policies. People also disagree about ends.

Ethics can help to frame some policy controversies but fastening our attention on what we think matters. Often, an expression of our fundamental values is a view that certain options are out of bounds—especially for a legitimate democratic state. Ethics can help us to understand what those boundaries might be. Of course, people often disagree about fundamental values. Making those differences explicit can help us to frame the disputes about policy.

Much of what is at stake in policy controversies depends on the findings of social science. If, for instance, social scientists could establish that children reared in families headed by same-sex parents had substantially diminished life prospects over those with alternative arrangements, that might crucially affect policy options. This is assuming social scientists somehow reached a consensus about the findings. Of course, even that would not settle the issue of what policy should be about same-sex marriage and parenting. Some persons will insist that significant liberties are at stake and should not take second place to concerns about overall well-being—even for those of children.

It turns out that in the case of same-sex marriage, as well as with the bulk of other themes the book has discussed, social scientists are uncertain about the causes of events, what is currently happening, and what might result from alternative policies. This uncertainty calls for guidance about how to proceed—if at all—in conditions of limited knowledge. Ethics can offer some guidance here. It helps us to understand how we might proceed, for even when social scientists furnish definitive findings about policy possibilities, they do not resolve for us what we may do, what we must not do, and what we must do.

Fashioning public policy (or abstaining from policy) is particularly fraught for states. Contemporary nation states claim a monopoly on the use of coercive force in a given territory. They claim the right to impose obligations on residents. Public policies thus seem to call for a special form of justification. They should be justifiable by considerations that no reasonable person can reject. The policy domains this book surveyed pose distinct challenges to justifying what states currently do, might do, or might not do. Sometimes, however, there might be a more widely acceptable justification available were states to have more modest aspirations. Perhaps it is easier to justify what states do when they attempt to do less.

Of course, this is but a sketch of a wider inquiry into public justification and public policy. Whether public justification is more forthcoming when states do less is partly a conceptual and partly an empirical question. Social scientists will be quick to point out that doing nothing can have consequences. Those consequences might not be justifiable.

Among the topics we surveyed that might lend themselves to policy improvements with less policy are those about marriage, education and intelligent design, immigration, and factory farming of animals. In each case there are frequently public policies in place that might seem inferior to available alternatives. Some policies needlessly impose uncompensated costs on others or prevent people from making choices that seem to harm no one. Perhaps instead it might be best to allow people to experiment to find out what works given their distinct histories and challenges. Sometimes imposing a single policy resolution will not be the best way for different-minded persons to achieve an acceptable resolution. Perhaps indeed there need not be a policy about a matter at all. Of course, being open to experimentation is not the sole province of nonstate actors. States can permit laboratories for alternative policies within their borders. The late Elinor Ostrom is widely hailed for having investigated alternatives people devise for handling certain collective action problems regarding shared resources. Sometimes private solutions work. Sometimes state policy is part of the solution. Often, however, different sorts of institutions and norms will work for different circumstances (Ostrom, 1990). These solutions are likely impossible to specify in advance. People need to discover them by exploring possibilities, including those among and within state policies.

At other times, states may not and perhaps cannot forbear policy-making in some way. Consider, for instance, the case of torture. What counts as torture and when, whether, and how to punish it are all matters that call for some policy resolution. Indeed, given that the matter touches on the rule of law and criminal justice, there may need to be a single set of clear guidelines about torture in a political community. People—especially state agents—need to know what they must not do. Relatedly, given that reparations and restorative justice frequently touch on how states grapple with their own unjust conduct and what they permit of others in the criminal justice system, policy silence or inaction might prevent important social, political, and indeed moral progress. Sometimes states need to figure out what to do given what they have done previously. They need rules and a plan to govern what they do.

Public policy is important because it can open people up to possibilities. But it is dangerous because it sets boundaries. Ethics can help us to understand much of the rich and perhaps permanent disagreement about the proper tasks of governance. The findings of social scientists help us to begin to understand causes and consequences. But such empirical conclusions do not begin to address the challenges of figuring out what is permissible, what is impermissible, and why people disagree about these issues. Bringing an ethical lens to the challenges of governance can help us to frame possibilities and prohibitions.

Public policy may yet increase opportunities for widely acceptable progress. But sometimes policy can open us to such progress when it permits people to explore what might work. What works in one context might not work elsewhere, partly because of different local conditions, and partly because of different values. Clarifying the ethical considerations rooting competing views on policy controversies can help us to gain clearer insight into what is at stake. We may even come to some consensus about how to overcome some of the controversy.

Reference

Ostrom, E. (1990). *Governing the commons: The evolution of institutions for collective action.* New York: Cambridge University Press.

Index

Lightning Source UK Ltd.
Milton Keynes UK
UKOW01f1108281215

265361UK00007B/193/P